Bottom-Up Enterprise

Insights from
Subsistence Marketplaces

Madhu Viswanathan

ISBN: 9781659837797

Cover Images

The front cover displays an iceberg upside-down. It is an apt representation of bottom-up enterprise – first in seeing the entire iceberg and its many levels, and second in turning it on its head to adopt a bottom-up approach. "Tip-of-the-(right-side-up)-iceberg" leadership is the antithesis of the approach presented here. Tipping the iceberg over on its head creates a rush of momentum and fresh perspective and insights.

The back cover displays the context from which our approach is derived – subsistence marketplaces.

Audience for this Book

This book is designed for two primary audiences – those interested in working in subsistence marketplaces, as well as those interested in applying the lessons learned (in such extreme contexts) to their own contexts, such as in advanced economies or in higher-income segments of developing economies. We aim to reach a diverse audience including practitioners in business, government, and social sectors; and researchers, educators, and students. We develop the notion of bottom-up enterprises learned through practice in extreme, i.e., resource-constrained, settings. Sometimes, the most insightful lessons for all settings come from such discovery.

The book begins with a journey of immersion and reflection in the first part, followed by explicit discussions of lessons learned in the second section. In the third and last part, we broaden the dialogue to include bottom–up applications to a variety of settings and operations. Even for those not working in subsistence marketplaces, there is significant value in understanding the implications of these bottom-up approaches to their own efforts. We illustrate a number of situations where our approaches have had impact in other domains.

Finally, our sequencing here is bottom-up as well, beginning with a deep understanding of subsistence marketplaces, followed by the design of solutions and enterprise plans for them. After this, the discussion turns to lessons in running a bottom-up enterprise before moving on to the application of these lessons in a variety of contexts.

There is an irony is writing a book about being bottom-up. The very act of writing about it is, in a sense, top-down. And so goes the dance between the bottom-up and the top-down that is detailed in this journey.

Acknowledgements

I have been at the intersection of so much positive and noble energy in the journey described here. I thank every community member, team member, student, staff, colleague, partner, friend, and relative for their role in the endeavors outlined here, spanning many countries and continents and many sectors of society. In a sense, writing a book is about baring one's soul. I am deeply indebted to the wonderful people who made this journey possible. It is a privilege to articulate the journey and the lessons learned. Whatever the metaphor, whether the elephant and the six men who could not see[1], or the tip of the iceberg, I feel truly fortunate to be able to see so much of the elephant or the iceberg and paint a picture.[2]

[1] "Blind Men and an Elephant." Wikipedia. Accessed April 18, 2016. https://en.wikipedia.org/wiki/Blind_men_and_an_elephant.

[2] Special thanks to Tom Hanlon, Anne McKinney, Srinivas Venugopal, Steven Morse, and Ron Duncan for their tireless efforts in copyediting the book.

Foreword

Raj Echambadi, Senior Associate Dean, College of Business, University of Illinois, Urbana-Champaign

I was born and raised in India. Although my family was not poor, I had seen poverty up close all around me when I was growing up. My first job after college was with a renowned tractor company as a service engineer in the southern Indian states of Tamil Nadu and Kerala working with subsistence farmers. So I firmly believed that I knew what there is to know about the nature and challenges of subsistence marketplaces – or so I thought until I read Madhu Viswanathan's work on subsistence marketplaces.

Marcel Proust writes "the real voyage of discovery consists not in seeking new landscapes, but in having new eyes." Madhu's work provided those new eyes for me. I was fortunate to discover new insights in old things that I had seen thousands of times before. More importantly, I was able to connect the lessons from subsistence marketplaces to my work that was steeped in the developed world. After all, the lessons from subsistence marketplaces appear to be universal. Therein lies the power of Madhu's work; it is rigorous yet relevant across various contexts.

Madhu is the epitome of an engaged scholar, one who has actively collaborated with subsistence communities around the world in order to create pioneering research at the intersection of poverty and business. Few people in the business discipline have examined the notion of poverty. The ones who did advised first-world companies on the vast market potential of the poorest consumers and suggested strategies to reach these consumers. Madhu's work is different. Through his research, he has created a solid framework for how researchers and policymakers should approach problems in subsistence marketplaces for their overall betterment. But that is only half the story.

What is impressive is that Madhu has used the bully pulpit afforded by his university affiliation and the insights from his research to make meaningful contributions to the lives of countless poor people. He has used the language of business and entrepreneurship to empower people. I saw this firsthand in a subsistence community in Uthiramerur, India, when a young woman proudly showed off to me her entrepreneurial venture, a small retail store of about 50 square feet. When I asked her why she started it, she said that she did it so that she could send her children to school so they could have better lives. She felt empowered after going through marketplace literacy education with Madhu's team in India. She is one of the countless people who are being changed for the better by the work done by subsistence marketplace initiatives around the world. Madhu's community-centered work – empowering people through education – is a message of hope.

Madhu's research work, grounded in a values-based framework, provides a serious template for approaching subsistence marketplaces. At a broad level, his work is design thinking at its best. Engage in a bottom-up approach to generate, test, and implement ideas. Treat people the way you would want to be treated. Study the problem from the outside but immerse yourself in the situation before embarking on a long-term solution. Do not look at any problem in a vacuum, but study the totality of life circumstances in order to create sustainable solutions. Create a feedback loop wherein you test, iterate, and learn in a continuous manner. The bottom line is clear: engage people in a context of partnership and reciprocity and mutually beneficial outcomes will follow.

One fascinating insight from this book is how the template from subsistence marketplaces is relatable to other contexts. When one thinks through the problem, the answer is self-evident. Subsistence marketplaces are marked by inordinately high levels of uncertainty. So when one learns to design creative solutions under extreme uncertainty in subsistence marketplaces, either by designing a product for a marginalized market in the developed world (i.e., reverse innovation), or designing a product for other contexts (i.e., higher education in the online market), it is a just a matter of using the same frame in a different context. The first principles are the same. The vantage point is the same. In a sense, the framework is a mindset that is adaptable to various contexts.

This book is a tour de force. It reflects serious scholarship that would benefit academic researchers, students, policymakers, managers, and community organizers around the world who can use these insights, whether for accumulating knowledge or for empowering the poor and the vulnerable. Given that billions of people are mired in poverty, enhancing the overall wellbeing of our communities is our collective compact toward achieving a global, civil society. This book takes a small, but significant, step toward achieving that goal.

Table of Contents

Part I: Understanding and Designing Solutions for Subsistence Marketplaces

Introduction

Every journey begins with a story, and every journey is a continuation of a story. Here is how my own story with subsistence marketplaces, marketplace literacy, and the bottom-up approach, began, and how it expanded to include many others.

The Bottom-Up Story

I came to a doctoral program about 30 years ago with some notion of conducting research that would impact people on a wider scale, including those in my country of birth, India. I recall thinking that using marketing communications might be one pathway to accomplish this. Over the next decade, I learned to crawl, walk, and run in a research sense and develop an academic career. Interestingly, my work revolved around the psychology of consumers' use of numbers and words and more generally, magnitudes, as well as how researchers themselves use numbers, through the dissection of measurement error. Studying the use of numerical and verbal nutritional labels as well as preference for numerical information provided a logical pathway to numeracy and literacy.

About two decades ago, I ventured into studying how low-literate, low-income consumers in the United States dealt with problems they faced in their everyday lives – especially in how they fared in the marketplace. **I was motivated by the almost complete lack of work on low literacy and its effects on phenomena such as decision-making.**

In one sense, this was the first attempt at a "bottom-up approach" to examine how vulnerable sections of society, in terms of income and literacy, interacted with the marketplace. **As my bottom-up journey continued, I wanted to learn from and reach vulnerable segments of society with some potentially useful research.** The research approach was also bottom-up – rather than have any specific theories or frameworks whether they are about poverty or from relatively affluent contexts, the idea was to generate understanding from the bottom-up. It was about moving from data to conceptual insights – being inductive rather than deductive, at least initially. Appropriately, we used the most open-ended of approaches, relying on interviews and observations. And our first impressions from almost two decades ago when observing low-literate individuals shop persist: the things we take for granted (that low-literate, low-income consumers cannot).

Image 0.01: Deep Engagement in a Few Places: Locations Where Our Teams Work With Communities.

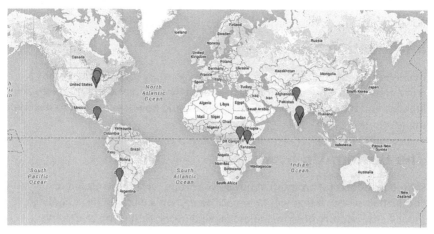

We began our research by studying how low literacy and low income influence the way people think, feel, negotiate the local environment, and interact with the marketplace. Over time, we moved on to studying ecosystems and deriving implications for developing products and business models. Thus, our research process reflects the bottom-up approach as we derived implications from data on the ground. Indeed, our approach was bottom-up in the sense of what we learned as well, which emerged from our work.

From the United States, our work expanded to contexts of poverty in India, where poverty is more extreme and widespread, and later to Tanzania and Argentina. (And more recently to Honduras and a refugee settlement in Uganda). **Our research approach centered on listening and learning.**

An element of bottom-up team building came into being here, as our team, other than myself, was comprised of people from the communities we studied. Our research through conversations with customers and entrepreneurs at the bottom of society was enhanced by the unique insights at the micro-level that came from my team. We have conducted our research with a field team consisting of members of the communities we studied, thus grounding us in these contexts.

In parallel, using such bottom-up insights, we have developed and scaled a marketplace literacy educational program that has provided a variety of insights.[3] We embarked on creating a marketplace literacy educational program that was developed bottom-up, from our research and with our team.

The path for our educational program gained through our research went from *what* to *how* to *why*. Unique to our program was a focus on the know-why in addition to the know-how and the know-what. We moved from observations to concepts, and stitched together concepts from the bottom-up, starting with people our study participants knew and how they were different. We gained additional insights through the delivery of the program and classroom experience as we observed and interacted with the participants. We developed this program based on our research with a field team, offered it in face-to-face settings, and scaled the education through a teacher-less educational approach. Over time, this program grew, and with our partners we have now reached tens of thousands of people, offering the program in six countries.

Image 0.02: Perspectives on Poverty.[4]

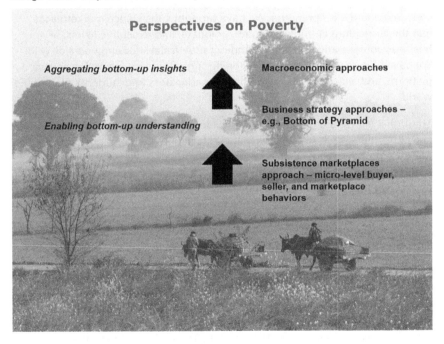

The term *subsistence marketplaces* was coined to reflect a bottom-up approach to understanding marketplaces of poverty to contrast with relatively macro-level approaches, such as macroeconomic insights about poverty or even a bottom-of-the-pyramid approach, which begins with organizations working in these contexts.[5] In contrast, we began by studying life circumstances, consumers, entrepreneurs, communities, and marketplaces in this realm. Bottom-up refers to the ground level of a phenomenon that we use as our foundation or starting point. Much of humanity engages in "business" and marketplace exchange in these settings; the subsistence marketplaces approach emphasizes the need to study them in their own right and not as a means for business, policy, or social initiatives by outside entities.

Our Work to Date

So what have we done so far? For almost two decades, we have conducted a lot of research on subsistence marketplaces. We have created social initiatives to teach people marketplace literacy education so that they can be better consumers and entrepreneurs. We have brought subsistence marketplaces into the curriculum at undergraduate, graduate, and executive levels, in business courses and through an undergraduate class for engineers as well. We have offered the course worldwide through Coursera, an online course platform, and also created a web portal for educators and students around the world.

Through it all, we are gaining micro-level insights about entrepreneurs and consumers, their relationships, their life circumstances, and so on. We are learning how people consume, how they buy or make (or sometimes forgo) products and food, how they build relationships, and how they run enterprises. We are seeing how they interact with others, with ecosystems, and how they confront environmental problems.

We gain understanding at this micro-level. And from this understanding of subsistence consumers and entrepreneurs, we learn how to design products and ecosystems, develop enterprises and business models, and, more broadly, how to facilitate sustainable development.

Our approach has always been deeply engaged in communities. We started with low-literate, low-income consumers in the United States and the problems they face in the marketplace. We moved on to subsistence consumers and entrepreneurs in India, using the word *subsistence* to denote poverty that is more extreme. Since 2001, we have had a team on the ground in India. This team is comprised of people who are from the communities that we work with.

---

[5] Viswanathan, Madhu. *Subsistence Marketplaces.* eBookPartnerships, 2013.

Similarly, we work in East Africa (Tanzania and Uganda) and in Latin America (Honduras and Argentina) as well, through deep engagement in the communities. We don't have widespread knowledge of subsistence around the world, and we do not pretend to, but we do have deep engagement in a few countries around the world.

Within this stream, a community of researchers, students, and practitioners has been created through a series of biennial conferences. Our efforts in research have generated more than 40 authored publications, and we have edited roughly 60 refereed publications through special issues. We have created learning experiences that reach almost a thousand students a year at the University of Illinois, spanning first-year undergraduate to graduate and executive levels in business, and disciplines such as engineering and industrial design. For a decade now, we have designed and delivered a year-long course on subsistence marketplaces with international immersion experience, involving some of the most challenging and impoverished areas of the globe. This learning experience was ranked one of the top courses on entrepreneurship and sustainable development by *Inc.* Magazine.[6]

In addition, we have taken our accumulated experiences and reached out globally to tens of thousands of students around the world through a course on the online learning platform, Coursera.[7] We also aggregate research and educational materials on subsistence marketplaces for educator, students, and practitioners, and disseminate it through a unique web portal.[8] In parallel, through a social enterprise that was founded, the Marketplace Literacy Project,[9] we have pioneered the design and delivery of consumer and entrepreneurial literacy education to low-income individuals. Through this organization and its partners, tens of thousands of individuals have received consumer and entrepreneurial literacy education.

As we move through Part I, the learning experience begins with understanding subsistence marketplaces and the bottom-up approach to designing solutions and then focuses on designing and implementing solutions for subsistence marketplaces and on sustaining bottom-up enterprises. In Part II, we then step back and derive lessons learned from our experiences which provide insights about running bottom-up enterprises.

---

[6] Buchanan, Leigh. "Best Courses 2011: Sustainable Product and Market Development for Subsistence Marketplaces." Inc.com. 2011. Accessed April 18, 2016. http://www.inc.com/magazine/20110401/best-courses-2011-sustainable-product-and-market-development-for-subsistence-marketplaces-at-the-university-of-illinois.html.

[7] http://coursera.org/

[8] https://business.illinois.edu/subsistence/resources/resourcesmlp/: Use the password *subsistence* to access materials on the web portal.

[9] http://www.marketplaceliteracy.org/

In Part III, we help you understand how to apply the bottom-up approach in non-subsistence contexts, including higher education, and we share the perspectives of students and co-laborers in our initiative. Thus, we aim to take the reader through a bottom-up experience from a variety of experiences and in a variety of contexts.

We aim to make this experience immersive, interactive, and hands-on, as if you are in a subsistence marketplace, and as if you are going to be taking part in an actual project.

You can use this learning experience to understand low-income contexts where you live. There are subsistence contexts and there are subsistence contexts. Each one is different. We cannot pretend to know about war-torn areas. We cannot pretend to know about areas that have suffered genocide. It is not easy to work in this arena. I don't want to convey the impression that solutions are easy by any stretch of the imagination. It is extremely challenging, but we must try. By empowering individuals and subsequently the community and marketplace surrounding them, we can provide opportunity, relief, and positive momentum for those who have not had a chance in life.

Beginning the Bottom-Up Journey

Since 1997, we have studied people living in poverty and how they function in the marketplace as consumers and as entrepreneurs. We have learned how people think, feel, and relate to each other in these subsistence marketplaces. Much of humanity lives in these marketplaces, making very little money, and barely making ends meet. We focus on understanding subsistence marketplaces and designing solutions for them.

And now, we are going to lead you on your own journey to discover how subsistence marketplaces work and how to design solutions for them, what lessons we have learned, and how they can be applied.

You are going to learn about subsistence marketplaces virtually, through a variety of means, including day-in-the-life videos, a movie, interviews, immersion exercises, and an online poverty simulation exercise. You will design a solution to meet a specific need. You can also create an enterprise plan to go along with it. Exercises are also interspersed through relevant parts of the book that can be completed both individually and in a group.

As you go through the learning experience and choose a topic to focus on and to design a solution for, you will consider who you and your potential team are, why you chose the particular problem, how you propose to address the problem, what challenges and opportunities you foresee, and how you plan to overcome those challenges.

Chapter 1: Life in Subsistence Marketplaces

Tanzania

Maria lives in a tribal community in Tanzania. She believes she is 62, but is not sure. She is also not certain of the ages of her three adult children, two sons and a daughter. She is more focused on what it takes to survive in a drought-threatened land.

She grew up a cowherd, taking her family's cow out to graze early in the morning and bringing it back in the evening. At age 20 she was married and looking after her husband's cow.

She has milk and porridge for her meals, and sometimes maize and beans, and as she has her whole life, she goes to the communal water tap to collect water for the day in a 20-liter bucket. "It takes me 30 minutes each way," she says. "Sometimes I balance the water on my head; other times I have use of a donkey." She sometime makes multiple water trips in a day.

She boils the water before drinking it, and drinks only a few glasses a day, using the rest to wash dishes and the *kalabus,* which are used to collect the milk from the cow. "To boil the water, and the milk from the cow, we rub dry wood together to spark a fire," she says.

For many years, only the men could buy and trade in the market, but in the last 12 years or so, women can do so as well, and Maria's husband has shown her how to buy in the market.

"Now I buy," she says, smiling. "I buy maize and sugar in the market, and I teach my daughter how to buy."

Hers is a life of hardship and survival. But she has survived, and her life, simple and laborious as it is, is better than it was as a child, when food and water were very scarce, and she would go many days with only a bit of milk to nourish her.

"I am thankful to God for my life and I am eager to learn how to be a better consumer and perhaps even how to run my own business," she tells an interviewer who has come to teach people how to do just that.

Argentina

Kiara is in the third year of her studies in social media in the Universidad de Mendoza in Mendoza, a city in Argentina's Cuyo region. Mendoza is the heart of Argentina's wine country, and its population is much larger than that of the small farming village she grew up in and still lives in. She commutes 50 kilometers a day each way. Most young people in her village drop out before they graduate from high school, but she has faced many privations and wants a better life for herself and sees education as the route to that better life.

"Education is necessary to generate, project, and transform ideas into reality," she says.

Her reality right now includes often waking at 3 a.m. to irrigate her family's small farm; they grow grapes to sell to local wineries and also have a grove of olive trees. In addition, they own a few goats.

She cares about the generation of students, of children, coming up after her. "I encourage them to get an education and to consume resources wisely," she says. "I tell them to be satisfied with what they have, to not yearn for what they can't or don't have, but to wisely use what they do have."

It is important to Kiara to keep her culture alive; while she strives for the education that most in her community do not attain, she is mindful and proud of her own culture. "I want to transmit that culture to young people, to keep it going," she says.

India

Kannan rises at 3 a.m. He moves soundlessly in his tiny, one-room apartment in Chennai, India, a bustling metropolis of more than 8.5 million people, so as not to wake his wife and his infant child, who are sleeping on a mat. They have no furniture in the room, and no electricity, but they do have a small burner in a corner in which to heat water and food. So he does not bump into anything, even in the dark, because there is so little to bump into.

He puts on his clothes and he heads outside, stepping carefully in the rain-soaked alley, watching for potholes. He gets on his motorbike, his prize – and nearly only – possession. He starts the bike and pulls out into the alley, making his way slowly to the street.

He operates the bike with one arm, because that is all he has. He lost the other arm many years back, in an accident in the village he grew up on.

This is Kannan's daily routine. He goes on his bike to receive the newspapers that he then delivers, door to door, throughout the neighborhoods surrounding his. He does so tirelessly, willingly, and with one thing in mind: to make enough money to pay for rent and food.

What a visitor most notices about Kannan is his effervescent, sunny personality. He is forever smiling. His smile is such that only later do you notice, oh, he is missing an arm.

And you learn from Kannan that when he proposed to his wife, he said, "Surely you must have noticed that I do not have a left arm, but in all this time you have never mentioned it." And she said, "Yes, of course I have noticed that you have no left arm. I am not blind. That does not bother me. I will *be* your left arm."

You had better believe that Kannan has had more than his share of bumps and bruises from learning to ride first a bicycle and then a motorbike. Life is not so easy with one arm.

Walking 30 minutes each way to carry home buckets of water while you are in your sixties. Commuting 50 kilometers each way, every day, to better your life while being mindful of conserving the resources you have. Rising at 3:00 in the morning to deliver on a motorbike, with one arm, newspapers to support your family. Maria, Kiara, and Kannan are like so many people we have met over the years who live in subsistence: hardy, determined, resilient, and ingenious in how they make do with the little they have.

Images from Subsistence Marketplaces

Let us begin with a few images to help you understand the process.

Image 1.01: A Woman Making Mud Cookies in Haiti.[10]

Here is a marketplace in Haiti where people are buying and selling cookies made out of mud. Now, these cookies have some nutritional value (salt and vegetable shortening are often added, and the clay may contain calcium),

---

[10] Photograph: Feed My Starving Children. https://www.flickr.com/photos/fmsc/6348144519.

but they are very harmful as well. These are the choices that people living in subsistence have to make on a day-to-day basis.

Image 1.02: Ghanaians Working in Agbogbloshie, a Suburb of Accra, Ghana.[11]

Here is a typical situation that you'll see around the world of people looking for reusable items, metals, and so on. Now, what they do is actually very beneficial to society, when we think about some of the environmental problems that we face and the wastage of resources, but what they do is really not valued at all.

Image 1.03: Women Carrying Firewood in Nepal.[12]

---

[11] Photograph: Marlenenapoli. https://commons.wikimedia.org/wiki/File:Agbogbloshie. JPG.

[12] Photograph: Engineering for Change. http://www.flickr.com/photos/44221799@ N08/4521897946/%22Flickr%E2%80%9D.

This is a scene where women are gathering wood for cooking. This is a scene that shows interconnectedness between livelihoods, the environment and people. Due to deforestation, there is less and less wood, and as a result, women spend more and more time looking for less and less wood. They use wood indoors for cooking, and that leads to smoke and lung ailments, and they send out girls to look for less and less wood, and as a result, girls don't go to school and get an education. As with many issues in subsistence marketplaces, choices are impacted by economics, by the environment, and by social aspects.

Image 1.04: Coffee Farmer Checks Latest Coffee Prices in Ethiopia.[13]

This is an optimistic image of a man in Ethiopia using a cell phone. It is amazing to see how people have adapted to different technologies, as long as it serves a useful purpose. People living in subsistence can communicate with missed calls because incoming calls are free, and sometimes entrepreneurs will close deals based on the number of rings. If there is one ring, it means "I agree to your price," and if it is two rings, it means "I don't agree," and so on.

The first of many relevant exercises interspersed throughout is below.

Exercise: Diary Entry

For this assignment, create your first-person profile and your broader impression of living in subsistence in the form of a diary entry. Focus not just

---

[13] Photograph: Pete Lewis and the Department for International Development. https://en.wikipedia.org/wiki/File:Knowledge_is_power_-_driving_a_hard_bargain_(5984450612).jpg.

on the economic realm as in product and market interactions, but more on life circumstances in subsistence where the marketplace is one part.

- Identify key life-changing circumstances.
- Reflect on what you learned about living in poverty – i.e., the types and nature of challenges that individuals have to face in different areas of subsistence such as food, etc.

Interviews can be found at our web portal.[14]

The Harsh Reality of Poverty

I have to first say that I have not experienced poverty, and I'm sure there are many readers who have. So keeping that in mind, how does somebody like me explain what poverty is based on my study of this whole area? I will describe a typical day today where I drove my car over to my university to teach. Everything I wanted worked very well. The roads worked fine, my car worked fine, my cellphone worked fine, and if something did not work, I always had a cushion; I had another way to achieve my goals.

But if I take away all that certainty, then I have poverty. If I'm uncertain about my next meal, I have poverty. **If I need to cook my next meal, but I don't know where the staple food is going to come from, if I don't know where the energy is going to come from, if I don't know the quality of the water with which I will cook, then I have poverty. Poverty is so much about uncertainty. And it is about the lack of a large margin of error or a cushion to fall back on.** So people in poverty have considerable uncertainty and not much room to stumble.

It comes down to the things we take for granted, the certainties we have in our lives. It comes down to the fallback options or things we have that cushion our fall during the down times. In poverty, there is simply little or no cushion in any tragedy that strikes. The very things we take for granted are missing in poverty – whether it be the larger infrastructure or institutional mechanisms, or basic necessities such as food and healthcare.

Poverty is about uncertainty on the most basic of dimensions. Such uncertainty is a chronic state of life that is exacerbated by transient shocks that occur during emergencies. In the face of the lack of cushion or fallback, outcomes can have a large downside. Thus, the risk involved in either unanticipated events or in actions taken can be large, in terms of negative outcomes.

---

[14] https://business.illinois.edu/subsistence/resources/resourcesmlp/: Use the password *subsistence* to access materials on the web portal.

The lack of cushioning of a fall makes the downside of actions quite significant. However, the chronic nature of uncertainty provides a push to take action. This constant tension between chronic and transient uncertainty creates the paradox of having everything to lose and having nothing to lose, rather than one versus the other. With very little to begin with, having everything to lose is a constant state of affairs. On the other hand, with such a large downside to small shocks to the system, getting out of the status quo appears like nothing to lose.

In such challenging conditions, we have the opportunity to create transformative solutions, such as the cell phone. For example, for me a cell phone is just a cell phone in most situations, but for somebody like an elderly woman in a remote village, it is much more. It can be a lifeline in the middle of the night when she has to call a doctor to find out what to do about her sick grandchild, and she lives in a village that is 30-40 miles away from a town with a doctor.

Image 1.05: Doing More With Less: Maasai Tribesmen in Tanzania.[15]

Here is an image that shows people doing a lot more with less as well. This is something else that we can learn from subsistence marketplaces, to do more with less, and that is a lesson that we all need.

---

[15] Photograph: Subsistence Marketplaces Initiative.

Exercise: Analysis of Buyers and Sellers

Read two more interviews covering buyers and sellers from our web portal[16] and write an analysis of the interviews. Your analysis may take one of the following forms:

- A comparison of people in all the interviews you have read
- A synopsis based on your inferences and interpretations of all the interviews
- A broader discussion of poverty based on the interviews
- Any direction you wish, highlighting turning points in lives, etc.

The Need for Sustainable Solutions

So why bother? Why do we care about people living in subsistence? In 2012, more than 2.1 billion people survived on less than $3.10 per day.[17] In 2011, more than 70% of the world's population lived on less than $10 per day.[18]

Considering the world's population, I was born in 1962, when the population of the world was about 3 billion. When I turned 50 (and it was actually exactly on the day I turned 50!), the official population of the world reached 7 billion. In about three decades, the population of the world will be about 9.5 billion. Many of the people who are going to be added to the world will be poor, trying to make it out of poverty.

That is one collision course we are on in terms of very basic needs such as drinking water and food and so on. And then we have environmental issues, natural resources and the harm that we may be doing to the environment in many ways; that is another collision course we are on. This book is really about these two challenges coming together and how we can try to solve some of the issues that arise.

---

[16] https://uiuc.qualtrics.com/jfe/form/SV_9Lz8nEapIPtIBxH: Use the password *subsistence* to access materials on the web portal.

[17] "Poverty Overview." Poverty Overview. Accessed April 21, 2016. http://www.worldbank.org/en/topic/poverty/overview.

[18] Kochhar, Rakesh. "Seven-in-ten People Globally Live on $10 or Less per Day." Pew Research Center RSS. 2015. Accessed April 21, 2016. http://www.pewresearch.org/fact-tank/2015/09/23/seven-in-ten-people-globally-live-on-10-or-less-per-day/.

Image 1.06: Poverty and Sustainability.

*People
Planet
Profit*

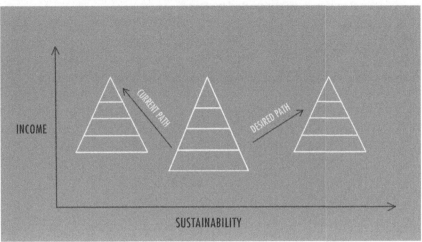

Now, here is an image of an income pyramid where people are coming out of poverty in countries like China and India on an unprecedented scale. But if they come out of poverty and imitate the way I consume, at the top of the pyramid, then we are in for really multiplying some of the disasters I talked about. **It is a very hypocritical thing to say, because I have the resources and I'm able to consume what I want, but at the same time, this is really necessary hypocrisy.** We have to talk about this because of the environmental issues we face. So what we need to do is to try to figure out a way to grow, to have people come out of poverty, but to do it in a sustainable way.

What do I mean by sustainability? You've heard a lot of definitions, such as how an initiative impacts people, planet, and profit. But we need to consider what is sustainable for people living at the bottom, for people living in subsistence. What is it that they are trying to sustain? It may be culture, livelihood, language, and so on, and we need to understand this as well. That is what we mean by a bottom-up approach.[19]

Exercise: Poverty Model   *People → Circumstances —Impli
cation*

Create an abstract diagram or conceptual map that expresses what you have learned from reading the interviews. This diagram should present the "big picture" about the lives of people in poverty (not just economic factors) and can take any form:

---

[19] As we note subsequently, this is also why our marketplace literacy program includes sustainability literacy.

- Causal diagram with boxes (with large category titles and a list of factors) and arrows supported by text
- A collage
- A more organic model

Take an angle and build a broader understanding beyond the individual interviews.

Chapter 2: Marketplace Perspectives

Next, we're going to look at how people live, think, cope, relate, and negotiate in the marketplace. We need to understand how people think before we can design solutions for them. Solutions that make perfect sense to us might make no sense at all in a different context. So we need to consider not only the person and the thinking, but the context as well. Such a holistic understanding will lead to more successful and satisfying interactions – on both ends – in subsistence marketplaces.

First, let's consider the thinking process of low-literate, low-income consumers and entrepreneurs.

Thinking in Subsistence Marketplaces

I want to start off with something I observed almost two decades ago. This was in a store in the United States, with a number of low-literate, low-income people. I asked them to buy five or six things for about $50. I will never forget my impression from what I saw then, which has not changed more than 15 years later. I was amazed at the things that I take for granted when I go through a store.

For example, when I'm in a store and need to buy something, I go in, I look through a few things, maybe two or three different brands of bread, and buy the one that I like. I trade off a few attributes and come up to the counter. If I don't have enough money, I'll put aside a product and I'll leave. But what I just described to you doesn't even begin to describe the experience of shoppers with a low level of literacy. Their shopping experience can be confusing, embarrassing, and time-consuming.

Low Literacy and Seemingly Mundane Tasks

Having enough money at the counter can be cause for celebration, and not having enough money can be cause for despair. I described how I may have forgotten a few things and left them behind, and that really is not a big deal for me; I forgot. But for people who do not have enough money at the counter and are low-literate, the issue is not that they forgot. The issue is that they cannot count, and they do not have enough literacy, and as a result, they are not attributing the lack of money to being forgetful but to not being literate. The simple task that I gave those shoppers, a task that I take for granted, was challenging and time-consuming for them.

For example, **locating a product can take a long time if I cannot read the product signs and do not want to ask somebody every time I need to find a** product. It can be frustrating and embarrassing to find a product – and once I find it, I may be so relieved that I simply put it in my cart. I may have used up all my energy just looking for the product, leaving little energy to try to figure out if it is the best product, the best price, and so on. Locating a final price on a price display, in fact, can be difficult as well. There are so many different prices – sale prices, percentage-off signs, and so on, and those numbers can be confusing if I am low-literate.

Low Literacy and Consumer Behavior – "The Things We Take for Granted"

The following observations are based on shopping trips with low-literate, low-income consumers.

- Considerable amount of effort is spent in basic tasks:
    - o Locating a product
    - o Locating a price display
    - o Locating the correct packages and volume
    - o Computing the price for two if the price for one is known
    - o Computing final prices based on percentage-off sale signs
    - o Computing total cost in a shopping trip
    - o Allowing for taxes
- Magnitudes not easily interpreted in terms of meaning
- Nutritional labels not understood
- Unit prices similarly not comprehended

Locating the correct packages can also be an issue. For example, if I need 150 candles, I need to find a package of 100 candles and a package of 50 candles. That sounds easy to you and me, but it can take a lot of effort for somebody who cannot read. Or if one product costs $1.50, how much does two cost? Often, people need to manually compute this, because they cannot add it up in their minds.

I once noticed a person stayed away from any product that had a percentage-off sale sign, and I asked him why. He said (paraphrasing), "I don't know how to compute, so if it is 70 percent off or 30 percent off, I don't know what the price is." If it is half off, he told me, maybe he can figure out the price, but he didn't seem sure even with that computation. So he stays away from all sales, and he said that it was humiliating to ask somebody at the counter what the final price is.

Computing the total cost on a shopping trip can be difficult. The way we conducted this research is by observing people and talking to them. We received people's permission to accompany them around the store, we observed them from a distance, and then we sat down and asked them some questions. I recall a person who seemed like a very safe shopper, until she provided a clue otherwise. She was checking everything she bought, and we had given her a $10 gift certificate for her participation in the research. She had about $30 to $40 dollars' worth of items in her cart, and she looked at me and said, "Will this be about $10?" So her problem was computing the total on a shopping trip.

Another concern is figuring out how to allow for taxes. Some low-literate people might say, "I don't know how much the tax is going to be, so I'm just going to say if I buy one thing, it is going to cost me $5; I hope I have enough money for the taxes." Magnitudes are not easily interpreted. If you ask me to buy something for $50, and let's say I had six items to buy for $50, and I bought one item for $1.50, in most cases I would know I have enough money for the remaining items. But low-literate people will oftentimes not be sure if they have enough for five more items.

And finally, low-literate people have trouble understanding nutrition labels and unit prices. Labels like sugar content are very abstract, and people don't know what exactly they mean. Unit prices are also very abstract. They relate to what the price per ounce is, and things like unit of measurement are difficult to follow as well.

Concrete Thinking

Low-literate people often use what we call concrete thinking or concrete reasoning. A low-literate person might say, "I look to see which costs the most and which costs less, and I just get the smaller one because it costs less." Now, that could be because that person is poor, and as a result he buys the cheapest item available. But then I ask, "Let's say you buy a packet of bread that is half the size. You are getting less bread for the money. How do you try to make sure it is the cheapest in terms of how much you are getting?" And he responds, "I just look at the tag and see what is cheapest. I don't look by their sizes."

So this is one of the issues with low literacy; people have difficulty abstracting between pieces of information, between price and size and synthesizing that information. If I've expended a lot of effort just to find where the bread is in the store, I'm just going to buy the cheapest. Because I have difficulty with abstractions, I engage in concrete thinking or concrete reasoning.

A Russian psychologist, Alexandr Luria,[20] conducted a study on low literacy in the 1920s. He showed peasants in Central Asia a hammer, a saw, and a hatchet and asked them for the word that describes them. The word that he was looking for was *tools*. This comes naturally to me, because I have literacy, I have a good education, and I know that a saw, a hatchet, and a hammer are tools. Now, the peasants responded by saying not the word *tools*, but by saying (and I paraphrase), "Well, if there are trees, then I can chop them and I can use firewood and I can keep my family warm." So they thought in terms of the immediate visual graphic world of here and now, and "How can I use something," rather than in terms of the concepts that are represented by words like hammers and saws and hatchets. That is what we mean by concrete thinking.

So if I'm low-literate and I'm in a high-tech store and I need to buy something and I see all this complex information coming at me – price and calories and all of that – how do I negotiate through the store? I buy the cheapest item that I need.

In a tribal community in Tanzania, women sometimes spoke of buying the largest item, as they had a 20-mile walk to the marketplace once a week. Running out of things was a big concern. However, combining different pieces of information such as price and size was still difficult.

Now, concrete thinking manifests itself in different ways. For example, interest rates are an abstraction. I do not know how to compute a particular interest rate, and I don't know what it means to me, and so, very often, non-collateral loans are described in terms of number of rupees or number of dollars or whatever the currency may be.

Health or healthiness is also an abstraction. What does healthiness mean to somebody who is low-literate? Well, it may just mean something as concrete and extreme as not being in the hospital. Nutrition is an abstraction; a nutritious product can be something quite abstract. We really need to understand some of the things that we take for granted, and realize that low-literate people think more concretely, and design solutions accordingly.

The notion of a business or an enterprise can be an abstraction. What people understand intuitively is exchange. And the notion of a value chain, where I buy from a supplier far away from me and sell to someone far away, can be an abstraction as well.

This is not a matter of being more intelligent or less intelligent. There are many low-literate people who are very intelligent, very resourceful. They

---

[20] Luria, A. R. *Cognitive Development, Its Cultural and Social Foundations*. Cambridge, MA: Harvard University Press, 1976.

simply did not have access to a good education. As a result, they live through these constraints, within which they do the best they can.

The notion of concreteness here refers to how information is combined to reach a higher-level abstraction. But we can also think about other aspects, such as knowing what to do versus why, or understanding cause and effect at different levels of abstraction. For instance, a symptom such as numbness in the arm may indicate a deeper health issue that is often difficult for low-literate, low-income people to grasp. In other words, there is sometimes "flat" cause-and-effect thinking at a concrete level. Similarly, people may know what to do and how, but articulating why may be more difficult. In fact, this notion could be pushed further. If I grew up in essentially random circumstances, then why would I believe that if I do this, it will lead to this? If I live in day-to-day uncertainty, then why would I believe that planning will cause better outcomes?

Image 2.01: Concrete Thinking: Focusing on Price, Not Size.[21]

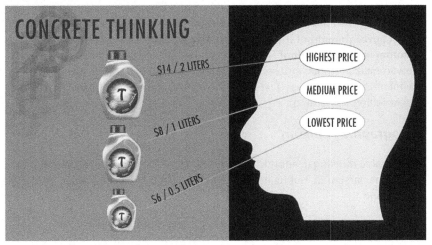

Thus, concrete thinking is relevant in many aspects - in what information is gathered, in how information is combined, in how cause and effect is inferred, in knowing how versus why something is done a particular way, and in how goals are set.

Ultimately, it comes down to lack of exposure wherein, say, the notion of a business that spans across wide geographies or that buys from one place and sells elsewhere becomes relatively abstract and difficult to envision. Education and relative affluence enable exposure and thinking across spatial

---

[21] Image: Bob Dignan, Christina Tarn, and Killivalavan Solai for the Subsistence Marketplaces Initiative.

boundaries, across time, across different peoples, and across different settings and scenarios – some imaginary as well. On the other hand, people in subsistence marketplaces who lack exposure elsewhere may run circles around outsiders in terms of their local expertise.

In the entrepreneurial context, this issue is related to the notion of understanding what an enterprise is beyond intuitive notions of exchange. Thinking beyond the immediate in terms of time frame, spatial, social, and possible versus real are some ways to consider it. Can I envision my enterprise six months from now? Or in terms of how it will grow? Can I envision my enterprise buying and selling in spatially-dispersed ways in a spatially-dispersed value chain? Can I envision my enterprise transacting with others who are not like me? Can I envision scenarios that are not real but possible?

The notion of what is abstract can be surprising for those of us who take it for granted. One women who took our marketplace literacy education has now started comparing prices across shops and become a more informed customer. **When I asked why she bought in the past without checking, she said, "I never thought of myself as a *customer*." Indeed, the notion of a customer is an abstraction!** This notion comes with rich and related concepts of awareness of rights, and self-confidence, and skills. But to a low-literate, low-income person, it may just be about buying something (from someone who is selling something).

Pictographic Thinking

Pictographic thinking is another form of thinking. For example, a person told me that he can count, but he cannot read. He also told me he always buys the same brand.

> **Consumer:** *When you go back to the store, you look and see oh, this is the brand I bought before – I ain't gonna get this, I'm gonna get that other one.*
>
> **Interviewer:** *How do you tell that it's the brand you bought before?*
>
> **Consumer:** *Ain't nothing wrong with my eyes.*

This was a very good response, because the brand name, for that person, is an image or an object in a scene. It is not a word to be read; it is a bunch of wiggly signs and colors that this man remembers as an image.

Some people describe this as sight-reading; they just look at a word and remember it as an image. Some people can navigate from one town to another, even two or three hours away, and drive through the streets of both towns without being able to read a single sign. This is pictographic thinking. What you see is what you get. You rely on your sensory ability – in this case, the visual sense.

If my literacy level is very low, I cannot even read numerals. Now, that is quite rare, because typically people can tell a higher number from a lower number, no matter how low their literacy is. I recall one young woman who served tea from a teashop to a factory nearby and was paid Rs. 500 in five one-hundred rupee bills as a monthly salary. One month, she received one five-hundred-rupee bill and started crying because she thought her salary had been cut. This is among the lowest levels of literacy I have encountered. Usually, people are able to use numerals and know which is higher and which is lower.

If I cannot read numerals and I have to catch a bus, I look at the shape of the bus and at the shape of the number of the bus rather than read the bus's number. So here comes bus 17A, and it looks like bus number 17, and I get on it and I go to the wrong place.

Image 2.02: Pictographic Thinking: Pattern Matching to Select a Bus for Travel.[22]

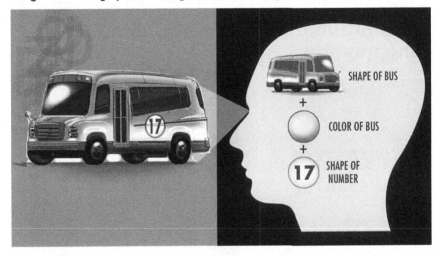

Pictographic thinking also means that people come up with ingenious ways to add and subtract while they are shopping. One woman who had very little education found an ingenious way to try to add and subtract to keep track of the total in her shopping basket. As she went through the store, she pictured about ten $5 bills in her mind, and every time she bought something, she would take a $5 bill off. To her, adding and subtraction with symbols are abstract. She doesn't know how to add and subtract, but she can manipulate images in her mind. That is what we mean by pictographic thinking.

_____
[22] Ibid.

Image 2.03: Pictographic Thinking While Shopping.[23]

Image 2.04: Pictographic "Adding" While Shopping.

Pictographic Thinking – "Adding" While Shopping

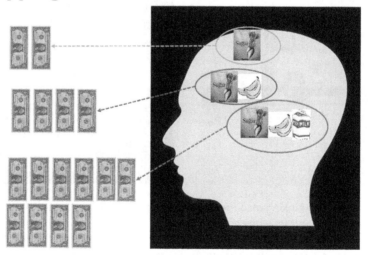

By pictographic thinking, we also mean that I'm not going to look at the amount of sugar to buy or the amount of salt to buy, because those units of measurement are abstract. I'm going to imagine how I'll use the sugar, I'm going to imagine myself pouring the sugar when I'm baking a cake, I'm going

---

[23] Ibid.

to imagine how much sugar I poured, and I'm going to buy the package that corresponds to the amount of sugar that I pictured in my mind.

That is pictographic thinking. If you want to understand people living in subsistence and design solutions for them, you have to understand how they think, and you have to adapt to it. They think concretely and they think pictographically. In many ways, I think I'm not well qualified to try to design a solution for people living in subsistence, simply because of the amount of education I've been fortunate to receive. So I have to try to think the way somebody living in subsistence does, even for a short time, to try to design solutions.

Exercise: Comparing and Contrasting Consumer Thinking

How is thinking among low-literate consumers different from the way you think as a consumer? Write your comparisons and contrasts into 3-4 bullet points.

Feeling in Subsistence Marketplaces

We discussed how people think; but what about how people feel? As I described earlier, if I don't have enough money at the counter, it is not a big deal to me, but for somebody who is low-literate, they feel that they have been exposed in front of everybody for their low literacy, and it can be devastating.

People who are low-literate do all they can to maintain their self-esteem through shopping encounters. They may be willing to pay a little bit more if they are treated kindly, if there is a friendly relationship in the store rather than the store manager saying, "Just buy what you want and get out of here." So the relationship matters to them, and they may be willing to pay a little bit more because they are respected. Here is a quote from a low-literate woman on how she felt in a shop:

> *So, how to make the purchases if I go to a shop? How to ask the seller? How much would they say the price is? Should I ask the rate or price first, or should I ask about the item or product? These are all problems. If I had studied well, up to eighth standard or grade... You see, sometimes they ask me what my educational qualification is. I feel bad. I wouldn't have such feelings if I had studied. I could state my qualifications proudly. All this happens only because I have no education, doesn't it? I agonize about why I didn't study, about why my family did not provide me the education. I have such feelings. I have fears due to lack of education, you see, that they may ask me something at the store,*

I mean they would ask me the rate, state the price of a particular item. We don't know how to repeat it and we don't know how to speak about money. I have such fears.

Low-literate people are typically very passive in the marketplace, and they sometimes are willing to pay more rather than be exposed for their low literacy. They are willing to ask a question, but they are afraid, because if they are asked a question in return, they might not know how to answer it. So there is a big difference between somebody who is poor and low-literate and somebody who is poor and has some level of literacy. Feelings and self-esteem may be involved in the most mundane of buying tasks, something that may not even occur to those who are relatively affluent and educated. In one's own town or city, people may hesitate to go to larger stores for fear of being exposed for their low literacy and low income. Emotions of fear and shame are close to the surface in shopping encounters.

The issue of feeling and emotional constraints was brought home to us starkly in a refugee settlement in Uganda. Here, the issue is more than subsistence, it is poverty following tragic events, and violence against those near and dear to oneself. This can mean dreading thinking of the past and the future, bringing on emotional constraints in addition to cognitive constraints. The same happens in a less extreme way in other subsistence contexts where there are emotional constraints to dwelling on a very difficult past or in hoping for a much better future that may be beyond reach. We have seen this in how subsistence consumers process advertisements, filtering out things beyond their purchasing power for purposes of consideration, while still being entertained by them. Thus, emotional constraints can lead to cognitive focus on the immediate as well.

Exercise: Comparing and Contrasting Consumer Feeling

How is the feeling among low-literate consumers when something does not work in the marketplace (like not having enough money at the counter) different from the way you feel as a consumer? Write your comparisons and contrasts into 3-4 bullet points.

Coping in Subsistence Marketplaces

How do people cope? Given the way they think and they feel, and the very difficult experiences they have, how do they cope? Well, they use many strategies, some of which are ingenious. For example, we talked about a woman who pictured $5 bills as she shopped, taking away a bill in her mind as she put an item in her cart.

One person we talked to told us, "My daughter did all the shopping, and when I was a daughter my mom did the shopping." As a result of her low literacy, she delegated the shopping responsibilities to her daughter or to her mother. And the same person whom we met earlier, who talked about being able to count but not read, who bought the same brand by just looking at the brand rather than reading it, has a different way to cope in trying to hide the fact that he cannot read. He usually tells somebody, "You know what, I don't have my glasses. I cannot see, so can you read this out for me?" So he comes up with a different way to cope as well.

This is how consumers and entrepreneurs think, feel, and cope in subsistence marketplaces. They may give up money and economic value to preserve their self-esteem and to go to a shop where somebody is friendly. And finally, in terms of coping, people come up with various ways – some rudimentary rules, depending on others, and so on – to cope. Buying one item at a time from a menu, approximating five dollars per purchase, buying small quantities, and so forth are some of the many rudimentary rules that people come with for themselves.

Image 2.05: Thinking, Feeling, and Coping in Subsistence Marketplaces.[24]

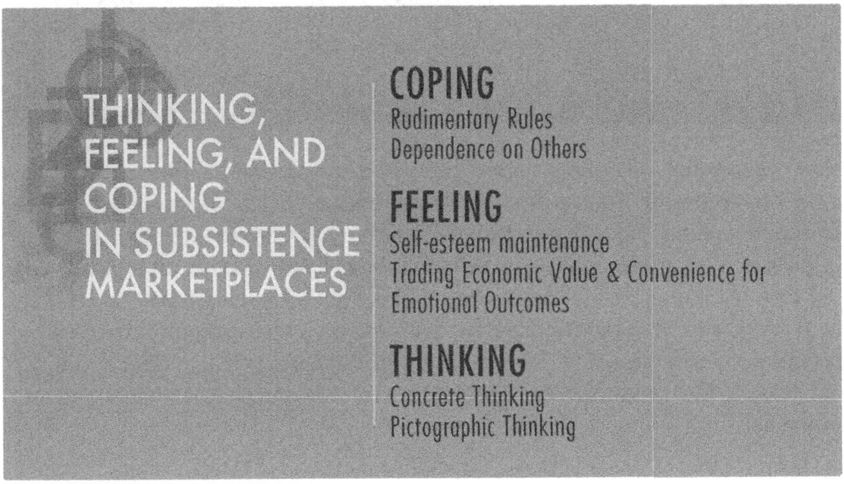

THINKING,
FEELING, AND
COPING
IN SUBSISTENCE
MARKETPLACES

COPING
Rudimentary Rules
Dependence on Others

FEELING
Self-esteem maintenance
Trading Economic Value & Convenience for
Emotional Outcomes

THINKING
Concrete Thinking
Pictographic Thinking

[24] Ibid.

Subsistence Consumers and Entrepreneurs

Image 2.06: Neighborhood Retail Store in a Rural Village in Tamil Nadu, India.[25]

Next, we discuss subsistence consumers and entrepreneurs. Here is a picture of a neighborhood retail store and a large reseller. If I live in a poor urban community, I may have the choice of either buying from the neighborhood retailer or a large reseller. The large reseller has lower prices, but typically will not give me credit, and is two or three miles away. The neighborhood retailer is much closer, has higher prices, but will also give me credit and charge a bit more for offering credit. The neighborhood retailer will also offer some services. One of those services is to secure money and charge a small fee for doing so.

---

[25] Photograph: Anne McKinney for the Subsistence Marketplaces Initiative.

Image 2.07: Large Reseller in a Flower Market, Chennai, India.[26]

Now, this may seem strange, but if I'm a poor woman and I live in this neighborhood, I may need to secure the money from an alcoholic husband or from a thief, because I live in a hut. My choice in this setting is to buy either from the neighborhood retailer or the large reseller – and I often will choose the neighborhood store for the advantages it offers, even though it will cost me a bit more.

Marketplace Relationships

I'm going to give you an extreme example to illustrate a point about marketplace relationships. Here is a woman who buys from the neighborhood retailer on credit. The shopkeeper maintains a record of her purchases, and he marks a price on certain products, particularly generic products like eggs and so on, because he knows that he is giving her credit as well. I asked this woman if she checks prices at the neighborhood retail store, and she gave me a very surprising answer. She said, "No, imagine how the store owner would feel if I checked prices."

Now, why is that? Well, if I am from the outside and I'm looking in, I'm going to say, "Wait a minute, you shouldn't be buying there. That is not rational. You

---

[26] Ibid.

should save up at the beginning of the month and you should stock up on items by going to the large reseller. That is the rational thing to do."

Well, here is the problem. I may be an expert on many things, but I'm not an expert on how to live in a subsistence context. She is an expert on survival, and so when I go into this setting, one of the first things I need to do is to put aside what I think is rational, what I think is right, or how I should behave based on what I'm used to. **I have to be willing to adopt a *mutual learning mindset* and to acknowledge that the people living there are experts in survival.**

So let's go back to what I said. I said it is rational to go to the large reseller at the beginning of the month and buy all that you want and stock up, but actually that is not the rational thing to do. Why? Well, the time frame of monthly assumes that I get regular income at the beginning of the month, and that may not be the case. Stocking up may be the last thing that a poor person in this neighborhood wants to do. Why? Because if I stock up and I have a much bigger need, maybe a health emergency, maybe my child's school fees, I am willing (and have the resilience) to starve, but I have to pay my child's school fees, and so stocking up is not the answer. It is not the rational thing to do for somebody who is surviving.

And finally, if I have to buy at the large reseller, what do I do? Well, I walk past the neighborhood retailer, go to the large reseller, buy the things I need, and come back. Now the neighborhood retailer is going to call me and say, "Well, repay my loan, don't come back for credit, and you can buy wherever you want."[27] Now what happens when I have my next crisis? I'm not going to get credit from the large reseller. So even though I'm poor and low-literate, and even though I engage in concrete thinking and pictographic thinking and so on, I have to think about relationships in the medium term. I have to think about the next crisis, and I have to live my life planning from one crisis to the next. That is why the woman feels that the relationship with the neighborhood retailer is more important than checking prices.

Again, this is a very different way of thinking, and this is why it is so important to have a mutual learning mindset. We go in assuming we don't know, and we try to understand the person's context. Once we do that, we can try to figure out what is new and what is not. Everything you learn there will not be new, but when you go in and try to understand, keep an open mind and don't assume you know what is right.

In this context, buyers and sellers are two sides of the same coin, so a small buyer learns about being a small seller when he or she goes shopping. Sometimes, for the buyers, a way out is to be sellers themselves, and so they learn, they share adversity. Consumption and entrepreneurship are

---

[27] If the shopkeeper is kind, he may say, "Buy a few things here and a few things there."

closely intertwined, blurred. One (entrepreneurship) happens due to extreme constraints in the other (consumption). Moreover, individuals consume what they produce or what is left over from their enterprise or from what they produce.

This is not a relationship where people are buying from a large company. They are buying from others who are similar to them, so elements such as trust become extremely important. We also see this in the context of farmers and intermediaries they know who lend money in times of need and who take ownership of crops.

The notion of buying from someone you know comes naturally in a setting where the one-on-one human relationship and trust are paramount. We see this in tribal communities in East Africa as we do in rural parts of Latin America. Relationships sustain in these settings. When teaching marketplace literacy, we emphasize how participants can get cheated. They, in turn, often point out the need to buy from one shop, to develop the relationship. While we don't want them to be cheated, the point is well taken, relationships are central. We caution them to be aware of prices in general while maintaining their relationships, in other words, be informed in carrying out their roles as customers.

Negotiating the Marketplace Environment

Image 2.08: An Emphasis on Relationships – Buyers and Sellers as Two Sides of the Same Coin.[28]

Buyers and Sellers as Two Sides of the Same Coin

---

[28] Photographs: Darrell Hoemann for the Subsistence Marketplaces Initiative.

Many one-on-one interactions happen in the marketplace. In this context, what does a subsistence entrepreneur do? I use the term *subsistence entrepreneur* very deliberately. **These are people with few resources who do amazing things. They may not produce a product that is new to the world, but they are amazing in how they use resources. They are "means entrepreneurs."**

Image 2.09: A Subsistence Entrepreneur Makes Pickles to Sell.[29]

How does a subsistence entrepreneur go about negotiating the environment? In the image above, you see a woman who makes pickles, and that actually is almost her entire house. It is the main room, and there is a small kitchen on the other side, and she makes pickles and packs them and sells them in the neighborhood and to stores. In doing so, she has to manage a number of different domains or entities. She has to manage her customers; some of them may want to buy on credit, and some of them are storeowners, and these relationships have to be managed. She has to manage her suppliers and make sure she gets ingredients to make the pickles, and she has to manage her family as well. She does this by having her family as her cushion. She might say, "I'm going to make sure and pay the supplier and get my supplies. If the customer wants credit, the customer gets credit and the family suffers. That is why I'm in business, in order to survive, and so the family has to suffer."

But along comes an emergency where the family is scrambling for a child's school fees or for hospital fees, and at that point the entrepreneur goes to the supplier to ask for credit or goes to the customer and says, "I cannot give you credit anymore. You really need to pay up because I have an emergency."

---

[29] Photograph: Subsistence Marketplaces Initiative.

So the entrepreneur is constantly moving resources between these three domains of family and suppliers and customers.

The reason I went into this in detail is to show you how important it is to have bottom-up understanding. It is so important to go beneath terms like social capital and marketplace negotiations and understand what is going on. For example, microfinancing institutions often talk about the need to make sure that the money they lend to entrepreneurs is used for the business. That is a valid and understandable point. But money doesn't stay in separate compartments; resources move between these domains of family, supplier, and customer. Resources are fungible, and they are moved around these different domains, and it is important to understand this when designing solutions. **In fact, the very notion of compartments assumes resources – for example, with resources, I can compartmentalize my physical surroundings, my mental activities, my typical day, and so forth.**

One-size-fits-all is not going to suit this entrepreneur. This entrepreneur needs flexibility, and very often the community lenders are able to give her that flexibility. They know her life circumstances, and they are not going to say, "You have to follow this one set of rules." They are going to bend and make sure that their lending works for her. So this is something to keep in mind as well. Moneylenders in the same community, such as women who lend to other women, may be more understanding, as they see each other in a variety of day-to-day situations and share adversity.

Image 2.10: Subsistence Entrepreneurs – Managing Family, Suppliers, and Customers.[30]

---

[30] Photograph: Darrell Hoemann for the Subsistence Marketplaces Initiative.

Subsistence Marketplaces in Action

How do these marketplaces work? Let's look at exchanges, the relational environment in terms of people relating to others, and the larger context. Exchanges have many aspects: there is a constant demand for customization, there are fluid transactions, and buyers and sellers are quite responsive.

Image 2.11: Exchanges in Subsistence Marketplaces.[31]

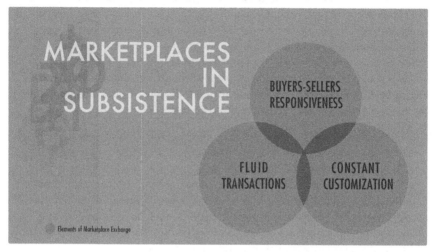

Exchanges: Customized Transactions

Here is an example of constant customization. A woman who runs an enterprise points out that if somebody asks for a different price, she can say that the item or the product can be different but there is no difference in the price. Why is that? "We can't encourage this, others may follow it," she says. "They may go and announce to others that she is changing her prices."

What she is saying is that you have to be careful about customizing the price for each and every person. Everybody is going to ask you for a special deal and a special product and so on. If you do give them a special deal, it is good to have a reason for it. Maybe it is somebody who is extremely poor or who is elderly or who bought a lot of volume, and so on, but otherwise, if you don't have a reason for providing a special deal, everybody is going to come and ask for it.

In this particular person's case, she also sells in installments, and once in a while somebody would take possession and not pay her some of the

---

[31] Image: Bob Dignan, Christina Tarn, and Killivalavan Solai for the Subsistence Marketplaces Initiative.

installments. She goes to the buyer's house and says, "You must pay." The buyer says, "I won't pay," and an argument ensues. Whether the buyer pays or not, the entrepreneur cannot just say, "Well, never mind," because everybody else will start doing the same thing. So she needs to adhere to some general principles in spite of this tremendous pressure to customize.

At times, she has to customize as well, and this is what we mean by constant customization. In the case of the woman who makes pickles, a number of stores come to her and say, "You are giving us very little pickle. I know you are packing in these particular quantities, but the people in our neighborhood are construction workers. They only eat once a day. Give us more pickles." So she says, "Well, you know what, I'll try to figure something out for you, all right?" And she packs a little bit more pickle every time she supplies to them. Now, the word can get out, but she has to customize a little bit so that they can survive as well and they can have a good product.

Exchanges: Fluid Transactions

Transactions are very fluid. To give you an example, one entrepreneur says, "It is the same price. I would have given them a bit more quantity; that is why I quoted a slightly higher price."

You can try this out, where you go and bargain heavily and try to buy a pound or a kilogram of grapes. Sometimes when you weigh it elsewhere, you may not get what you bargained for, literally. So, you may not get your pound of grapes, and then if you go back and ask the shopkeeper and say, "You know what, you didn't give me a pound, you gave me less than a pound." The shopkeeper may say, "Well, that is the weighing you'll get for the price that you bargained. You bargained a very good price, so I weighed it a little differently." Similarly, installments may not be paid if the product stops functioning. So much is decided on the spot and varies from day to day or even hour to hour.

Exchanges: Responsive Transactions

In this one-on-one environment, buyers and sellers are often responsive to each other. It is not the type of relationship where a buyer deals with a large organization. A seller says, "If they prefer a particular brand, I'll buy it and keep it in stock. I would arrange it immediately. I will notice it in the morning, I'll rush immediately and make arrangements to have the parcel ready within the evening."

While buyers and sellers are responsive to each other, that doesn't mean that there is no exploitation. Quite the opposite – there is a lot of exploitation. Sometimes there is just one store in a remote village, and whatever the storekeeper says goes. Or a storekeeper is very well connected to the political power structure. But there is also some responsiveness, because, if you want to engage a small group of customers whom you see every day, you have to be responsive as well. When you are so close to where the people live, some degree of responsiveness becomes essential.[32]

Relational Environment: Enduring Relationships

In terms of the relational environment, there are two things to keep in mind: relationships tend to be enduring at a one-on-one level, and there is what we call interactional empathy.

Here is an example of enduring relationships. A customer says, "We will not change the shop. We will buy in a single shop. The things in the shop will be good. We will boldly go and ask if these things are not good. For me, he'll give the best goods after weighing. I would say 'I am buying it from you continuously, how can you give me this?'"

A poor customer multiplies her value through these small purchases by buying from the same store. As a result, she may get credit or other special consideration, and it helps her small seller as well, because that seller knows that she will have definite business from this particular customer.

So that is what we mean by enduring relationships. Noteworthy is that even though they possess very little, subsistence entrepreneurs have the ability to adapt and be flexible in offering services, a potential strength in competing with much more well-financed alternatives.

That doesn't mean that enduring relationships exist in every setting. If I'm a small flower seller and I go to a large wholesale market that deals with big shops, they may not give me the time of day. But in a one-on-one interactional setting within a neighborhood or between small sellers and small buyers, people emphasize enduring relationships.

Such relationships may lead to cheating as well. As noted earlier, during our educational programs, we ask participants to be aware and informed without taking away from forming mutually beneficial relationships.

---

[32] To view videos related to buyers and sellers, please visit our web portal at https://business.illinois.edu/subsistence/resources/resourcesmlp/: Use the password *subsistence* to access materials.

Image 2.12: Relationships in Subsistence Marketplaces.

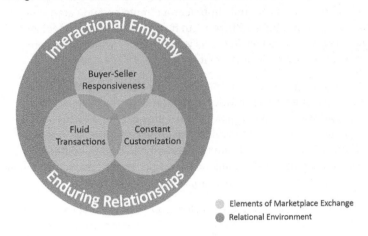

Relational Environment: Interactional Empathy

Interactional empathy is illustrated by this particular flower sell who says, "Business is important, but the human being is more important." What do we mean by this? First, understand that this is a very harsh environment. We are not trying to paint a rosy picture or romanticize poverty. We are saying that marketplace exchanges and relationships become blurred. It is really about relating human being to human being.

Image 2.13: The Larger Context of Marketplaces in Subsistence.[33]

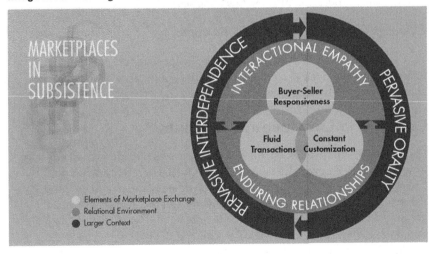

---

[33] Image: Bob Dignan, Christina Tarn, and Killivalavan Solai for the Subsistence Marketplaces Initiative.

We often hear this argument in bargaining: "You have to make a living; I have to make a living." If I have a coconut shop near a temple and you start one right next to me, I'll start a fight with you, but if you start a shop 50 feet away, I'll say, "Well, you have to make a living as well." In other words, there are norms about what is acceptable and what is not.

People are not engaging in the marketplace for some abstract principles of competition. They often don't know or understand abstract principles. Moreover, these principles are perhaps a luxury they cannot afford. They are engaged in the marketplace to survive. Nevertheless, there are norms of behavior at a human level. So they don't necessarily discern the difference between the economic and the human; those two get blurred as well, and that is what we are conveying through the term, *interactional empathy*.

In subsistence marketplaces, there are no clear compartments between the economic and the social. As discussed earlier, to have compartments requires resources, whether in terms of physical compartments such as how we organize our homes and workplaces or mental compartments in how we think about things.

Larger Context: Interdependence and Oral Communications

Finally, all of this is happening in the larger context of pervasive interdependence and pervasive oral communications. Everything in the marketplace plays out in this larger context. People are very dependent on each other and are continuously communicating with one another, whether face to face or, more recently, over cell phones.

Exercise: Transactions and Relationships

How are the transactions and relationships in subsistence marketplaces different from the ones you are used to? Write your comparisons and contrasts into 3-4 bullet points.

Comparing Low-Income Contexts

Having discussed how people think, feel, cope, and engage in marketplaces, it is interesting to compare consumer skills in the United States with developing contexts where there is more extreme and widespread poverty. In the US, there is quite a bit of low literacy and poverty, but the poverty is not as extreme. In developing contexts, people interact and learn to negotiate in a one-on-one marketplace. They learn to count verbally as they buy generic products, called *mouth arithmetic* in some places, and they are themselves often vendors as well. They have very severe income constraints – so if they don't make the right decision, they won't get their next meal.

Image 2.14: In-Depth Interviews, Tamil Nadu, India.[34]

In comparison, in the US, people deal with large stores, with technology that is difficult for them, and there is a lot of symbolic information on packages that assumes a certain level of literacy. So, ironically, what we find is that for, say, a second-grade-educated person in a developing country versus the US, the person in the former may be more functionally literate in the marketplace (have higher marketplace literacy), because they can learn through their one-on-one interactions. In the US, because of these large stores and the technology and the information that assumes a certain level of literacy, people may have a very difficult time improving their skills in the marketplace. People in the US who are low-literate can become quite isolated as well.

Now, obviously we are speculating and making a sweeping generalization based on our experience. There are differences between the urban US and the rural US as well as urban, semi-urban, rural, and tribal settings in developing countries. But it is quite ironic that you can be more functionally literate in the marketplace when you can rely on others and have a rich social network when compared to a more advanced economy with a well-developed infrastructure and institutional mechanisms where poverty is not as extreme. People in subsistence marketplaces are, of course, resource-poor, but may be quite rich in terms of social relationships and networks, which help develop skills.

---

[34] Photograph: Subsistence Marketplaces Initiative.

What are the differences and similarities between low-literate, low-income consumers in the US and subsistence consumers in developing countries? Write your comparisons and contrasts into 3-4 bullet points.

Needs & Products, Relationships, and Markets

What do we know about needs and products, relationships, and markets in subsistence? A key element of poverty is, of course, resource constraints. By definition, that is what poverty is, and that is what living in subsistence is. As a result of resource constraints, people lack the ability to buy many products, yet they need to fulfill their basic needs: water, food, shelter, and so on.

Needs and Products: Bettering Life Circumstances

In a subsistence context, people may produce their own soap and medicine, rather than buy these items, as they cannot afford to. Sometimes they make their own because they find packaged products are stale. For example, they may make spices on their own, and that allows them to make it cheaper and fresher and to customize it for different members of the family.

Making your own, when possible, can be a better option for many reasons, although it can take considerable effort. We find that people in many countries are slowly moving away from making to buying, and products that were sold in a generic way, wrapped in a newspaper or a leaf, are now sold in packages as well. Soap may be one of the first things that tribal communities buy when they come in contact periodically with marketplaces.

In addition to making or buying, somebody who is poor has the resilience to forgo. If they cannot afford it, they're going to forgo, even if it means they have to starve. The ability to forgo is counterintuitive in relatively resource-rich settings. It means a poor customer has the resilience to forgo and will not waste resources on a product that is not of good quality, unless she has no choice, and very often she doesn't have a choice.

When you take these three aspects of needs and products – lack of affordability, immediacy of basic needs, and making versus buying versus forgoing – it all boils down to the idea that, at the product level, it is really about bettering life circumstances. That is what a product has to be about, bettering life circumstances. This means we have to first, understand life circumstances, and second, we have to think about product offerings in a broader way to see if they can really better these life circumstances. We will discuss this issue in greater detail when we delve into how we design solutions.

Image 2.15: Enterprises in Subsistence Marketplaces: Products.[35]

Exercise: Developing a Model of Needs, Products, and Market Interactions

Use the variety of material in the web portal.[36] Graph a model that captures categories of needs, categories of products that satisfy these needs, and market interactions. Focus on buyers, sellers, needs, products, and markets. Categorize needs as you see fit, ranging from the physiological to the spiritual.

If you wish to display additional elements beyond these three circles that help you express yourself, please feel free to do so.

Relationships: The Human Dimension in the Marketplace

In terms of relationships, the resource constraints lead to interdependence among people. The woman you met earlier who buys from the neighborhood retail store builds on that relationship because she gets help in times of need, and buying from the same store helps that storeowner as well. Interdependence is pervasive in these settings. As we saw earlier, **marketplace relationships are strongly influenced by one-on-one interactions and word-of-mouth. People quickly develop consumer skills as they interact one-on-one in the marketplace.**

---

[35] Image: Bob Dignan, Christina Tarn, and Killivalavan Solai for the Subsistence Marketplaces Initiative.

[36] https://business.illinois.edu/subsistence/resources/resourcesmlp/: Use the password *subsistence* to access materials on the web portal.

This places great emphasis on the human dimension. People don't isolate the economics from the human or the business from the social. It is really about the human dimension. That is what the relationships are about, and that means fairness and trust and similar values are very important. It means that when you design a solution, you have to be trustworthy, and you have to think about how to improve individual and community welfare in order to be trusted. Can I trust you? Will you be fair to me? These are the types of questions that you will have to answer.

Image 2.16: Enterprises in Subsistence Marketplaces: Relationships.[37]

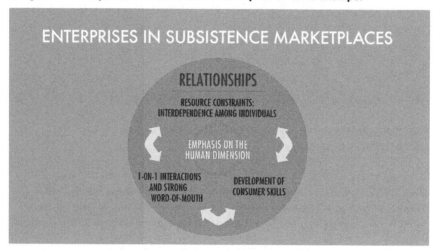

Markets: Negotiating the Social Milieu

Moving to markets, there are resource constraints and dependence and lack of mobility, even in an urban area. If I buy from a neighborhood retail store, there is a dependence there, and it is hard for me to buy at some other place because it costs me to move from one place to the other. In a rural setting that dependence is even more accentuated, as I have to think about the stores or often the one store or reseller around me and buy from there because the nearest town is 20 or 30 or 50 miles away.

There are many fragmented and distinct small markets. Each village can be quite different from villages around it, each cluster of villages can be quite different from others, and group influences vary from marketplace to marketplace. The primary influence might be the local authority, the social class, or the NGOs that are operating there. So it is important to know how to negotiate the social milieu.

---

[37] Image: Bob Dignan, Christina Tarn, and Killivalavan Solai for the Subsistence Marketplaces Initiative.

You cannot separate the complex social milieu from the marketplace. It is important to work with different groups when you are designing solutions, just as it is important to consider the social good, the good for the community, as the common denominator that these different groups can relate to.

Image 2.17: Enterprises in Subsistence Marketplaces: Markets.[38]

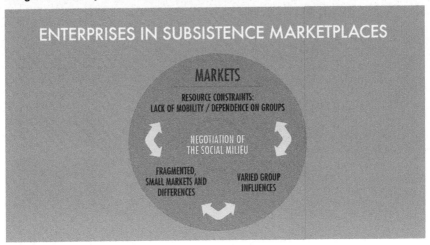

Summary

To summarize, products are about betterment of life circumstances, which means we have to understand life circumstances and we have to think about offerings that really improve those life circumstances. Relationships are about emphasizing the human dimension. This means, "Do I trust you? Are you going to be fair to me? Are you going to leave without telling me?" And it means we need to emphasize individual and community welfare. Finally, markets blur into the social milieu, which means we have to learn how to work with very different groups and view social good as the common denominator.

---

[38] Ibid.

Local Environments in Subsistence

Image 2.18: What Bottom-Up Insights About Subsistence Marketplaces Mean for Enterprise-Level Processes.[39]

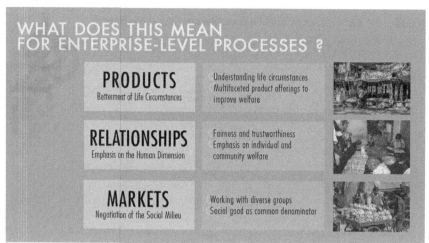

People living in subsistence face many environmental challenges, occurring at different distances. Some are immediate, right in the household or the workplace. Some are at a near distance, such as within the neighborhood. Some are farther away, at a societal level. And some are even more distant – global issues such as climate change and so on. We will discuss how people try to cope and gain some control over their local environment. Finally, we discuss what people try to sustain in their day-to-day lives.

---

[39] Image: Bob Dignan, Christina Tarn, and Killivalavan Solai for the Subsistence Marketplaces Initiative. Photographs 1 and 3: Darrell Hoemann; Photograph 2: Subsistence Marketplaces Initiative.

Image 2.19: Pollution in the Alamar River in Mexico.[40]

This image shows how the local environment is intertwined with day-to-day living. Unlike in resource-rich settings where environmental issues can be compartmentalized, people in subsistence live in the day-to-day environment. Throwing out plastic bags means the sewage will be blocked, which means disease in the neighborhood.

Image 2.20: Displaced Persons Outside a Temporary Shelter in Kibati Camp, Rubavu, Province de l'Ouest, Rwanda.[41]

---

[40] Photograph: Romel Jacinto. http://www.flickr.com/photos/37degrees/3481734401/.

[41] Photograph: Julien Harneis. http://www.flickr.com/photos/julien_harneis/302740941.

You see in this image that what people do in their local setting affects their environment as well. With respect to environmental issues in subsistence contexts, people often face a difficult trade-off between consuming for the immediate, like firewood, and conserving for the longer term. Consuming firewood for the immediate means deforestation. Sometimes, there are norms to not cut trees that are green within a community, to conserve for the longer term. People rely on the environment to live and they know what it means to harm the environment. It is amazing how, in subsistence contexts, people do so much with so little, finding ways to cope with a lack of resources. They reuse materials and use the natural resources in ingenious ways.

Learning About Subsistence Environments

Going into a subsistence environment, we are not the experts. The people who live there are. We need to learn from them about the issues they face. In our years in the field, we have gained marketplace insights about the environment and subsistence by asking people about:

- The problems they face, the challenges, and what they think about the next generation
- The environment in terms of their day-to-day lives
- How they think we are affecting nature
- How they think nature is affecting us as well
- Issues such as climate change and global warming

Climate change and global warming are abstract concepts that are removed from the day-to-day lives of people living in subsistence; we did not start off by asking about such issues. These are some of the methodological issues that we deal with in doing this kind of work and in gaining insights regarding the environment and subsistence.

Environmental Challenges

When it comes to environmental issues that are close at hand – affecting the household and the neighborhood or village – listen to this person:

> Nobody is disposing the garbage properly. It is spread everywhere. The air passes through the garbage, bringing a foul odor. It is inhaled by everyone, including the children. Then there is the smoking of cigarettes. People smoke in public and it affects everyone.

This person describes what happens in the local environment and how it affects the household and the neighborhood. This is another aspect of subsistence living. Another person, in talking about the environment, said:

> Even today I saw a plastic bag containing garbage that was thrown in the street by someone. They pack their domestic waste and garbage in a plastic bag and simply throw it on the corner of the street. And the plastic blocks the water flow.

In rural settings, there is a deep connection to the land, as people relate closely to the environment around them.

> We cannot compare farming with business, because we put our faith in the land. We ask it to take care of us and we take care of it equally like our child.

Here is an example of what happens with unsustainable practices and how they immediately affect the community. A key characteristic about subsistence and the environment is that all ecology is local; all environmental issues right away affect the people living there, so they have to be careful about how they interact with the local environment. In thinking about the societal level, people talk about how construction of houses has eroded the family system, and how social networks are eroding as well, how people don't know what is going on in the next apartment, and so on.

People talk about how it is important not to destroy forests, because they are beneficial to human beings. People have an intuitive sense of how natural resources and the natural environment are useful to them, because they live in the natural environment. In terms of the farthest distance and the global level, people talk about having heard of the hole in the ozone layer, and they talk about global warming and other global environmental issues.

Exercise: Group Presentation on Subsistence and Ecology

Using interviews and other material from the web portal[42] such as environmental videos, examine the intersection of subsistence and ecology:

- What are the unique ecological issues that subsistence marketplaces face?
- How do these issues affect their daily lives?
- What are some directions to take to find solutions?

---

[42] https://business.illinois.edu/subsistence/resources/resourcesmlp/: Use the password *subsistence* to access materials on the web portal.

The questions above are merely examples – please take the assignment in any direction you wish, bringing in images and providing insights.

Coping with Environmental Challenges

We discussed challenges in terms of different distances: the immediate, the near, the far, and the farthest distance. People also cope in terms of what they do, particularly at the immediate distance. They often only control their own household and, to a much lesser extent, the local area, the neighborhood. So they try to reuse materials, plant a number of trees around their house, not waste water, and so on. They try to get fresh air around their house. With these different issues that occur at different distances, people try to cope, but they focus most of their coping at the household level, having little control about what happens sometimes even in their neighborhood, let alone at farther distances.

We can compare and contrast this with what happens in a resource-rich setting in terms of the distance of some of these environmental problems and what people are willing to do about them. In resource-rich settings, environmental issues seem to be quite far away, and people are often indifferent about some issues. In subsistence contexts, people are immersed in the same environment where garbage, pollution, and other issues cause problems that they don't have much control over. Ironically, while they are more aware of, and affected by, the environmental problems on a day-to-day basis, they lack much control to be able to do something about it.

Image 2.21: Distance, Control, and Motivation.[43]

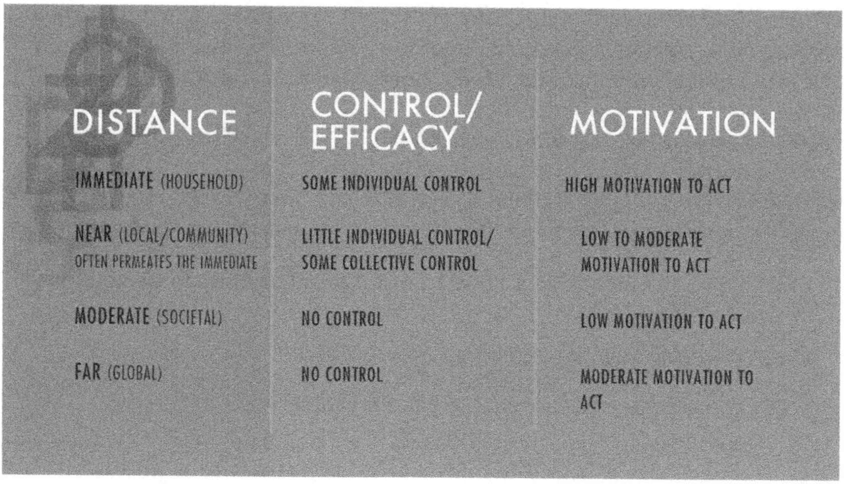

DISTANCE	CONTROL/ EFFICACY	MOTIVATION
IMMEDIATE (HOUSEHOLD)	SOME INDIVIDUAL CONTROL	HIGH MOTIVATION TO ACT
NEAR (LOCAL/COMMUNITY) OFTEN PERMEATES THE IMMEDIATE	LITTLE INDIVIDUAL CONTROL/ SOME COLLECTIVE CONTROL	LOW TO MODERATE MOTIVATION TO ACT
MODERATE (SOCIETAL)	NO CONTROL	LOW MOTIVATION TO ACT
FAR (GLOBAL)	NO CONTROL	MODERATE MOTIVATION TO ACT

[43] Image: Bob Dignan, Christina Tarn, and Killivalavan Solai for the Subsistence Marketplaces Initiative.

Image 2.22: Resource-Rich Versus Subsistence Contexts: Indifference to the Environment.[44]

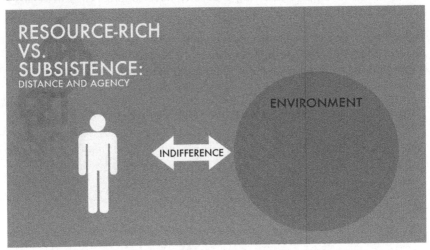

Image 2.23: Resource-Rich Versus Subsistence Contexts: Lack of Control.[45]

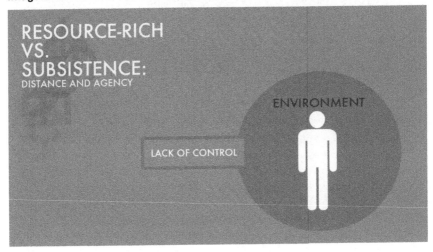

What do people try to sustain in these subsistence contexts? Well, fundamentally, what we see is people trying to survive, to relate to others and to the natural environment, and to somehow grow and get out of poverty. *Survival* means basic physiological and safety needs, food, water, sanitation, and so on. *Relatedness* means a need for belonging, a sense of community, and also a need to relate to the natural environment. And *growth* really means

---

[44] Ibid.

[45] Ibid.

education, particularly for the next generation, so the children don't suffer the same lives that their parents, living in poverty, have suffered. Growth means somehow finding a path out of poverty.

Growth is not so much self-actualization in terms of realizing potential, which seems like a luxury in a lot of these settings. It is about trying to grow in such a way that the next generation can at least get out of poverty be on a path of upward mobility.

Image 2.24: Sustainability from the Bottom-Up – Survival, Growth, and Relatedness.[46]

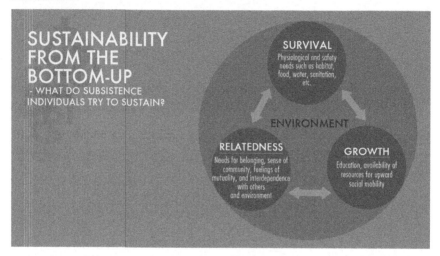

[46] Viswanathan, M., K. Jung, S. Venugopal, I. Minefee, and I. W. Jung. "Subsistence and Sustainability: From Micro-Level Behavioral Insights to Macro-Level Implications on Consumption, Conservation, and the Environment." *Journal of Macromarketing* 34, no. 1 (2013): 8-27. doi:10.1177/0276146713499351. Image: Bob Dignan, Christina Tarn, and Killivalavan Solai for the Subsistence Marketplaces Initiative.

Image 2.25: Sustainability from the Bottom-Up and the Hierarchy of Needs.[47]

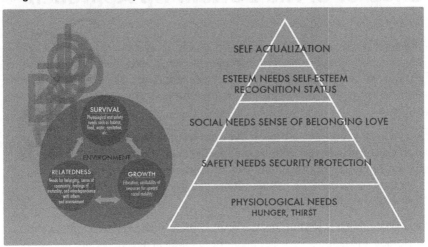

In summary, this chapter focused on understanding subsistence consumers, entrepreneurs, and marketplaces at the micro-level, examining how individuals, think, feel, cope, relate in marketplaces and negotiate their environment. This understanding is the foundation we will build on to design solutions.

---

[47] Ibid.

Chapter 3: The Bottom-Up Approach

There are many ways to look at poverty and economics in the marketplace. You can take a macroeconomic approach, which is like an airplane flying at 30,000 feet. You can take more of a mid-level approach, like the bottom-of-the-pyramid approach, where you look at organizations that are working in these contexts.

But we take a different approach. **We start from the bottom-up, not with organizations, but with the people living in poverty, with their life circumstances, with consumers and entrepreneurs and the marketplaces they operate in, with the communities they live in. And we build our understanding from there.**

So our approach is bottom-up. We want to understand the psychology, the sociology, the cultural aspects, the anthropological aspects of people living in subsistence or poverty, and we want to use this understanding to design solutions. We deliberately call it the *subsistence marketplaces approach*. The subsistence marketplaces approach starts from the bottom-up. We try to understand how people think and feel and act, and from this we try to derive implications for how to design solutions, how to design products, how to design enterprises, and so on.

The word *subsistence* is important, because it connotes the qualitative nature of life circumstances, of people barely making ends meet, and that could mean a wide range of low income. The word *marketplaces* is also important. We use *marketplaces* rather than *markets*, because markets may connote that I already have a product and I'm going to sell it in a new market. *Marketplaces*, on the other hand, emphasizes that there are preexisting marketplaces where people are already involved in exchange. The approach is first to understand these marketplaces and then to design solutions for them, and those solutions may end up being useful for us as well. Our aim is to be bottom-up – we want to gain micro-level understanding, and then move *up* in terms of using such understanding to design products and solutions.

Image 3.01: The Bottom-Up Approach.[48]

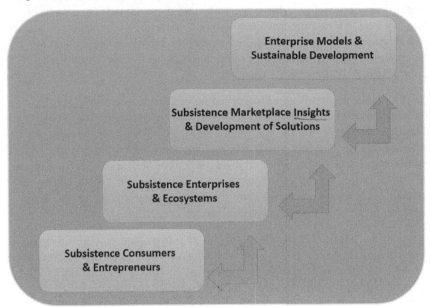

Bottom-Up Vs. Top-Down

We can contrast bottom-up versus top-down approaches in many ways. A perceptual example relates to looking at something with a conception of what to expect (top-down) versus letting the experience come to us, while reducing preconceptions to begin with (bottom-up).[49] What the eye sees is a good example, where perception can lead to new insight (bottom-up) or previous conceptions can guide what is seen (top-down[50]). **Thus, one connotation of a bottom-up versus a top-down approach relates to mindset – bottom-up is immersive during understanding, emersive in terms of learning, and emergent in terms of solutions.** This fits perfectly with contexts we are unfamiliar with, which are different in many ways, and are fraught with resource constraints and uncertainty.

---

[48] Viswanathan, Madhubalan, and Srinivas Venugopal. "Subsistence Marketplaces: Looking Back, Looking Forward." *Journal of Public Policy & Marketing* 34, no. 2 (2015): 228-34. doi:10.1509/jppm.34.2.86.

[49] Gioia, D. A., K. G. Corley, and A. L. Hamilton. "Seeking Qualitative Rigor in Inductive Research: Notes on the Gioia Methodology." *Organizational Research Methods* 16, no. 1 (2012): 15-31. doi:10.1177/1094428112452151.

[50] Gioia et al, 15-31.

deductive vs Inductive

Variations on this theme relate to theory-driven (top-down) versus data-driven (bottom-up) approaches to learning, while understanding of that data itself may have been based on previous theories.[51] In considering this interpretation of bottom-up and top-down, the universal human tendencies of selective perception suggest a natural limit to our capacity to engage in bottom-up approaches.[52]

Another facet of bottom-up versus top-down as it relates to mindset is in being deductive versus inductive, closely related to theory-driven versus data-driven approaches. Our notion of bottom-up emphasizes the need to overcome our preconceptions. This is particularly relevant due to many unique aspects of subsistence – many people have not experienced it and are at a distance from the phenomena; learning about the context is challenging in itself; we tend to assume we know the solutions stemming from our own state in life; and a variety of related factors.

Bottom-up is a term that has been used to denote piecing together of systems to give rise to larger systems, wherein the larger systems emerge organically, or using data to piece together perceptions.[53] Top-down, in turn, refers to the reverse, beginning with the larger system and moving toward subsystems or beginning with previously conceived concepts and moving toward data. Top-down versus bottom-up manifests in a variety of enterprise aspects. Fundamentally, one of the senses in which we use the term *bottom-up* here is to reflect an emergent process that is built on the foundation of deep insights about customers, communities, and the larger context.

Learning through the Bottom-Up Approach

Our approach recognizes the need for the bottom-up to meet the top-down. Our point is simply that, for the most part, current approaches are inherently top-down, and the subsistence marketplace, by amplifying this fundamental problem, provides a way to understand how to envision and implement bottom-up innovation and enterprise.

---

[51] Rosenthal, Robert, and Ralph L. Rosnow. *Essentials of Behavioral Research: Methods and Data Analysis.* New York: McGraw-Hill, 1991.

[52] Sarter, Martin, Ben Givens, and John P. Bruno. "The Cognitive Neuroscience of Sustained Attention: Where Top-down Meets Bottom-up." *Brain Research Reviews* 35, no. 2 (2001): 146-60. doi:10.1016/s0165-0173(01)00044-3.

[53] Strauss, A., and J. Corbin. "Grounded theory methodology." *Handbook of Qualitative Research*, 273-85. 1994.

To capture the bottom-up approach, we move through three stages of learning:

- First, **we move beyond sympathy for subsistence marketplaces to informed empathy** through systematic exercises designed to create virtual immersion and emersion experiences;

- Second, we use a deep bottom-up understanding to design solutions for subsistence marketplaces; and

- Third, we learn from subsistence marketplaces as we design solutions for all contexts.

What can we learn by adopting a bottom-up approach and why is it so critical? Bottom-up learning helps us to gain insights from "data" rather than viewing situations through previously-held concepts. Bottom-up learning is ongoing, as cognitions, knowledge structures, and future learning are impacted through virtual immersion, emersion, actual immersion, and reflection.

Through the bottom-up approach, we begin with micro-level rather than macro- or meso-level foci, thus anchoring ourselves in this vantage point. **With a bottom-up perspective, we analyze needs and problems from the viewpoint of the subsistence consumer or entrepreneur rather than purely or largely from the vantage point of an organization.** We stitch together marketing and other business responses from the bottom-up – i.e., bottom-up planning and implementation – rather than use a traditional top- down approach. We initiate change from the bottom-up in coevolving pathways with local communities.

Bottom-Up: A Neglected and Necessary Orientation for Poverty Contexts

The theme here is not that bottom-up approaches are superior to top-down approaches. Rather, the theme is that bottom-up is often a neglected and more difficult approach, and presents a gap that becomes a canyon when working with unfamiliar and fundamentally different, resource-constrained contexts fraught with uncertainty – for example, a poverty context. Our top-down knowledge has been created in contexts we know well, and it applies to these more familiar contexts, but not to poverty contexts. These more familiar contexts are developed, and share commonalities of progress and development often tied together by material needs that apply to middle and upper classes globally. They share educational commonalities that bridge differences, infrastructures that draw on progress in science and technology, and institutional mechanisms that are based on some degree of shared knowledge. Shared language is one such example of commonalities across contexts that enable understanding at different levels of abstraction.

But we don't know much about subsistence marketplaces, and we often form preconceptions based on what we take for granted. Moreover, subsistence marketplaces do not have infrastructure and institutional mechanisms that are shared or part of common knowledge in relatively affluent parts of the world, and don't share the degree of education that the developed world does. Depending on the degree of isolation, tribal communities more so than, say, other rural communities or semi-urban communities, do not have the same shared knowledge that comes from education. Geographically-dispersed small villages lacking exposure to shared knowledge in turn lead to myriad differences between each subsistence context, making top-down approaches less effective.

Thus, the inherently distinct nature of each subsistence context, and the often extremely high degree of unfamiliarity with as well as the resource-constrained challenging nature of these contexts, combine to accentuate the need for bottom-up approaches. Finally, the connectedness within these communities represents an amplified version of any word-of-mouth communication in relatively affluent communities, particularly before the onset of the virtual world. In such a world of one-on-one interactions, top-down approaches need to be combined with bottom-up ones as well.

Bottom-Up: Counterintuitive and Effortful

Bottom-up approaches are fundamentally counterintuitive in at least one sense. A top-down approach begins with us, our organization, our knowledge base, our assumptions, and our goals.[54] It comes naturally. It is inherently easier to pursue than the opposite, not that achieving our knowledge base and our goals is easy in an absolute sense.

A top-down approach appears more efficient in a number of ways. It draws on what we already know and builds on our existing infrastructure to achieve goals. We draw from our existing knowledge all the time. We form impressions based on what we know. We communicate through traditional media channels using "universal" language. We conduct market research using a sample selected from a universe, a predetermined population based on, say, demographics. We design products to be optimal based on how we know they will fit into people's lives.

People who develop products with a top-down approach may have some level of understanding of how consumers will use products and can optimize them in advance. For example, a designer may know what a typical kitchen in a middle class household looks like for the most part, and employ a top-down approach. In one sense, the notion of planning followed by implementation or

---

[54] Gioia, D. A., K. G. Corley, and A. L. Hamilton. "Seeking Qualitative Rigor in Inductive Research: Notes on the Gioia Methodology." *Organizational Research Methods* 16, no. 1 (2012): 15-31. doi:10.1177/1094428112452151.

specific stages in product development assumes sufficient knowledge. So do optimal notions of design.

Something happened to these top-down approaches to business or development when the world became interconnected through technology. With technological trends and increasing connectivity around the world, governments and commercial and social enterprises are moving away from top-down, centralized, command-and-control approaches to more organic, bottom-up approaches. Examples include crowdsourcing and open innovation processes or promotional campaigns that depend on social media.

A sense of community is being recaptured through texting, Facebook, Twitter, and so forth. Social media is bottom-up and broadcast media is top-down. In fact, social media now allows individuals to broadcast. Top-down is unidirectional, whereas with bottom-up, consumers, entrepreneurs, and organizations are communicating with each other. Technology has greatly increased the scale of word-of-mouth and other consumer-to-consumer communications. Small subsistence communities represent the off-line, and now mobile phone, interactions that are as old as humankind itself and that the next generation in other contexts is recapturing virtually. These interactions are creating contexts and communities that top-down approaches are not ideally suited to address.

None of this is to suggest the superiority of one versus the other. Rather, it is to point out the shortcomings of top-down approaches and show where a bottom-up approach can serve to complement a top-down approach or even be more dominant. It is also to point out what bottom-up can be, how we go about adopting this approach, and why we can benefit from doing so.

Differences Between Top-Down and Bottom-Up Approaches

Top-Down Approach	Bottom-Up Approach
Going in with a preconceived notion	Going in with an open mind, expecting to learn
Current perception based on past understanding	Current perception open to new insight
Entrenched in familiar environment and culture	Immersed in new environment and culture
Theory-driven	Data-driven
Deductive	Inductive
Macro-level focus	Micro-level focus
Unidirectional	Multi-directional
Economies & Organizations	Marketplaces

The Bottom-Up Approach

Stages in Bottom-Up Innovation

We have talked about the advantages of the bottom-up process. Now let's take a look at the stages of the process.

We show the unique stages for bottom-up innovation in Image 3.02. The stages, in sequence, are:

- Virtual immersion
- Emersion
- Preliminary idea generation and evaluation
- Preparation for field research
- Actual immersion
- Reflections about immersion
- Focused concept generation and selection

Image 3.02: From Virtual Immersion to Focused Concept Generation.[55]

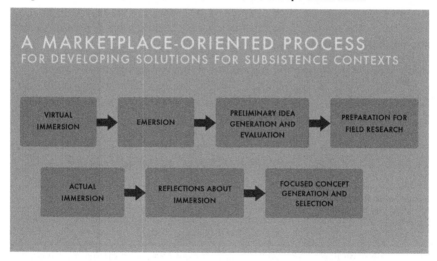

Concept detailing, concept testing, prototyping, ecosystem design, and business plan development are steps that follow, some of which can be divided more finely.

We'll take a closer look at each phase.

---

[55] Image: Bob Dignan, Christina Tarn, and Killivalavan Solai for the Subsistence Marketplaces Initiative.

1. *Virtual Immersion*

Using poverty simulations, analysis of interviews, model-building using data, multimedia-based immersion exercises, day-in-the-life videos, and a movie, we sensitize students, managers and researchers to the deeply distinct context of subsistence. Virtual immersion serves to efficiently bring the unfamiliar context to the individual. We draw on our extended micro-level research to paint a picture of how consumers and entrepreneurs negotiate the marketplace, covering domains such as thinking, feeling, and relating, as a function of extreme resource constraints. These exercises are at the core of our bottom-up approach.

To view a video that illustrates the concepts of understanding needs of individuals in subsistence, please visit our web portal.[56]

To cover different domains of poverty, we begin with broad life circumstances, through such means as writing a first-person profile of people living in subsistence and developing a model of poverty and its causes and effects, or a model of the local environment and basic necessities (example in Image 3.03).

Image 3.03: Virtual Immersion Exercise – A Model of Poverty.

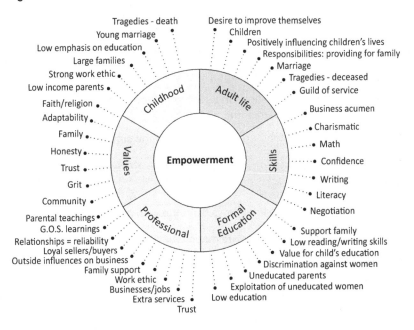

---

[56] https://business.illinois.edu/subsistence/resources/resourcesmlp/: Use the password *subsistence* to access materials on the web portal.

The first-person profile is particularly powerful, as participants adopt the perspective of the interviewees and relate their life stories. We then focus on the marketplace domain by developing a model of needs, products, and markets. Virtual interactions through online interviews are another dimension we have brought into our educational experiences. Day-in-the-life-videos are powerful tools to provide the kind of detail that is so important to gaining bottom-up insights. Sometimes, we can use a specific day-in-the-life video to drill deep into the need-drivers-context and consider solutions. This learning process is bottom-up in that participants extract insights from raw data from a variety of sources, based on content provided with exercises and open-ended search.

During virtual immersion, we compare and contrast poverty across contexts. We have set our poverty simulation in a US context, to begin with, a setting that participants may be somewhat familiar with. Playing the role of a family member in a setting where each week in real life is represented in 10-15 minutes, and making financial decisions while interacting with banks, pawnbrokers, and so forth, compel participants to imagine themselves in the shoes of the poor at more specific and deeper levels. Online poverty simulations based in the US or in India are other ways of creating the virtual immersion experience. We have created an online poverty simulation.[57]

Exercise: Poverty Simulation

Complete the online poverty simulation. Consider three levels:

- What happened in the simulation
- Your psychological reactions in terms of feelings, decision-making, and perceptions of others, to name a few
- Your overall understanding of poverty from the simulation

Exercise: Virtual Immersion – Understanding Subsistence Context and Needs

View one of the immersion slideshows from the web portal.[58]

- Select a specific slide and write down what you see
- Repeat for two other slides

---

[57] https://business.illinois.edu/subsistence/resources/resourcesmlp/: Use the password *subsistence* to access materials on the web portal.

[58] https://business.illinois.edu/subsistence/resources/resourcesmlp/: Use the password *subsistence* to access materials on the web portal.

- Run the slideshow and jot down your reactions for each slide as follows, focusing on the unique needs, drivers, and larger context

  o Write down any responses that come to mind as you view each slide

  o Capture any thoughts – they may be observations or deeper thoughts

Through virtual immersion exercises, we cover poverty in a variety of contexts. Moreover, we use broad immersion into poverty to have participants identify needs, drivers, and the larger context – akin to needs, their immediate causes, and their more distal causes (Image 3.04).

Image 3.04: Project Overview.[59]

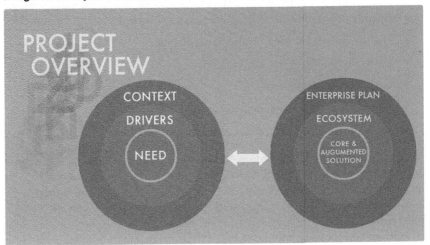

This multilevel consideration of life circumstances is a prelude to similar exercises at idea generation and concept detailing phases. It emphasizes the need to look beyond needs and understand their drivers as well as the larger contexts in which they occur. As such, virtual immersion teaches us about unfamiliar contexts where larger life circumstances mingle with the manifestation and satisfaction of needs that could be considered in isolation in relatively resource-rich contexts.

One purpose of virtual immersion is to move from sympathy, a naturally-evoked emotion that arises with normal exposure to poverty, to informed empathy, which arises from a deeper dive into the life circumstances and

---

[59] Image: Bob Dignan, Christina Tarn, and Killivalavan Solai for the Subsistence Marketplaces Initiative.

marketplace interactions. Such a deeper dive requires sustained analysis of data in a variety of forms.

Exercise: Problem or Need Selection

- Complete a virtual immersion (slideshow, interviews, day-in-the-life videos, etc.)
- List 3-4 needs on a sheet of paper
- Analyze the needs and identify one need to focus on

Exercise: Understanding Needs, Drivers and Context of Subsistence

- Describe your chosen need
- Specify geography, demographics, usage situations
- List drivers of this need (immediate causes)
- Show interlinkages between drivers
- List larger context elements
- Show interlinkages between context elements
- Draw out in concentric circles with labels

usage cases [handwritten annotation]

Informed empathy leads to a more comprehensive understanding, necessarily coupled with unlearning preconceptions. For instance, implicit notions associating poverty predominantly with lack of hard work are challenged by the information coming from simulated experiences where, despite very hard work, it is extremely difficult to make ends meet. The anxiety and stress associated with poverty and the clouded decision-making under survival threat are important realizations as well. Whereas sympathy reflects a natural human emotion in response to what is observed, informed empathy forms the connections with cognitions. Informed empathy is, perhaps, more sustained than sympathy as well.[60]

Virtual immersion also serves to change the vantage point to be truly bottom-up, thus anchoring the participant at the ground level from which to view phenomena and develop solutions. As discussed subsequently, while this vantage point cannot be the only consideration, it is often one that is assumed or taken for granted and not addressed explicitly. Although we illustrate virtual immersion using the fundamentally different context of subsistence, it can also be applied in familiar settings, where implicit

---

[60] Miller, T., M. Grimes, J. McMullen, and T. Vogus. "Venturing for Others with Heart and Head: How Compassion Encourages Social Entrepreneurship." *Academy of Management Review*, 2012. doi:10.5465/amr.10.0456..

assumptions prevent detailed understanding. Virtual immersion is an efficient way of gaining bottom-up understanding.

2· *Emersion*

The next step in the bottom-up innovation process is emersion, which is akin to submerging oneself in an entirely new context and reemerging to compare and contrast what has been learned with previous knowledge. Thus, the specialist in business, engineering, or design gets an opportunity to reassess existing concepts and assumptions developed in resource-rich settings and how generalized and misplaced these concepts and assumptions may be in the context of subsistence.

Emersion involves reflection on what is new here and requires revisiting disciplinary concepts and insights. In this phase, we use methods such as discussions of case studies, of commercial and social enterprises, and reflective exercises. Additionally, we move the project forward through idea generation and screening, adding another source of emersion in terms of hands-on tasks in this radically different context. Most importantly, an assignment explicitly involves reflection with a view to emersion – in terms of insights and a tieback to one's discipline or functional area. Essentially, the assignment is as follows.

Exercise: Emersion

You came into this experience knowing concepts in your areas of expertise. But with the radically different context of subsistence, have new concepts emerged in your thinking? Have you thought about how you need to change or extend existing concepts?

For example:

- In design: What is unique about designing for subsistence marketplaces?
- In marketing: What is unique about communication strategies?

Ultimately, the questions to answer are these: How has your understanding of subsistence changed the way you think about your discipline and related disciplines (e.g., marketing and business in general)? What are specific examples of concepts that need rethinking?

Emersion typifies the bottom-up process, as insights emerge after examining data. This reflection phase allows for the bottom-up to meet the top-down as new data leads to adjusting previously-learned concepts and assumptions. Emersion in many ways closes the loop on informed empathy, unlearning assumptions, tying cognitions to preexisting concepts, and examining the need to stretch them or even create new concepts to address the unique characteristics of subsistence marketplaces.

In this phase, exposure to the unfamiliar and radically different leads to learning of new information, which, in turn, is reconciled with preexisting knowledge. For example, a designer may realize the limitations of designing for optimality in a setting where she does not have knowledge of needs, usage conditions, or possible uses, when compared to designing for familiar consumers living in similar settings and assuming a similar infrastructure. Whereas empathic design focuses on the user, our approach incorporates the community and larger context as well with a simultaneous multi-level focus.[61]

The immersion-emersion iteration is at the heart of adopting a bottom-up approach. When virtual immersion occurs without emersion, preexisting concepts may continue to be employed in a purely top-down manner. Without immersion (virtual or actual), the shift in vantage point and anchoring from the egocentric self or organization to one that is psychologically and physically distant[62] (socially, physically, and hypothetically – as in the likelihood of finding oneself in the same situation), does not happen. The immersion-emersion iteration fundamentally addresses the issue of how to bridge large distances efficiently while changing one's cognitions and underlying knowledge structures.

3. *Preliminary Idea Generation and Evaluation*

In tandem with emersion or soon after, participants engage in idea generation for their respective projects. Here again, we use a variety of immersion exercises, with multimedia content customized to the general problem area. In this iteration, we tie the need, drivers, and context elements closely to the problem arena and anchor them in the bottom-up vantage point. We use repeated iterations, starting with the general need and developing drivers and the larger context elements.

---

[61] Leonard, Dorothy A., and Jeffrey Rayport. "Spark Innovation through Empathic Design." *Harvard Business Review* 75 (1997): 102-15.
Viswanathan, M., S. Venugopal, I. Minefee, J. S. Guest, B. J. Marinas, V. Bauza, L. Valentino, R. Kupaza, and M. Jones. "A Bottom-Up Approach to Short-Term Immersion in Subsistence Marketplaces: Methodological and Substantive Lessons on Poverty and the Environment from Tanzania." *Organization & Environment*, 2016. doi:10.1177/1086026616633255.

[62] Trope, Yaacov, and Nira Liberman. "Construal-level Theory of Psychological Distance." *Psychological Review* 117, no. 2 (2010): 440-463.

Image 3.05: Context, Drivers, and Needs.

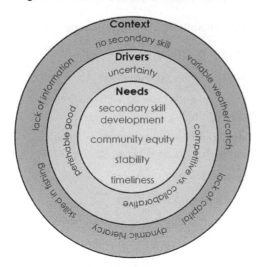

Next, we use immersion exercises to generate fine-tuned needs and then develop drivers and the larger context element for these more specific needs. To stimulate need generation, we combine top-down exposure to current solutions or technologies with bottom-up use of multimedia materials, such as video analysis and image analysis.

Exercise: Bottom-Up Approaches to Idea Generation

- Mine images to come up with ideas

- Review videos to come up with ideas

- Dive deeply into one context to come up with ideas – e.g., use videos in the web portal

- Finely tune needs or break up needs into smaller dimensions (associated drivers) of associated context to come up with ideas to address using the need, each driver, or each context element to stimulate

    o Freeze one of the following and come up with ideas:

        a. Customer group – e.g., children

        b. Geographic location – e.g., South India

        c. Usage situation – e.g., household versus workplace versus transportation

        d. Consider what, whom, where, when, and how

        e. State the problem from the perspective of the end-customer and come up with ideas

Exercise: Top-Down Approaches to Idea Generation

The following steps refer to the top-down approach to concept generation.

1. Review technologies and use to come up with ideas

2. Review current solutions and use to come up with ideas

3. Review functions of current solutions and come up with ideas (e.g., personal grooming – different functions)

4. Review current processes in delivering solutions and come up with ideas (e.g., nutritional additive to what, in what form, etc.)

5. Review data and use to come up with ideas

6. Review country descriptions and come up with ideas

7. Review parallel products for different needs/industries and come up with ideas

We use bottom-up and top-down exercises in need generation, writing about a need or problem as the end-beneficiary or as the manager of an organization and then breaking it into more specific statements as shown in Image 3.06.

Image 3.06: Bottom-Up Need Deconstruction Exercise – Amputee in Subsistence Marketplaces.[63]

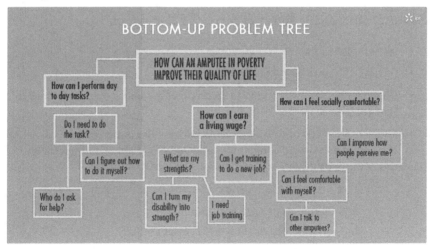

---

[63] Image: Bob Dignan, Christina Tarn, and Killivalavan Solai for the Subsistence Marketplaces Initiative.

Exercise: Bottom-Up Needs Deconstruction

- List needs as statements in first person as the end-beneficiary
- Eliminate/combine redundant/identical statements
- Group cards according to the similarity of the need they express
- For each group, choose a label to generalize the need
- Review and revise groups
- Generate and evaluate ideas based on this exercise

Exercise: Top-Down Needs Deconstruction

- List needs as statements in the first person as the manager of an organization
- Eliminate/combine redundant/identical statements
- Group cards according to the similarity of the need they express
- For each group, choose a label to categorize the need
- Review and revise groups
- Generate and evaluate ideas based on this exercise

Idea generation focuses on the core design aspect, although we also list ideas that fall into augmented design, ecosystem, or even enterprise plan elements. Participants also develop criteria to evaluate and screen ideas. This task as well can be approached bottom-up in addition to top-down, by ranking products and articulating why.

Exercise: Core Solution Generation

Step 1: Observation

- Take notes individually when going through immersion exercises on the web portal

Step 2: Idea Generation and Selection

- Focus on a chosen problem / need
- Generate ideas
- Narrow down to one idea

Step 3: Concept Detailing

- Draw out details of concept

Exercise: Idea Generation and Evaluation

- Generate ideas that address needs or sub-needs
- Rank the ideas
- Draw out a chosen idea or combination of ideas as a concept, in detail that addresses the need
- Draw additional concepts but keep the focus on getting some detail down
- Evaluate the concepts on the attributes or criteria you developed

Exercise: Developing Criteria for Evaluation

- Rank your concepts
- Consider the ranking and articulate why
- List criteria
- Consolidate criteria

Criteria are reasons people will opt for your solution. They illuminate the ways in which people's needs are being served.

For example, consider Image 3.05 from the viewpoint of the potential beneficiary.

- I need to survive. I need to provide for my family. So one of the criteria is to **function in certain occupations**.
- Similarly, I need to feel comfortable in social settings, so **social acceptance** is another criterion for this particular solution.
- I need to feel content with myself, and self-image matters as well, so the *appearance* of the prosthetic matters as well.

One way to get at criteria is to rank a set of ideas and then work back, reverse engineer, or deconstruct why you ranked the ideas in this way. This is bottom-up as well.

Exercise: Identifying Criteria to Evaluate Concepts

This exercise will help you consider your focused need and identify the criteria to evaluate your ideas.

- Draw a bottom-up figure of what you expect the end user to think about in terms of need and sub-needs. What is the need being served?
- Develop criteria or attributes representing how you will satisfy different aspects of the need.
- Consolidate the list attributes to be collectively exhaustive and mutually exclusive.

An example of an outcome of idea generation is shown on the next page.

Sample Evaluation Matrix

Criteria	Accessibility of Technology	Ease of Use, Maintenance, Education		Sustainability		Communication		Trust			Draws on Fractal's Strengths	Draws on Team's Strengths	Fairness to the Community	Overall Score
Rationale	Easy Access to Technology	Easy to learn	Easy to use	Demand/ Supply	Energy Use	Timely	Completed/ Updated Information	Buyer/ Seller	Completion of Sale	System				
Ideas/ Weights	1	1	1	1	0.5	1	0.8	0.8	0.5	0.8	0.5	1	1	
Cell-Phone-Based	4	4	3	4	3	5	5	3	3	2	4	3	4	40.3
Radio-Based	1	4	3	4	3	4	4	3	3	5	4	4	3	37
Stationary Kiosk	4	4	5	4	4	3	3	3	3	2	4	4	5	41.2
Mobile Kiosk	3	2	4	2	1	3	3	3	3	2	1	1	2	26.2
Call Center	4	3	4	3	2	4	4	3	3	3	3	3	4	37
Modified "Morse Code"	0	2	2	5	5	1	2	3	3	5	1	1	1	23.9
Fishing Database	3	5	3	3	3	3	3	3	3	4	4	4	3	36.7
Weather Insurance	3	3	4	5	3	3	3	3	3	2	4	4	4	37.7

This level of engagement in the problem domain before actual field research is grounded in virtual immersion and helps think through solutions to some degree before embarking onto field research. This phase also allows input from stakeholders that refines the core domain area, albeit from a relatively top-down perspective.

Preparation for Field Research

Preparation for field research is another distinct step. Here, participants develop plans relating to what they would like to observe (e.g., parts of the value chain), whom they would like to talk to (e.g., different stakeholders), stimuli they would collect and/or show during interactions, rough scripts of in-depth interviews, and methods for recording (e.g., diaries, field notes). We emphasize unstructured qualitative interviews that paint a picture of the ground reality of subsistence, rather than structured approaches that presume a high degree of knowledge of the context. These open-ended approaches allow methods to evolve through the course of the actual immersion. For instance, early in the process, broader approaches aim to paint a big picture of life circumstances with goals becoming more specific over time. Input from stakeholders can veer the project in a different direction.

Exercise: Field Research Plan

- Whom to talk to
- What to observe
- Items you need
- What products/items would you want purchased at field research locations in advance for your trip
- Roles you will play
- Interview plan
- Script outline
- Stimuli
- Key ideas developed into concepts to show
- Other stimuli to show
- What questions you want answered on the trip – script in detail
- What stimuli you will show – example concepts but other things as well
- Whom you want to talk to
- What you want to see
- Some strategies you will use to observe and record

5. *Actual Immersion*

Actual immersion provides a bottom-up perspective and experience in two central ways – through deep, unfiltered conversations with end-users, including those at the bottom of the power hierarchy, and through ground-level observations of households, marketplaces, and communities. Seeing and hearing for oneself with as little filtering as possible is central. In this regard, a mutual learning mindset becomes very important – we acknowledge our own expertise, yes, but we also learn from those who are experts at survival. The person from outside this survival context who adopts this mindset is at an advantage in not carrying the baggage of those "familiar" with the context, who may have difficulty seeing things in a different way or appreciating the merits of new solutions. The person who learns from the survival experts is the one who ultimately develops marketplace literacy.

Image 3.07: Understanding More Than the Customer.

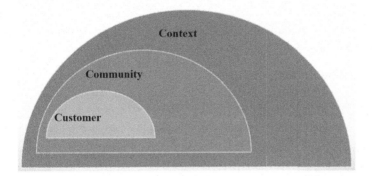

Actual immersion involves bridging physical and psychological distances in a real sense and adopting the bottom-up vantage point as an anchor. Deep conversations and seeing for oneself enable understanding the reality of living in a subsistence environment. Trying out solutions can also be part of this process. Actual immersion should also allow for the possibility of throwing out previously developed ideas and insights and starting from scratch. This represents bottom-up innovation in its truest sense.

Exercise: During Your Actual Immersion

- Keep a diary
- See, hear, experience
- Soak in experiences that money cannot buy
- Write, draw, photograph
- Record what you saw, what you felt, what you did

- Reflect at the end of the day
- Minimize electronics

6. *Reflections About Immersion*

Reflection is an important phase after actual immersion. It enables revisiting and absorbing new information from an intense experience. It serves these purposes:

- Observers can adjust and sometimes correct factually inaccurate interpretations, often in the domain of cultural understanding
- They can compile data, put various insights in perspective, and gather and reassess information
- They can avoid premature fixation on solutions or unquestioned insights that may follow an intensive, often both shocking and exhilarating, experience

Reflection following actual immersion is akin to emersion following virtual immersion in affecting cognitions, knowledge structures, and future learning.

Exercise: Reflection on Immersion

- The essence of what you learned in a sentence or two
- An image, an event, or an interaction that exemplifies what you learned
- Clarifications
- What you learned about yourself

Exercise: Crystallizing Insights

- Review notes, images, etc.
- List key insights from immersion
- List key insights that represent a change from previous beliefs

7. *Focused Concept Generation and Selection*

We follow reflection with a phase of focused concept generation. This phase serves to avoid premature fixation on a solution that may arise as a reaction, or overreaction, to an intense actual immersion experience. In this phase, participants step back into the domain in which they will develop solutions. In previous iterations, they have been somewhat restricted in their ability to forge a solution; now, they are armed with more understanding and bottom-up knowledge that will guide them in creating a solution.

Participants evaluate concepts and select a concept to focus on. Variants of the concepts are also developed using the same method to generate ideas and concepts.

8. *Subsequent Steps*

The process continues with selecting a concept and detailing it, while considering different variants, and developing customer needs, technical specifications, metrics, and benchmarks, and creating a prototype. You will see that our bottom-up approach is intertwined throughout the process. The exercise of understanding needs, drivers, and contexts is repeated throughout the process, with the added insights coming from actual immersion and from analysis. Furthermore, we initiate a bottom-up deconstruction of the problem, listing sub-needs in hierarchical form. These exercises feed into a deeper understanding of needs, drivers, and context from a bottom-up perspective.

Exercise: Variants of Single Concept Generation

- Select one concept
- Write down variants of concept
- Create multiple variants (4+ per person)
- Write each variant down on a sheet of paper
- Analyze key design elements
- Go back to the problem and key issues as needed

Exercise: Developing needs, metrics, technical specifications, and benchmarks

- List needs and sub-needs
- List metrics for each need
- List technical specifications
- List benchmarks

In this phase, participants also engage in top-down problem deconstruction, top-down need deconstruction, and forming a hierarchy of needs (see Images 3.09-3.12).[64] The aim is for this traditional top-down approach to meet the bottom-up approach (see Image 3.09). These processes provide the foundation for systematically spelling out needs, metrics, benchmarks, and specifications. They also keep the designer grounded in the bottom-up insights, rather than

---

[64] Bagozzi, Richard P., and Utpal Dholakia. "Goal Setting and Goal Striving in Consumer Behavior." *Journal of Marketing* 63 (1999): 19. doi:10.2307/1252098.

moving to a different compartment called "the design of solutions" without integrating bottom-up insights at every step.

As you come up with your ideas and narrow them down to a concept using the criteria, it is important to gain insights about the idea or the concept that you choose. So apply the learning about gaining marketplace insights. Prepare for your interaction with end beneficiaries by developing pictures representing your ideas or your concept, and some questions as well. Think about the end beneficiary in terms of their thinking, their feelings, and the way they relate to the marketplace and cope. Ask about the need. Ask about current solutions. Ask about shortcomings and what an ideal solution would look like.

In other words, be very open-ended at the beginning, allowing people to give you a sense of what the ideal solution looks like. Then show them the concept in pictorial form and obtain an open-ended response. This is very important – you don't want to lead people to respond to certain aspects of the solution. Start out broadly and then narrow down to more specific questions after you've given the respondent a chance to provide an open-ended response.

Ask specific questions such as:

- How would you change the solution?
- What additional features would you like to see?
- What support would be helpful for this product?
- How much would you pay for this product?
- How would you like to learn about and receive communications about this product?
- Do you have any other suggestions?

Now, don't stick to this script, but be creative! Just as we want to give people open-ended questions to respond to, we want to be open-ended in our approach. We are not giving you an exact recipe to follow, but guidelines to help you along the way.

Most importantly, adopt a mutual-learning mindset. Set the stage for the interaction where the end beneficiary, the low-literate, low-income subsistence person feels empowered and like an expert (that he or she is about the life circumstances) in responding to your questions. That is very important because of the difference in status between you and the respondent. Often, people are going to come into the setting thinking that there is a right or a wrong answer and that they may be scolded for giving the wrong answer. This is where the mutual-learning mindset is very important. We are experts in certain things, but they are experts on survival. And they need to be deeply involved in shaping the solution.

Exercise: Concept Testing

Prepare the following:

- Drawings
- Respondents Needed
- Questions for Concept Testing
    - Current Way of Meeting Need?
    - What They Think of Concept?
    - How to Change It?
    - Additional Features? Support?
    - How Much They Will Pay?
    - How Would They Like to Receive Communications?
    - Any Other Suggestions?

Moving beyond the core solution, the design of the augmented solution (referring to features over and above the core functionality of the solution), and the ecosystem (aspects in the community realm extrinsic to the solution, such as education, social networks, and service centers) is informed by bottom-up understanding, very critical for settings lacking basic infrastructure.

Image 3.08: Bottom-Up Needs Deconstruction (Sangam Project in the Web Portal).[65]

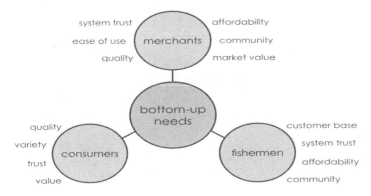

---

[65] https://business.illinois.edu/subsistence/resources/resourcesmlp/: Use the password *subsistence* to access materials on the web portal.

Image 3.09: Top-Down Needs Deconstruction (Sangam Project in the Web Portal).[66]

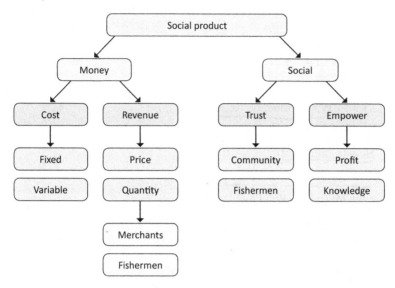

Image 3.10: Bottom-Up Problem Deconstruction (Sangam Project in the Web Portal).[67]

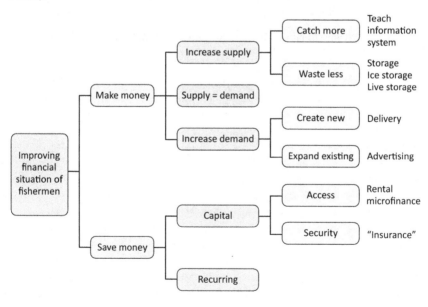

---

[66] Ibid.

[67] Ibid.

Image 3.11: Top-Down Problem Deconstruction (Sangam Project in the Web Portal).[68]

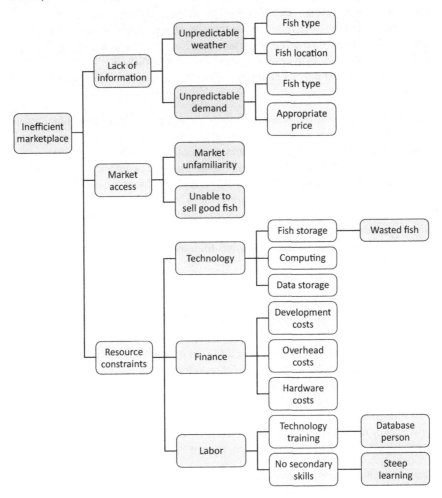

Bottom-Up Design of Augmented Solutions and Ecosystems

The outcome of this approach is not restricted to the design of a good or a service, but to an augmented solution and a supporting ecosystem. Thus, the goal is not restricted to transactional value to the customer, but is focused on a holistic, sustainable value proposition that covers augmented product elements as well as elements of the larger ecosystem.

[68] Ibid.

In this regard, we aim to design solutions that are not in isolation from the life circumstances that impinge on them. As noted earlier, the designer is not familiar with, or even able to, envision life circumstances and related usage situations in subsistence marketplaces. Usage situations are fraught with uncertainty and a myriad of variations. From the vantage point of the end user, uncertainty is the defining characteristic of daily life. Products can be used for different purposes and in different, sometimes unpredictable situations.

In contrast, design for relatively resource-rich settings involves relative certainty of current circumstances and an assumed infrastructure, a point we make without understating the uncertainty relating to such issues as future trends and technological advances. For example, you can design solutions for a typical kitchen in a middle-class US household based on certain assumptions. But in subsistence marketplaces, deprivation at the household level is on multiple fronts, such as, say, basic literacy, thus requiring augmented solutions, such as through incorporating education as it relates to the product into the packaging, rather than assuming a minimal level of knowledge.

An augmented solution is still part of the product offering, whereas an ecosystem is extrinsic to the offering but related to it. At the marketplace level, people lack infrastructure, institutional mechanisms, and traditional customer support (such as through dealer networks). Combined with individual and household level deprivations, these add up to great constraints in the lives of people living in subsistence. These constraints highlight the need for developing a larger ecosystem to serve functions ranging from education about the product to after-sales service. We cannot narrowly focus design on a functional product solution assuming reliable energy supply or dealer networks or educational systems. Uncertainty extends beyond the household to the larger environment where products are used, serviced, and repaired.

Thus, the value creation process has to reflect and capture these needs as well. The value proposition extends beyond the good or service to include augmented elements that address deprivation at the household level and enable people in subsistence to experience and realize value. Ecosystem elements address deprivation at the marketplace and larger context levels, enabling value networks.

Summary: Steps in Concept Detailing and Design of Solution

- Learning from Field Research
- Concept Generation
  - o Process
  - o Concepts

- Evaluation
  - o Discussion of Criteria and Rationale
  - o Discussion of Ranking
  - o Matrix of Concepts and Criteria
- Chosen Concept
- Needs-Drivers-Context
- Bottom-up Problem Deconstruction
- Needs – Metrics – Benchmarks – Specifications
- Top-down Problem Deconstruction
- Detailed Concept
- Detailed Drawings
- Core Product and Core Process
- Packaging
- Ecosystem and Process
- Technical Specifications
- Customer Needs/Attributes – Technical Specifications (Metrics/Values)
- Preliminary Cost Analysis
- Benchmarking
- Process Design (Ecosystem)
- Concept Testing
- Prototyping – Timeframe and Goals

Developing Enterprise Plans

The bottom-up approach takes on a different sense in permeating the enterprise plan. Literally every element of a typical process of developing marketing strategy from the top-down takes on a bottom-up version. Market research, typically conceived of in implementation as starting with a universe and appropriate samples, gets turned on its head, as insights have to be stitched together from the ground up from opinion leaders, social groups, and so forth. Top-down market segmentation has its bottom-up counterpart in stitching together groups of customers and geographic locations (sets of villages) based on ground-level understanding of cultural, linguistics, and other differences and similarities.

Product design is grounded in bottom-up insights. Communications that would normally begin with a top-down focus on media outlets and reach and other such considerations are flipped to create ground-level communications and spreading positive word-of-mouth. Distribution networks that assume basic infrastructure have to be completely rethought. Even scaling has to be rethought in terms of radially moving out from villages or clusters of villages by failing small at distinctly different locations and learning how to increase reach and word-of-mouth.

Individual and the community good as they relate to the need being addressed are an inherent part of the value creation process. As noted elsewhere, in a multilevel analysis of subsistence marketplaces,[69] organizations need to understand how to better basic life circumstances and enhance individual and community welfare through basic and augmented products. In terms of relationships, organizations need to consider the human dimension in exchanges in addition to the economic by engendering fairness and trust. At the marketplace level, organizations need to negotiate the complex social milieu, using individual and community good as the common denominator.

Design Reflects the Reality of the Marketplace

Resources enable compartmentalization and specialization, whether at a personal level for a customer or entrepreneur or at an organizational level. Design thinking can assume a somewhat compartmentalized orientation as well, reflecting the reality of the marketplace. The ability of a customer to have a need satisfied without impinging on other needs reflects an underlying ability to allocate resources for that need.

Thus, something as seemingly normal as a kitchen, a space allocated for specific functions, is an example to design for. Dividing up life circumstances into the workplace and family or professional and personal is another example. For an entrepreneur, separating the enterprise from the personal sphere is another example that assumes resources.

In contrast, needs and usage situations or the workplace and the home can impinge on each other in subsistence marketplaces due to the lack of basic resources that are implicitly assumed in relatively resource-rich settings. Simple day-to-day activities such as cooking or eating occur in shared spatial areas that are very close to the local environment. The household representing the immediate spatial distance often blurs into the local environment and community representing the near spatial distance. In turn, the local environmental issues permeate into household space.

---

[69] Viswanathan, 2013.

Earmarking resources for specific activities is another arena with key differences. Resources are moved around between family and work. For example, a subsistence entrepreneur moves resources between family, customer, and supplier to meet day-to-day responsibilities.

Bottom-up thinking in such settings requires understanding of the blurring of spatial, functional, and psychological arenas, and we need to anticipate varied means by which needs are fulfilled or unfulfilled in different settings (usage situations) that blur seemingly distinct domains, such as the household and the community.

So, viewing a need and a consumption activity in isolation or even in relative isolation is not likely to lead to effective solutions. Rather, an understanding of larger life circumstances has to precede design, and the value creation process has to blur the basic functional solution with the augmented solution as well as elements of the ecosystem.

An Inside-Out Approach to Wider Deployment

This approach is also germane to what is traditionally referred to as scaling – a term that is inherently top-down from our vantage point in assuming some sort of multiplication or replication of what is done in smaller scale, with the household being a typical unit of analysis. Rather, with the holistic, sustainable value proposition that we describe, we take an inside-out approach that begins at the community level and spreads organically. Distinctly different clusters of communities would be the starting point for the core and augmented product and ecosystem elements to create value. Positive word-of-mouth at the ground level in turn can enable a radial spread of the reach of the value proposition. We prefer terms such as wider deployment to scaling in subsistence marketplaces, given the connotations of multiplication or replication that come with the latter.

Why The Bottom-Up Approach is Ideal for Subsistence Marketplaces

The bottom-up approach is germane to subsistence marketplaces because of the characteristics of these marketplaces:

- They are geographically fragmented and often isolated
- They have distinct and myriad cultural and linguistic differences
- They are relationship- and community-centric, influenced by numerous groups
- They lack access to shared knowledge and related technology and to infrastructure and institutional mechanisms

When the distinctiveness of each context is combined with the uncertainty inherent in these contexts and the unfamiliarity of an outside entity, a bottom-up approach becomes essential.

Deficits relate to infrastructure (e.g., roads and transportation for distribution) and to individual and societal capabilities (e.g., education, literacy, skillsets, institutional mechanisms) in subsistence marketplaces. Lack of traditionally-developed distribution channels, media outlets, sampling frames, and related market research infrastructure lead to the need for bottom-up implementation as well as bottom-up learning and perspective-taking. Less acknowledged is the capabilities deficit *about* subsistence marketplaces among outside entities. Lack of understanding of radically different contexts and unfamiliar settings in turn lends itself very well to bottom-up learning, phenomenal focus, and perspective-taking.

Perhaps the most important trait to implement a bottom-up approach to innovation is a mutual learning mindset – one that acknowledges that subsistence consumers and entrepreneurs are experts at survival, just as those from the outside have expertise of their own. Openness to learning going into subsistence marketplaces is particularly critical; you need to suspend preconceptions about rational behavior, because these preconceptions are based on implicit assumptions of relative affluence that revolve around what is taken for granted. Thus, issues such as what constitutes rational behavior need to be revisited.

Chapter 4: Understanding Subsistence Marketplaces

Having outlined the bottom-up approach in the previous chapter, in this chapter we continue our journey into understanding subsistence marketplaces as a basis to then discuss the design of solutions.

Gaining Insights in Subsistence Marketplaces

Many of our project assignments involve gaining marketplace insight. As it is important to learn about subsistence contexts, this is a central theme of ours. To gain marketplace insights, we need to understand how people think, how they feel, and so on, and, in turn, what it means for conducting research in these contexts. So we use simple tasks with people in subsistence, and show them products and advertisements that make things real for them.

The first part of this chapter is devoted to helping you understand how to best relate to people, build authentic relationships, and immerse yourself in the environment as you carry out your research in subsistence contexts. A number of factors should be considered in gaining marketplace insights as illustrated below.

Image 4.01: Gaining Marketplace Insights.[70]

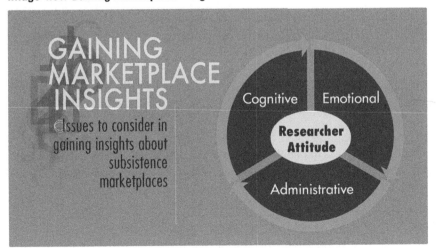

---

[70] Image: Bob Dignan, Christina Tarn, and Killivalavan Solai for the Subsistence Marketplaces Initiative.

Relating to People in Subsistence Contexts

When you relate to people in subsistence contexts:

- Use straightforward language

- Be realistic in what you ask them to do

- Do not have them read or write, but rather administer any survey yourself

We want to make people feel comfortable and at ease when they participate in this work. Perhaps the last time you took a school exam, you felt anxious about whether you knew the right answers. We don't want to put participants in that frame of mind, as they are not accustomed to this setting. So we do all we can to make them feel at ease.

Because we are of a much higher social status, and are asking individuals a number of questions, one of the first concerns they may have is whether we are testing them. They want to give us the right answers. So put them at ease and let them know that *they* are the experts and that you are there to learn from them. This is one of the first things I say when I'm having a conversation or doing an interview in these contexts, and I mean it! Consider their feelings and emotions, and have a sincere and respectful conversation with them that conveys that you want to learn from them and any answer they provide will be the right answer.

A few more keys to doing research in these contexts:

- Avoid judging people

- Avoid exploiting them

- Avoid making them feel anxious

- Be genuinely interested in what they have to say

In conducting your research, try to work with different organizations that can give you access to people who are at the bottom of society. Respect the participants and ensure their privacy just the way you would respect anybody in any research setting.

Go in ready to learn from people in this environment; immerse yourself in their environment. Do not think about what people cannot do because they are low-literate; think about what they do and what they can do. Emphasize their strengths in addition to noting their weaknesses, just as we all have strengths as well as weaknesses. That is why the mutual learning mindset discussed in Chapter 2 is so important in understanding what expertise they bring and what expertise we bring.

Building Authentic and Respectful Relationships

What are some generic issues in gaining marketplace insights? When you are dealing with subsistence or poverty, what you see is what you get. People don't have time for pretensions. Here are ways to build authentic relationships with the people you interact with:

- Don't try to act like you are poor
- Don't try to be somebody you are not, people will see through that, just be yourself; it is very important to be authentic in who you are
- When you don't know about something, ask, don't pretend you know the answer
- Don't try to maintain a distance
- Don't be status conscious
- Don't be so task-oriented that you focus only on trying to get what you want
- Engage people in a sincere conversation
- Help them gain something out of it as well, you will also gain more that way
- Understand the story of the human being across from you
- Seek out the powerless, even though this is very difficult to do

When you go to an NGO, they are going to take you on a tour, and sometimes you may not see or talk to the people who are at the bottom of the hierarchy. Seek them out. Try to talk to people, homemakers, farmers, and others who are at the bottom of the hierarchy.

When you engage in this work, respect, empathy, and sincere listening are critical. Don't just go through a laundry list of questions; listen to people's stories. Each person *is* a story, and has a very rich story. People open up their entire lives to us, and they are so generous, and in the end they enrich us in ways that we cannot describe. Some people have told us things that they say they only tell God in a place of worship. They've shared such things with us because they believe that we were there to learn from them and to create a solution that can help them. Our entire work depends on their generosity.

Resist the temptation to exploit, which may mean trying to confirm what you already believe, or to gain something at the cost of a respondent. A woman told me about her entire life and how she became an entrepreneur, and at one point in the interview she stopped and said, "I became an entrepreneur because my husband became dysfunctional." That was a very emotional moment. In such a moment, be empathetic and move on if it is the best thing to do so you don't exploit the situation, unless she wants to talk more about it. Remember that you have higher status, and there are many ways that you can exploit the situation, even if you are not intentionally doing so. Above all else, keep the welfare of the person you are talking to as your highest priority. Make sure that that person has a good experience. If you do that, you will have gained many insights as well, and more importantly, you will have gained a grounding based on the integrity of your research approach.

Immersing Yourself in the Subsistence Environment

Immerse yourself in the environment of the people you are interviewing. Do the groundwork, invest the time to understand the local context, and develop appropriate methods for your research. Don't go in necessarily thinking of the method as a survey or an interview. Be prepared to change your methods as you go along. Sometimes, as I mentioned earlier, it is good to observe people shopping, or living out their normal lives, and then ask them questions. Sometimes it is good to sit down and have them take you through their entire life. Sometimes it is good just to observe without asking questions. Maybe it is how they are cooking, or caring for their children, or working, and so on.

When you think about this kind of work, think about the longer term. Don't just think about a specific interview and what am I going to get out of it. Think about building a relationship with that community or similar communities elsewhere. Think about what that means and what you are going to give back. This may not always work out and we don't want to make promises we cannot keep. But it is good to have this mindset.

Develop diverse skills through local partnerships. Different people bring different skillsets. Some NGOs will be able to give you access to communities. Some may be able to help you to observe and to interview. So try to develop diverse skills by building partnerships.

Understand the motivations of the people you work with. Everybody is in it for something, and it is important to understand what that is, just as we are in it for something. This is extremely important in these very unfamiliar settings. What is that person in it for? What are you in it for? Articulate it, so they know who you are and they know what to expect from you. Communicate your motivations. Tell them where you come from, what you are doing, and why you are doing it.

When I do research I'm very clear about who I am and why I am there. I'm there to do research, but I'm also there because I would like to learn from the research and give back to the community by designing marketplace literacy programs. I'm careful not to make a promise I cannot keep. I'm going to tell them what I generally do. Sometimes when you leave a community, people will say, "Please help us with this," and these are very genuine pleas for help. But if I cannot do it, I have to be honest. I'm not going to make false promises.

Conducting Your Research

When you implement your research, engage in a healthy disbelief. Don't believe everything you hear, and don't believe that you have learned something right away. Be skeptical and refine your methods as you go along; try to understand things from different angles. For example, variables like income and age are difficult for some people to accurately talk about, so find different ways to get that information. Accuracy is very important here and sympathy cannot get in the way of obtaining accurate insights. This does not mean being rude and blunt; it means learning about an issue through different sources – for example, understanding sources of income someone may have beyond what is reported.

Make respondents feel that they know more about the topic, because they really do know more. Let them speak; be an attentive listener. It is okay if there are silences. Avoid leading questions and yes/no kinds of questions; rather, use a few broad questions and ask things such as "What was it like to do this?" or "How did you feel?" Avoid "why" questions when you can. Rather, ask people to tell you about a time when they did something. "Why" questions sometimes put people on the defensive, and also make the respondents answer the questions that you, the researcher, are trying to answer. It is better to let them tell you their story.

Start an interview by telling people what the topic is about. Begin with some broad questions: "What stores do you buy products from?" "Are there some stores that you like more than others?" "Why do you go to that particular store?" "What do you buy?" "Tell me about the last time you bought from that store." That is a very concrete way to ask a question – the last time you did something. "Think about the shopping experience. Can you describe what was noteworthy about the situation?" "What happened?" "How did it happen?" "For each product that you bought, how did you buy it? Did you look at the price? Did you look at the size?"

This principle of asking the broader questions is important. Ask about the last trip to the grocery store, and let people tell you which store they went to and what they did. Once they tell you, then ask, "What are some products you bought?" As they describe the products, ask how they bought them. Don't lead them, and don't ask a specific question until they tell you how they bought the products. Once they tell you how they bought the products or if the conversation needs prompting, you can ask more specific questions, such as "Did you check the price?" "Did you check for other attributes?" It's important to let people have a chance to give you an open-ended answer before you ask for something more specific.

Here is an example of a broad question about budgeting. You can start by asking for an example of the last time somebody ran out of money. Ask, "How did it feel to run out of money?" "What happened?" Interviewees can talk about their budget and what their typical monthly expenses are. They can talk about how they buy in installments, the interest they pay, and so on.

In terms of your field research, think about whom you want to talk to, what you want to observe, what items, products, and advertisements you need, what roles you'll play, what your overall interview plan is, and what stimuli you need to show to people.

Gaining Insights from Your Research

You can share ideas and concepts for solutions with participants, and try to get feedback. Seek feedback in an open-ended way before asking specifically about how participants would change the solution, what they would pay for it, what communication means would be best, and so on.

Try to gain broad insights about life circumstances and the community in general, rather than immediately homing in on your product or the need that you are focused on. You have to understand how that need interacts with other needs – for example, food, water, and sanitation. When people are deprived on multiple fronts, needs become interconnected, and it is important to first get a broader picture, and then funnel into one aspect or one need that you are focusing on.

It is also important to step back and see how that need plays out in terms of various other needs. If you are interested in how people cook, don't just focus on their stove. Think about where the stove is, if it is on the floor of a hut, if there are children running around it, how they cook, what kind of food they cook, how they cook as it relates to the rest of the houses in the community, and what the larger context is in terms of energy sources. You need to understand these different elements of the larger context.

Finally, keep a diary, because your thoughts are extremely important as you go along. One approach is to divide each page into two, with the top half for what you observe and the bottom half for your intuitive reactions and deeper thoughts.

Virtual Immersion

We discussed virtual immersion earlier. Now let us talk about the virtual immersion exercises that we have created for you. These exercises aim to enhance understanding without actually being there. You will look at a series of images and jot down some reactions as you go through.

For example, in the first virtual immersion exercise, we'd like you to focus on the larger context of subsistence and the unique needs that you see. As you go through, it is important to put down any responses that come to mind. Any thoughts and observations are worth putting down on paper. They may be your gut instincts, they may be an intuition, but that may lead to you seeing this particular context in a different way. You don't have to use the same terms that are typically employed, like health and education and so on. You may be able to put down something that is a different way of viewing this particular context. Once you are done with this, reflect on your observations with an open mind.

Virtual Immersion – Understanding Subsistence Context and Needs

The following instructions are given to students for a virtual immersion exercise.

> Use one of the immersion slideshows in the web portal.[71] During each slide, jot down your reactions as follows:
>
> - Focus on the unique needs, drivers, and larger context
> - Write down any responses that come to mind as you view each slide
> - Capture any thoughts - they may be observations or deeper thoughts

We will illustrate this with a few selected slides. For example, here is a slide with a person who is collecting aluminum cans.

Image 4.02: Makoko in the Water.[72]

---

[71] https://business.illinois.edu/subsistence/resources/resourcesmlp/: Use the password *subsistence* to access materials on the web portal.

[72] Photograph: Heinrich Böll-Stiftung. https://commons.wikimedia.org/wiki/File:Makoko_auf_dem_Wasser_(5209071096).jpg.

Now, you can see a number of different things. First of all, there are a number of dwellings in the background, and it seems like this is garbage that is thrown out from many of these dwellings. And you begin to wonder, "What problems arise when you have stagnant water with so much garbage in it? What kinds of diseases are caused by these conditions?" It also leads us to think how intermingled the local environment is with the dwellings. So right there you have the water, the garbage, and people throwing out garbage in the water, resulting in illness and disease. Perhaps, reusable things in the garbage are retrieved. What is the demand for them? What does a person do with them? How does a person clean them and sell them?

Image 4.03: Women Carrying Firewood in Nepal.[73]

This is an image you've already seen of women looking for wood for cooking. You can see the attire that they are wearing, you can see how far away they probably had to travel to collect this firewood, and how much firewood they are collecting as well.

I spoke to a woman in a marketplace in Tanzania who was selling this kind of firewood and feeling quite guilty about it. She said (paraphrasing), "I did not cut any tree, this was wood that was already fallen. It is very wrong to cut green trees; they need to grow." She also told me how it takes her seven hours to collect the firewood and return home, as she has to travel far to find the wood. A few years ago she could do all of this in two or three hours. With deforestation, there is less and less wood. With long-term drought, there are a number of issues with what happens with these local environments as well. And here's another problem she faces: cooking with firewood leads to indoor smoke and lung ailments, but she doesn't have a choice.

---

[73] Photograph: Engineering for Change. http://www.flickr.com/photos/44221799@N08/4521897946/%22Flickr%E2%80%9D.

Here are a set of images of neighborhoods from around the world. You can compare dwellings across geographic regions, such as what the roofs and walls are made of and how the houses are spaced. You can visualize what the layout of that small house is going to be like in each of these places. Issues to consider here include electricity and water supply. Put down your thoughts as they flow through your mind. Try not to censor yourself; your perspective is unique. There are no experts in this domain; if we did, why do we have these problems on this larger scale? You may be able to see something that somebody else doesn't see.

Image 4.04: Subsistence Dwellings in Chongqing, China.[74]

Image 4.05: Dwellings Built Over the Canals in Vietnam.[75]

---

[74] Photograph: Zhiqiang. https://en.wikipedia.org/wiki/File:Shibati_Yuzong_Chongqing_China_Slum_Shantytown_Area_Overview_November_2010.jpg.

[75] Photograph: McKay Savage. https://en.wikipedia.org/wiki/File:Vietnam_08_-_151_-_houses_over_the_canals_(3186477231).jpg.

Image 4.06: Dwellings Built on Swamp Land near a Garbage Dump in East Cipinang, Jakarta.[76]

Image 4.07: Dwellings of Villa 31, Retiro, Buenos Aires, Argentina.[77]

---

[76] Photograph: Jonathan McIntosh. https://commons.wikimedia.org/wiki/File:Jakarta_slumhome_2.jpg.

[77] Photograph: Aleposta. https://en.wikipedia.org/wiki/File:Villamiseria5.JPG.

In this regard, we earlier discussed the mutual learning mindset. We have some expertise, and we are observing people who have some expertise as well, certainly in survival. These two perspectives have to meet, and for that to happen, we virtually immerse ourselves in this context, through these images, and note what is unique about them. By doing that, we will be focusing on not just the need, but what drives that need. You'll begin to see how those drivers and that need play out in a larger context. So that is why it is important to put down all the thoughts that come to mind, and go through this immersion exercise, taking our time to go through each of these images.

Exercise (Repeated from Chapter 3): Virtual Immersion – Understanding Subsistence Context and Needs

View one of the immersion slideshows from the web portal.[78]

- Select a specific slide and write down what you see.
- Repeat for two other slides.
- Run the slideshow and jot down your reactions for each slide as follows. Please focus on the unique needs, drivers, and larger context.
  - Write down any responses that come to mind as you view each slide.
  - Capture any thoughts – they may be observations or deeper thoughts.

Understanding Needs, Drivers, and Context — frame the model

Why do we need to focus on the needs, drivers, and context? Because it is not enough to just understand a product or the need or the consumer. These are very unfamiliar contexts where life circumstances are blended with products, daily needs, routines, the relationships people forge in the marketplace, and much more.

If you are designing a stove solution for me in an advanced marketplace, you know what my kitchen looks like. You know the infrastructure I have. You know that I can count on electricity. You can assume many things about the way I live and the way I consume. As a result, you can focus on my need and figure out how to make a most efficient and effective gas stove for me. But in a subsistence setting you are talking about an unfamiliar context where people are going to be using your product to serve a need in ways that neither you nor they can anticipate.

---

[78] https://business.illinois.edu/subsistence/resources/resourcesmlp/: Use the password *subsistence* to access materials on the web portal.

Let's consider the stove in a subsistence context. It may be on the floor of a hut, with children running around it. So how do you design for that context? Moreover, it is not enough if you just understand the household, the need, and the product that will meet that need. You have to understand how that household interacts with the neighborhood, and how that community interacts with other communities. How do they cook in that community? What are the cultural values there? What are the different types of food that are cooked? It is not enough to understand the consumer alone. You have to understand not only the consumer, and the community, but the larger context as well. Issues of infrastructure, availability of fuel, and so forth become pertinent.

Image 4.08: Understanding the Consumer, Community, and Larger Context.

Understanding More Than the Customer

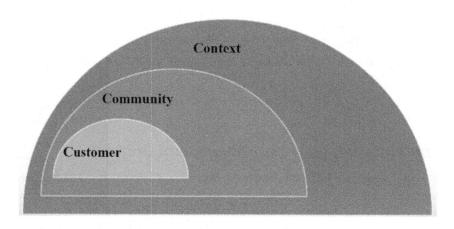

Drivers are the Causes of the Need

In relatively affluent settings, we are typically unfamiliar with a context where day-to-day living occurs with a lot of uncertainty. And that uncertainty is happening at a household level, at a community level, and playing out in a larger context as well. You have to think through what the consumer's needs are, what factors drive those needs, and what the elements of the larger context are in which all of these drivers happen.

What we are going to do in the entire project in terms of developing understanding is shown on the left side of the picture below. We are going to look at the need that you are going to focus on. We are going to understand what drives that need (to be so stark usually) in a subsistence context. What are the causes of that need? We cannot just think about the product and assume that everything else will fall into place. And finally, we are going to understand the larger context elements, the larger backdrop where drivers and needs occur.

Image 4.09: Project Overview.[79]

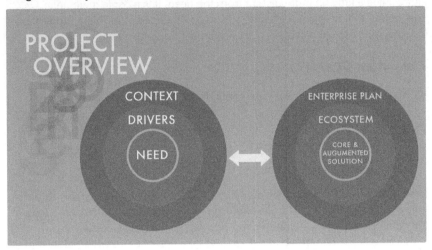

On the right side of the image below, we focus on designing the core and augmented solution in the innermost circle. We also have to design the ecosystem that goes around the core and augmented solution. And then we design the enterprise plan as well.

The augmented solution and ecosystem are important because, in subsistence contexts, people are deprived on multiple fronts. It is not enough to focus on the product (the core solution) alone. We have to think about how to augment the product, maybe with education. And we have to think about the ecosystem; this may include educational classes, or a network of farmers, or something else.

Using the next series of images, we discuss an example of a need for protection from parasite-carrying mosquitoes. This is a huge cost, in human and in economic terms, because of malaria in the African continent. What are the drivers of this need? In other words, what causes this need to be so stark? Among the factors:

- Inability to take preventive measures
- Affordability of the treatment

---

[79] Image: Bob Dignan, Christina Tarn, and Killivalavan Solai for the Subsistence Marketplaces Initiative.

- Lack of access to healthcare
- A poor public health infrastructure

So, all of these are drivers. A driver is anything that causes the need to manifest as it does. As long as it is closely related to the need, it is a driver. On the other hand, if it is a little bit more distant from the need, it is a context element. Ensure that the drivers are framed in terms of the need or problem rather than in terms of the eventual solution, as we are at the understanding phase now.

The Larger Context

So what is the larger context? Elements of the larger context could include:

- Climatic conditions
- Demographics and poverty
- The lack of infrastructure

Keep in mind that you can decide what a driver is and what a context is, as long as the context is the larger backdrop and the driver is more immediate to the need (see Image 4.10 below). You don't have to really wrestle with whether something is a driver or a context as long as you recognize what belongs in the larger backdrop, and what is a more immediate cause of a particular need. Thus, lack of access to healthcare could be a larger context element in some scenarios. *List needs → drivers → context*

Image 4.10: Example of Needs.[80]

---

[80] Image: Bob Dignan, Christina Tarn, and Killivalavan Solai for the Subsistence Marketplaces Initiative. Photograph: Alison Bird/USAID. https://commons.wikimedia.org/wiki/File:Health_care_for_sick_babies_(5686758533).jpg.

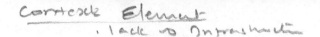

[handwritten: Context Element / lack of Infrastructure]

Image 4.11: Drivers of Needs.[81]

> **PROBLEM**
> Drivers of needs
> Malaria is known as the disease of poverty
> and a cause of poverty
>
> **POVERTY** | Inability to take preventive measures
> Affordability of curative treatment
>
> **INFRASTRUCTURE** | Poor public health infrastructure
> General availability of health care

Image 4.12: Context Elements.[82]

> **PROBLEM**
> Context elements
>
> **CLIMATE**
> Climatic conditions in Africa
> conducive for the thriving
> of vectors
>
> **DEMOGRAPHY**
> Area: 30.3 million km²
>
> Population: 888 million
> (250 million < $0.9 a day)
>
> 1 in 2 people have access to hospital or doctor
> in Sub-Saharan Africa

---

[81] Image: Bob Dignan, Christina Tarn, and Killivalavan Solai for the Subsistence Marketplaces Initiative.

[82] Image: Bob Dignan, Christina Tarn, and Killivalavan Solai for the Subsistence Marketplaces Initiative. Data: "Is African Poverty Falling?" *AfricaCan End Poverty*. 2009. Accessed April 19, 2016. http://blogs.worldbank.org/africacan/is-african-poverty-falling.

Exercise: Understanding Need, Drivers, and Context

To help you understand the need, the drivers, and the context, we have developed an exercise. Use the exercise to identify the need that you will focus on in your project.

- First, go through the virtual immersion. List needs that you find interesting on a sheet of paper.

- Identify the top three needs you would like to focus on for your project topic.

- Describe these three needs in terms of geography, demographics, and usage issues.

- List the drivers – the immediate causes – of the need.

- List the larger context elements.

- Draw all of this out in concentric circles with labels. The very act of drawing out what you have in your mind in the form of a big picture is important for you to see what your thinking is really about.

Bottom-Up and Top-Down Need/Problem Deconstruction[83]

We have created some exercises to help you deconstruct needs, from which you can then generate ideas and a concept to design your augmented solution and ecosystem. Remember, an idea is just something preliminary, piecemeal, any element of a solution. It could be the beginnings of a solution or some part of it. Nevertheless, it should be distinguished from ideas for aspects of the enterprise plan that involve implementing the solution, which can come later. A concept is more detailed. It is self-contained. And it is useful to represent the concept in the form of a picture or a figure.

Consider the example of a low-cost prosthetic social enterprise that was called IPT. The students came up with many ideas, which you can see in Image 4.13 below, for upper-arm prosthetics for people living in India who have amputations. How did they arrive at these ideas? They first developed a problem tree, both from the top-down perspective of their organization, and from the perspective of subsistence, consumers, communities, and stakeholders.

---

[83] Roozenburg, N. F. M., and J. Eekels. *Product Design: Fundamentals and Methods.* Vol. 2. Chichester: Wiley, 1995.

Image 4.13: Sketches of Students' Ideas for Prosthetics.[84]

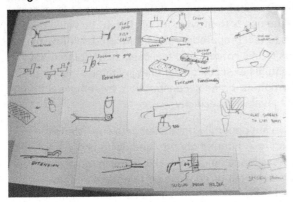

Exercise (Repeated from Chapter 3): Bottom-Up Idea Generation

- Finely tune needs or break up needs into smaller dimensions (associated drivers – associated context) and come up with ideas to address using the need, or each driver, or each context element to stimulate

- Freeze one of the following and come up with ideas:

   o Customer group – e.g., children

   o Geographic location – e.g. South India

   o Usage situation – e.g., household versus workplace versus in transit

- Consider what, who, where, when, and how

- State problem from the perspective of the end customer and come up with ideas

Bottom-Up Need Deconstruction

There are many ways to do this. We can deconstruct the need or the problem into questions through forming a problem tree.[85] Now, let us start with the person with an amputation in a subsistence setting. When we try to deconstruct his needs from the bottom-up, we start by taking on his perspective. So we talk about his need to survive. That is his most basic need. And that means he needs to be comfortable in social settings, provide for his family, and feel content. All of this has implications.

---

[84] Photograph: Subsistence Marketplaces Initiative.

[85] Bagozzi, Richard P., and Utpal Dholakia. "Goal Setting and Goal Striving in Consumer Behavior." *Journal of Marketing* 63 (1999): 19. doi:10.2307/1252098.

If he needs to be comfortable in social settings, he needs to have an inconspicuous arm to minimize being perceived differently. He needs an arm that will not hurt anyone. If he needs to provide for his family, he will need to maintain a job. He needs to feel prepared for the future. And self-image is important as well. He needs to feel content and feel capable of doing many things, while being realistic in his expectations, and enjoy things that he does. So this is what we mean by bottom-up need construction. It can have different starting points and different levels of specificity.

This is important because we are generally unfamiliar with subsistence settings. This is not like going to a different country and designing a solution for somebody in a middle-class household there. This is much more than that. In this setting, there is much uncertainty, so we need to understand not only the need, but the drivers and the context as well. We need to understand not only the consumer, but the community and the larger context as well. That is why we do this kind of analysis, to really push home on the bottom-up philosophy and enable proper grounding in the context.

Image 4.14: Bottom-Up Need Deconstruction – Amputee in Subsistence Marketplaces.[86]

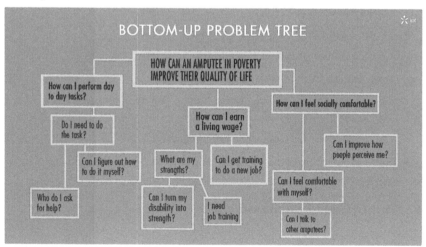

Exercise (Repeated from Chapter 3): Bottom-Up Needs Deconstruction

- List needs as statements in first person as the end-beneficiary
- Eliminate/combine redundant/identical statements

---

[86] Image: Bob Dignan, Christina Tarn, and Killivalavan Solai for the Subsistence Marketplaces Initiative.

- Group cards according to the similarity of the need they express

- For each group, choose a label to generalize the need

- Review and revise groups

- Generate and evaluate your ideas/concepts based on this exercise

Exercise: Need Listing

- List needs

- Eliminate/combine redundant/identical needs

- Group cards according to the similarity of the need they express

- For each group, choose a label to generalize the need

- Create a hierarchy of needs and sub-needs

Top-Down Need Deconstruction

We can also deconstruct needs from the top-down. So, IPT can look at its own needs. They need to provide solutions that improve amputees' quality of life. That means they need to identify amputee needs and expectations and tap into local expertise and support. They need partners for manufacturing and distribution, positive word of mouth from trusted experts, and so on. This is what we mean by top-down need deconstruction.

Image 4.15: Top-Down Need Deconstruction: How Can Low-Cost Prosthetics Improve Amputees' Lives?[87]

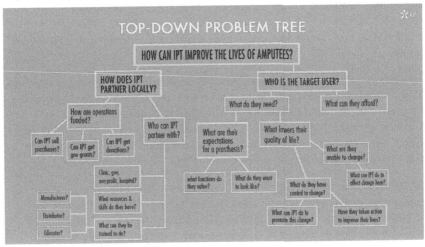

---

[87] Ibid.

Exercise (Repeated from Chapter 3): Top-Down Need Deconstruction

- List needs as statements in first person as manager at organization
- Eliminate/combine redundant/identical statements
- Group cards according to the similarity of the need they express
- For each group, choose a label to generalize the need
- Review and revise groups
- Generate and evaluate ideas/concepts based in this exercise

Exercise (Repeated from Chapter 3): Top-Down Approaches

- Review technologies and use them to come up with ideas
- Review current solutions and use them to come up with ideas
- Review functions of current solutions and come up with ideas (e.g., personal grooming – different functions)
- Review current processes in delivering solutions and come up with ideas (e.g., Abbott additive to what, in what form, etc.)

Bottom-Up Meeting Top-Down

We are not saying that we should just be bottom-up in our understanding. We are saying that the bottom-up is often neglected. *The bottom-up has to meet the top-down.* **If we just take our organizations' perspectives, then we are not going to understand the bottom-up needs.** We are not going to serve, for example, amputees with the proper solution. To do that, we need a bottom-up understanding of people in subsistence as well as top-down understanding of needs.

We can create a slight variation on need deconstruction by looking at problem trees. In this particular case, we start off with a question or a statement, and we break that question or statement into other questions and statements, and move down from there. We want to make sure that we cover all the different topics involved in the problem, but at the same time we want to make sure that there aren't overlapping questions as well.

So, for example, with a bottom-up problem tree in the form of a question, how can an amputee in poverty improve his quality of life? That is the fundamental problem that the amputee faces from the bottom-up. That breaks down into a number of questions. How can I perform day-to-day tasks? How can I earn a living wage? How can I feel socially comfortable? And so on. Personalizing the questions adds a level of depth that third-person descriptions don't. This is one more step toward bottom-up understanding and informed empathy.

This is just a variation of listing sub-needs. Here, we have written statements or questions to clarify sub-needs. Similarly, we could have a top-down problem tree. How can IPT improve the lives of amputees? And that can break down into a variety of questions as well. These sub-needs and this kind of deconstruction stays with us throughout as we think about the solution. Such deconstruction essentially keeps us honest using bottom-up understanding as a foundation.

Exercise (Repeated from Chapter 3): Identifying Needs[88]

This exercise will help you identify needs.

- Write need and sub-needs as statements in the first person, taking the role of the end beneficiary
- Write each statement on a separate card
- Combine these cards into groups, based on topic, and label these groups to identify specific needs based on those topics
- Review and revise these groups repeatedly until you have covered all the sub-needs involved in that larger basic problem or need that you are serving

This will help you analyze the need and begin to see the different, smaller needs that it breaks into (i.e., the sub-needs).

Keys to Understanding Subsistence Marketplaces

We present the keys to understanding subsistence marketplaces from previous chapters in list form. Then we will briefly explain each key.

1. The bottom-up approach is unique.
2. We have to unlearn our assumptions about life in subsistence marketplaces.
3. We need to understand how low-literate people think, feel, and cope.
4. We need to understand how exchanges and transactions work.
5. Relationships are paramount in subsistence living.
6. People in subsistence focus on survival, relationships, and growth.
7. We can gain great insights from people in subsistence marketplaces.
8. The process for developing solutions is multifaceted.

---

[88] Watkins, Ryan, Maurya West-Meiers, and Yusra Laila Visser. *A Guide to Assessing Needs: Essential Tools for Collecting Information, Making Decisions, and Achieving Development Results.* Washington, DC: World Bank, 2012.

9. To design solutions, we need to know the need, the drivers of the need, and the larger context.

1. The Bottom-Up Approach Is Unique.

Our bottom-up approach is very different than a macro-level or even a mid-level approach. We start at the micro-level, with people, their life circumstances, and how they engage in the marketplace as consumers and entrepreneurs, and we build up from there. That is why we focus on the one-on-one interactions, the thinking, the feeling, the coping and so on, as well as issues such as the local environment.

2. Unlearn Our Assumptions About Life in Subsistence Marketplaces.

It's vital that we understand how people think, feel, and cope in the marketplace. Fundamentally the way they think is different in terms of concrete thinking and pictographic thinking. To understand people living in subsistence and then design solutions for them, we have to unlearn assumptions based on how we think and try to understand how *they* think and react in different situations.

3. Understand How Low-Literate People Think, Feel, and Cope.

People living in poverty have cognitive in addition to material constraints due to low literacy and lack of exposure. They have unique patterns of thinking, feeling, and coping. For example, low-literate people try to maintain their self-esteem in seemingly mundane situations, such as being at a store counter. It may not be a big issue for me, but it is for them, because their literacy is involved. And their low literacy is often the cause for their lack of income and life circumstances. People cope, sometimes in ingenious ways, to get around extreme constraints that they have faced all their lives. So it is critical to start out at that micro-level of understanding how people think, how they feel, and how they cope, to design solutions for people living in subsistence marketplaces.

4. Understand How Exchanges and Transactions Work.

Subsistence marketplaces are unique in terms of their exchanges, their relational environment, and their larger context. There is a constant demand for customization. Everybody wants a special deal. And how that is managed is critical for the entrepreneur. If you give a special deal, you need to have some logic, some rationale, for it. Sometimes you cannot give a special deal, because everybody will come and ask you the same thing. Transactions are very fluid. People will not pay for installments if the product is not good. And buyers and sellers are often quite responsive in this one-on-one interactional environment.

5. Relationships Are Paramount in Subsistence Living.

Relationships mean a lot in subsistence marketplaces. People multiply their value to the seller or to the buyer through relationships. This happens through oral language, through people talking to each other, and through people who are interdependent on each other. And it all happens in the human context of survival, so we cannot separate the economic element from the human element. That is why we discuss the notion of interactional empathy.

6. People in Subsistence Focus on Survival, Relationships, and Growth.

We talked about environmental issues and subsistence and the irony that, in resource-rich settings, people could do something about their environment, but often feel indifferent about it. In subsistence settings, people live their environment, they suffer the consequences from environmental problems, but they have very little control over the problems.

People in subsistence try to sustain themselves in terms of survival, relatedness, and growth. They focus on basic needs, on relating to each other and to the natural environment, and on aspiring for a better future for themselves, and particularly for their children, through education and other means.

7. Gain Great Insights from People in Subsistence Marketplaces.

We can gain marketplace insights in terms of how people think, how they feel, and so on by learning how best to conduct research in these settings. We consider thinking, feeling, and administrative issues in conducting research. Reach out to many people in subsistence settings. For example, don't just interview the person who shops at the store, interview the shop keeper as well. Everyone has a unique perspective and insights can come from the most unexpected people or places.

8. The Process for Developing Solutions Is Multifaceted.

The process for developing solutions includes virtual immersion, emersion (which is a compare-and-contrast in terms of the concepts you already know and the new or modified concepts you need), preparation for field research, actual immersion, reflection, focused concept generation, testing, and subsequent steps.

9. To Design Solutions, Know the Need, the Drivers of the Need, and the Larger Context.

To understand subsistence marketplaces and design solutions, we have to understand the life circumstances around the needs. We are dealing in an unfamiliar setting, where needs get blurred with life circumstances and with community-level issues. We need to frame projects in terms of the problem, which is about the need, the drivers, and the context.

Chapter 5: Designing Bottom-Up Solutions

In the previous chapter, we considered many aspects that aid you in understanding subsistence marketplaces as a basis for designing bottom-up solutions: building authentic relationships with people in subsistence contexts, immersing yourself in the subsistence environment, conducting and gaining insight from your research, understanding the needs, drivers, and context, and so on.

In this chapter, we are going to move into actually designing the solution itself. We will consider how to identify needs, design and augment your core solution, create your enterprise plan, and understand, position, communicate, and deliver your value proposition. We will also look at some examples of bottom-up solutions that we have developed.

Designing Solutions for Subsistence Marketplaces

To start, let us briefly consider four aspects of designing solutions for subsistence marketplaces:

- Understanding subsistence marketplaces
- Identifying critical product needs
- Designing products
- Developing products

Image 5.01: A Marketplace-Oriented Process for Developing Solutions for Subsistence Contexts.[89]

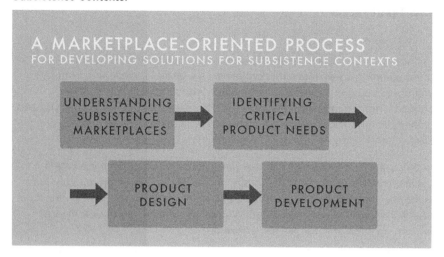

Understanding Subsistence Marketplaces

Image 5.02: A Marketplace-Oriented Process for Developing Solutions for Subsistence Contexts: Understanding Subsistence Marketplaces.[90]

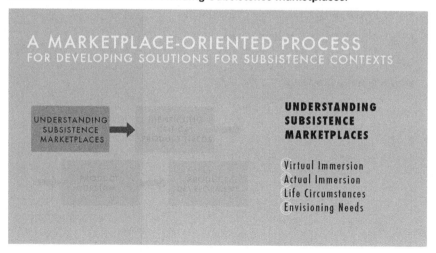

Virtual immersion and actual immersion are critical steps in understanding subsistence marketplaces. We can't assume we already have the answer

---

[89] Image: Bob Dignan, Christina Tarn, and Killivalavan Solai for the Subsistence Marketplaces Initiative.

[90] Ibid.

simply because we are more literate or we have a higher income than those we are trying to serve. We should strive to understand the broader life circumstances and not just the need that we are focusing on, because these life circumstances impinge on the need, and people living in subsistence are deprived on multiple fronts. We have to not only understand the consumer, but the community and the larger context as well. Our own unfamiliarity comes face-to-face with a complex context where the marketplace is blurred with many other realms of life and where each context is unique.

Identifying Needs

Image 5.03: A Marketplace-Oriented Product Development Process for Subsistence Contexts: Identifying Critical Needs.[91]

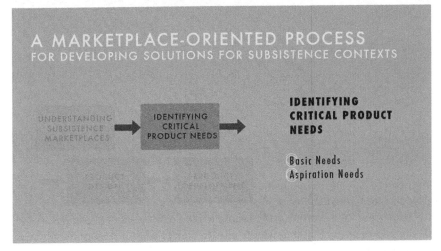

It is difficult to envision needs and usage situations if we have not experienced poverty. We must understand what the needs are and how they are being fulfilled in various usage situations. We cannot anticipate all of these usage situations, but as we design solutions we must try to understand the life circumstances and the usage situations in which these needs are being fulfilled.

In identifying critical product needs, there are basic needs and there are aspirational needs. Sometimes we think that, because people are living in subsistence, all they care about are basic needs. There are a number of aspirational needs, particularly as they relate to the next generation. They may be about healthy products for children or education for children, and so on. People aspire to have a better future for their children. People want their children to not go through the same hardships that they have. And people

---

[91] Ibid.

aspire to own products and brands that give them a source of pride, rare as this may be. Indeed, there are both life aspirations and marketplace/brand aspirations.

Designing Products

Image 5.04: A Marketplace-Oriented Product Development Process for Subsistence Contexts: Product Design.[92]

We need to be culturally sensitive, a recurring theme. We should design products for harsh usage circumstances. In one sense, we almost have to "user-proof" the product and assume it will be misused. It has to be designed assuming that the user is low-literate. It has to be designed to be locally sustainable, which may mean having a distributed source of renewable energy, or providing an entrepreneurial opportunity, a livelihood opportunity for the local community. Ideally, we should design products to be customizable and to serve multiple purposes because of very scarce resources. People constantly ask for a customized product in a one-on-one world, so we have to design products that are customizable at the point of purchase or usage.

---

[92] Ibid.

Developing Products

Image 5.05: A Marketplace-Oriented Product Development Process for Subsistence Contexts – Product Development.[93]

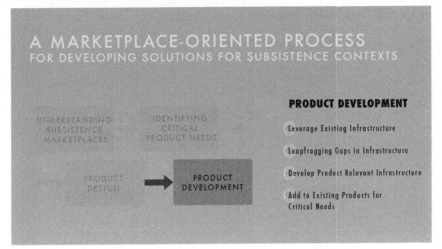

Leveraging the existing infrastructure is an important consideration in developing products. Sometimes we have to leapfrog the infrastructure, such as with a different form of energy solution or a different form of communication. We need to develop product-relevant infrastructure, such as education about the product, and the need. The solution has to add on to existing products to conserve resources.

---

[93] Ibid.

Framework for Understanding Problems and Opportunities, and Designing Solutions and Enterprise Plans for Subsistence Marketplaces

Image 5.06: Details of the Project.[94]

PROJECT DETAILS

1. PROBLEM
NEED AND ISSUES
DRIVERS OF NEEDS
CONTEXT ELEMENTS

2. OPPORTUNITY
GEOGRAPHY
BENEFICIARY/CUSTOMER
USAGE SITUATION

3. SOLUTION
CORE SOLUTION
AUGMENTED SOLUTION
ECOSYSTEM

4. ENTERPRISE PLAN
SUSTAINABLE VALUE PROPOSITION
COMPARISON WITH ALTERNATIVES & POSITIONING MAP
STORYBOARD OF VALUE CHAIN
COMMUNICATING THE VALUE PROPOSITION
DELIVERING THE VALUE PROPOSITION
DEVELOPING THE EXCHANGE MODEL

5. SUSTAINABLE OUTCOMES
SOCIAL
ENVIRONMENTAL
ECONOMIC

We present above our framework for understanding the problem and opportunity, and designing the solution as well as an enterprise plan to implement it. The rationale for this flow:

- It begins with a deep, bottom-up understanding, using the need-drivers-context exercise.

- This is then followed by the selection of the end-beneficiary or customer, the geography, and the usage situation(s).

- The next step follows from the iterative application of the need-drivers-context exercise that helps to narrow down and make choices.

- Finally, this is followed by the design of the solution, the development of the enterprise plan, and the outcomes that we aim for.

To gain a more practical understanding, let's now examine a complete example below and then discuss a number of phases involved. We'll look at the Development of a core solution, augment it, develop an ecosystem around it, and test the concept.

Our core solution generation exercise has a number of different parts. We start off by observing images and writing notes, as we have in earlier exercises. Then we generate ideas, without censoring any of them no matter how silly

---

[94] Ibid.

or crazy they may seem. Then we choose one idea and flesh it into a concept (a concept is simply a more detailed idea to serve a particular need). To help complete this exercise, we provide a number of actual solutions in categories such as agriculture, energy, health, education, finance, and communication in our web portal.

Designing the Solution and the Enterprise Plan

The entire solution and enterprise plan is summarized using a specific example below – the issue of preventing the spread of malaria, which we introduced in Chapter 4. The first three slides are repeated here to refresh your memory, before we show the solution and enterprise plan designed to address that issue.

Image 5.07: Example of Needs and Issues.[95]

[95] Image: Bob Dignan, Christina Tarn, and Killivalavan Solai for the Subsistence Marketplaces Initiative. Photograph: Alison Bird/USAID. https://commons.wikimedia.org/wiki/File:Health_care_for_sick_babies_(5686758533).jpg.

Image 5.08: Drivers of Needs.[96]

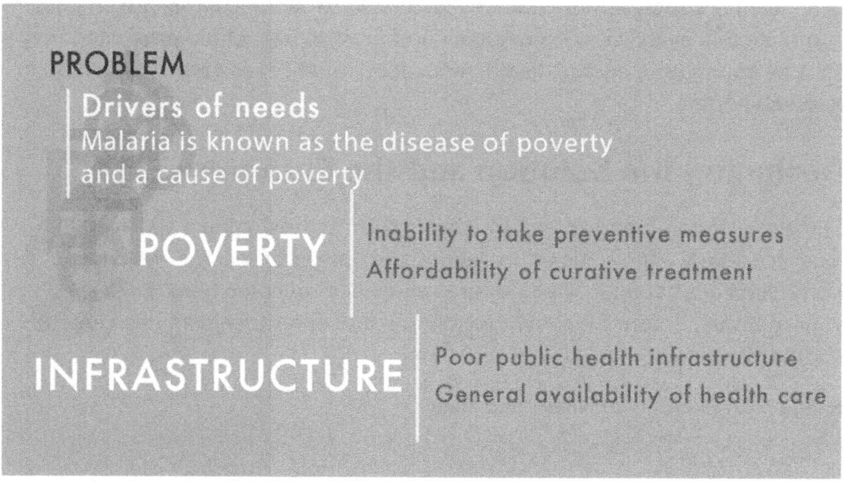

PROBLEM
Drivers of needs
Malaria is known as the disease of poverty
and a cause of poverty

POVERTY
Inability to take preventive measures
Affordability of curative treatment

INFRASTRUCTURE
Poor public health infrastructure
General availability of health care

Image 5.09: Context Elements.[97]

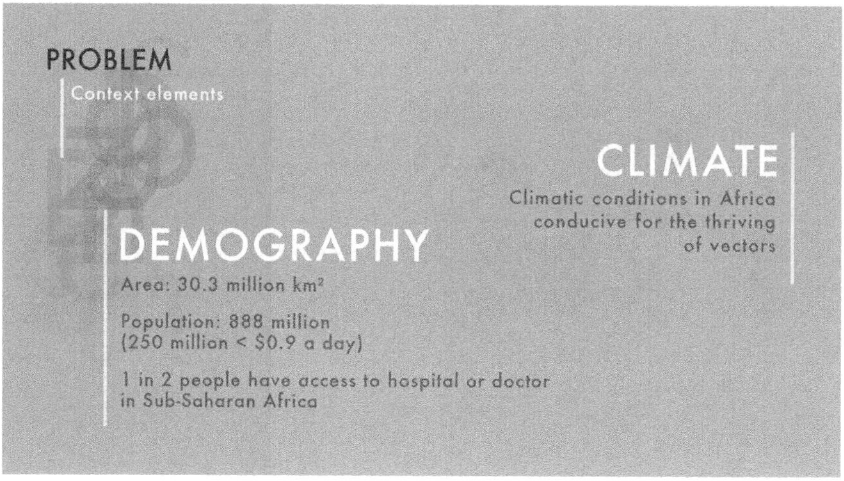

PROBLEM
Context elements

CLIMATE
Climatic conditions in Africa
conducive for the thriving
of vectors

DEMOGRAPHY
Area: 30.3 million km²

Population: 888 million
(250 million < $0.9 a day)

1 in 2 people have access to hospital or doctor
in Sub-Saharan Africa

---

[96] Image: Bob Dignan, Christina Tarn, and Killivalavan Solai for the Subsistence Marketplaces Initiative.

[97] Image: Bob Dignan, Christina Tarn, and Killivalavan Solai for the Subsistence Marketplaces Initiative. Data: "Is African Poverty Falling?" AfricaCan End Poverty. 2009. Accessed April 19, 2016. http://blogs.worldbank.org/africacan/is-african-poverty-falling.

Image 5.10: Opportunity – Geography.[98]

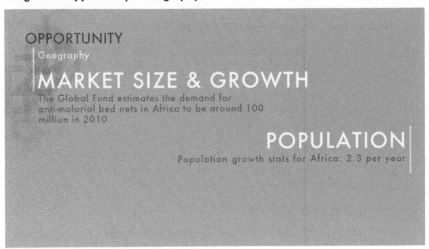

Image 5.11: Opportunity – Beneficiaries / Customers.[99]

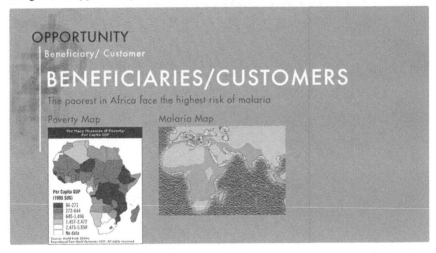

---

[98] Image: Bob Dignan, Christina Tarn, and Killivalavan Solai for the Subsistence Marketplaces Initiative.

[99] Ibid.

Opportunity – Usage Situations

- During sleep at night for infants and children

Solution – Core Solution

- Mosnet
  - o Durable, low-cost, organic, insecticide-treated, anti-malarial bed nets
- Product Features
  - o Effective: Reduces deaths in children by one fifth and episodes of malaria by half
  - o Durable: Lasts five years and is tear resistant
  - o Eco-friendly: Made of recyclable organic material
  - o Safe: Organic insecticide eliminates health hazards

Image 5.12: MosNet Augmented Solution and Ecosystem.[100]

---

[100] Image: Bob Dignan, Christina Tarn, and Killivalavan Solai for the Subsistence Marketplaces Initiative. Photograph: Presidents Mosquito Initiative. https://commons. wikimedia.org/wiki/File:Malaria_prevention-Insecticide_treated_bed_net-PMI.jpg.

Chapter 5

Image 5.13: Competition and Alternatives for MosNet.[101]

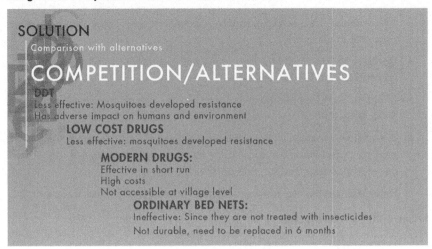

SOLUTION
Comparison with alternatives

COMPETITION/ALTERNATIVES

DDT
Less effective: Mosquitoes developed resistance
Has adverse impact on humans and environment

LOW COST DRUGS
Less effective: mosquitoes developed resistance

MODERN DRUGS:
Effective in short run
High costs
Not accessible at village level

ORDINARY BED NETS:
Ineffective: Since they are not treated with insecticides
Not durable, need to be replaced in 6 months

MosNet – Comparison with Alternatives

Merits	Demerits
High efficacy	Costly
Affordable	Patent protected
Locally produced	Multiple shots required
Easy to use	Mosquitoes develop resistance over time
Easy to distribute	Low life span
Reduce deaths in children by 1/5 and episodes of malaria by 1/2	Do not contain repellant
More affordable than vaccines and DDT in the long term	Health hazards
More effective than non-treated nets	
More durable than ordinary bed nets	
No harmful effects on the environment throughout the product's life cycle	
No health hazards (organic insecticide)	

---

[101] Image: Bob Dignan, Christina Tarn, and Killivalavan Solai for the Subsistence Marketplaces Initiative.

MosNet – Value Proposition

- Affordable: Priced at $3.50, MosNet is cheaper than comparable products in the market
- Durable: MosNet lasts for four years without having to be retreated with insecticide and is tear resistant
- Effective: Reduces deaths in children by one fifth and episodes of malaria by half
- Accessible: MosNet is accessible at the village level through various channels (mobile distribution, local retailers and wholesalers, government care centers, and partner NGOs)
- Safe: MosNet has no adverse effects on humans or the environment

Image 5.14: Positioning Map.

Comparison with Alternatives (Access, Availability and Affordability)

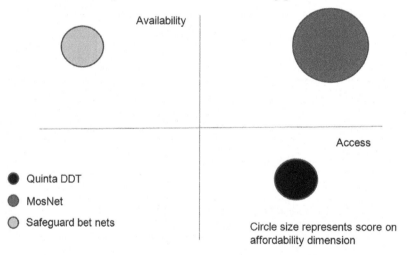

MosNet – Enterprise Plan

- Sustainable Value Proposition: Affordably priced at $3.50
- Communicating the Value Proposition: Community radio, street plays (awareness and usage training)
- Delivering the Value Proposition:
  - o Community health workers, local entrepreneurs, weekly village markets

- o Community-level production centers in 30 villages of Nigeria and Zimbabwe
- o Relationships with local suppliers of raw materials
- o Relationships with existing transportation partners in these locations
- o Partnerships with grass-root NGOs and government agencies for promotion and distribution
- o 10 local personnel per center hired and trained to manage the expansion process

Image 5.15: Communicating the Value Proposition – Sample Pamphlet.[102]

Because a healthy child means a happy household.

We'll protect you and your family for 4 years, no side effects.

MOSNET

mosquito bed nets

Available at your nearest primary health care center.

---

[102] Photograph: Presidents Mosquito Initiative. https://commons.wikimedia.org/wiki/File:Malaria_prevention-Insecticide_treated_bed_net-PMI.jpg.

Image 5.16: Delivering the Value Proposition.[103]

MosNet – Story Board of Value Chain

- A rural consumer receives awareness messages and the value proposition through community radio, health care workers, or street plays

- The consumer approaches local entrepreneurs, weekly markets, or primary health care centers to purchase the product

- The consumer is given product usage training in his/her local language, paid installments are worked out between buyer and seller

- The consumer uses the product at home in the manner suggested, the seller periodically follows up with the consumer

- The product is returned after four years for recycling; a 25% discount is given on the returned product

---

[103] Photograph, Left: Park, Joe Slovo. Cellphone repair shop photo, Cape Town, South Africa. 2013. https://commons.wikimedia.org/wiki/File:Cellphone_repair_shop,_Joe_Slovo_Park,_Cape_Town,_South_Africa-3384.jpg. Top Right: Benggriff. Street outside Makola Market, Accra, Ghana. 2013. https://commons.wikimedia.org/wiki/File:Street_Outside_Makola_Market,_Accra,_Ghana.JPG. Bottom Right: khym54. Home-based care workers, Lilongwe, Malawi. 2008. https://www.flickr.com/photos/51132506@N00/2427196867.

Image 5.17: Exchange Model.

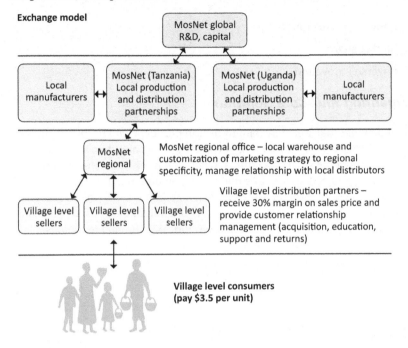

MosNet – Social Impact

- Reduced rates of disease, leading to better quality of life
- Higher household income
- Economic development of the region (malaria costs Africa $12 billion USD)
- Employment creation in the economically backward regions of Nigeria, Congo, and Zimbabwe

MosNet – Environmental Impact

- Made out of recyclable material
- Insecticide made out of organic extract
- No adverse effects on humans
- No adverse effects on the environment
- Ecologically sustainable

MosNet – Economic Impact

- Return on investment
- Market share
- Reverse innovation

Augmenting Your Core Solution

We noted earlier that it is important to design products with multiple uses. When you are designing a solution, you want to think about how to augment the basic product design. For example, when you think about the prosthetic solution, are there certain features that you could add to it, maybe for storage, maybe for certain types of features that will help in the workplace? Are there certain needs that you've left out, that you could not address, which you can now address by augmenting your core solution? With limited resources, enabling multiple functions from a single solution becomes very important.

Image 5.18: Sample Prototype (of Prosthetic).[104]

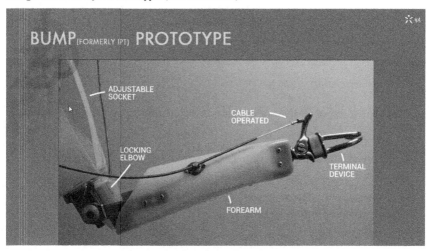

Image 5.18 shows the IPT prototype from a class project, and while it has many features, it may be useful to think about ways in which it could be improved. Is the appearance satisfactory? Will it be socially acceptable? Is the solution meeting some of these basic criteria? Bottom-up and top-down exercises can help you understand how to augment the basic solution.

---

[104] Image: Bob Dignan, Christina Tarn, and Killivalavan Solai for the Subsistence Marketplaces Initiative. Photograph: Subsistence Marketplaces Initiative.

Exercise: Augmented Product Design

- Add elements to the core concept that address needs.

- Reconcile elements:

  o Develop an augmented concept and represent it visually

  o Use bottom-up problem deconstruction and need deconstruction as bases

  o Add elements around the concept that address needs

  o Reconcile elements

  o Iterate above

Developing an Ecosystem Around the Solution

We can use the same analysis to develop an ecosystem around the core and augmented solution. The ecosystem is not intrinsic but extrinsic to the product, and represents the contextual support to enable the communication, delivery, use, or disposal of the core and augmented solution. The ecosystem is important because people living in poverty are deprived on multiple fronts, and it is not enough just to offer them a solution. They are missing or lacking the infrastructure, institutional mechanisms, education, and so on. They are missing all the things that we take for granted in relatively resource-rich settings, and, therefore, the ecosystem has to be considered as well.

In the case of IPT, they used the same bottom-up and top-down analysis to develop a resource network. So, because a person wants to be part of a social network, wants to be socially accepted, and needs education about the product, the IPT student team came up with a resource network. People can call into the network, get information, have their product repaired, and feel connected to a larger community of people with amputations. So IPT's solution was not just about the core product: the prosthetic. It was also about the community in which the person will be using the prosthetic, and the need for a network for that person.

This is the way to think about an ecosystem. It could be in the form of a network of farmers, a network of women who exchange information, and so on. But you have to figure out what the ecosystem is that will go around your solution to enable people to use your solution. These kinds of ecosystems are taken for granted in other settings. But very often, they are missing or sorely lacking in subsistence marketplaces.

Image 5.19: Proposed Ecosystem (for Prosthetic).[105]

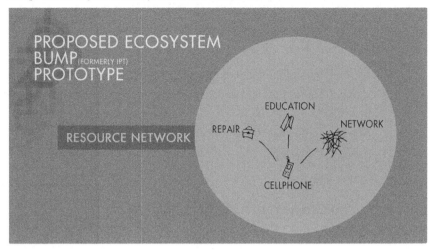

Exercise: Ecosystem and Process Design

Use bottom-up problem deconstruction and need deconstruction as bases for these exercises.

- Add elements around the concept that address needs
- Reconcile elements

    o Develop an ecosystem around your core concept and represent it visually

    o Storyboard customer moving through process

    o Iterate above

Creating the Enterprise Plan   *Most Important*

We now discuss elements of the enterprise plan, beginning with a storyboarding exercise that is fundamental to many things that we will be doing relating to the value proposition. We'll then talk about designing the value proposition, positioning it with respect to other solutions, communicating it, delivering it, and finally developing the exchange model.

---

[105] Image: Bob Dignan, Christina Tarn, and Killivalavan Solai for the Subsistence Marketplaces Initiative.

Storyboarding

Storyboarding is an intuitive exercise where we take the product through from beginning to end – from supply to assembly to purchase to usage to disposal, with particular emphasis on the aspects involving the customer where any amount of detail is perhaps not too much.

Image 5.20: Sample Product Prototype (Almost Home Disaster Shelter).[106]

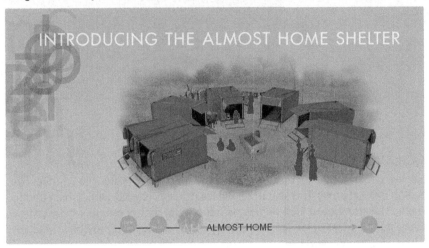

Let us take the example of the Sample Product Prototype (Almost Home Disaster Shelter), as seen in Image 5.20, one of our class projects. This is a solution for disaster-prone areas. As mentioned, the storyboard begins with the assembly – in this case, one that will be done under high-stress conditions. It ends with how the product is used, and in this case, important factors include a sense of community, a place to secure valuables, a place where people can worship, and so on. Deployment of the preassembled parts in disaster areas is another aspect that could be included in the storyboard.

---

[106] Image: Bob Dignan, Christina Tarn, Killivalavan Solai, and the Subsistence Marketplaces Initiative. To view a series of illustrations for assembly of the prototype (Almost Home Disaster Shelter, please visit our web portal at https://business.illinois. edu/subsistence/resources/resourcesmlp/ and enter the password *subsistence*.

Image 5.21: Sample Product Prototype (Deployable Kiosk for Vision Testing).[107]

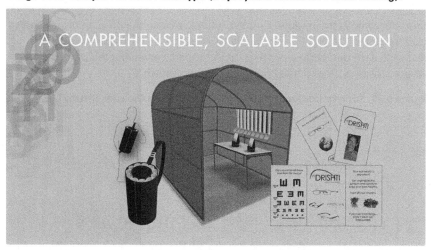

Another example, shown in Images 5.21–23, features a storyboard and displays a bag for vision entrepreneurs and a deployable kiosk to conduct eye testing in rural areas. This is part of a class project called Drishti, which means *vision*. The storyboard here begins with the vision entrepreneur who receives the materials to go to villages and conduct eye testing and provide spectacles. It involves the following:

- Traveling
- Unloading the materials
- Assembling the kiosk
- Unpacking the inventory bag with its spectacles and eye-testing equipment
- Setting up the kiosk
- Conducting eye-testing
- Providing the spectacles

Of particular importance in this storyboard are the steps that the consumer goes through:

- In learning about the product
- In purchasing it
- In using it

---

[107] Ibid. Illustrations for assembly of the deployable kiosk for vision testing are also at the link above.

- In repairing or maintaining it
- In disposing it

Image 5.22: Sample First Step in the Storyboard (Drishti [Vision] Project).[108]

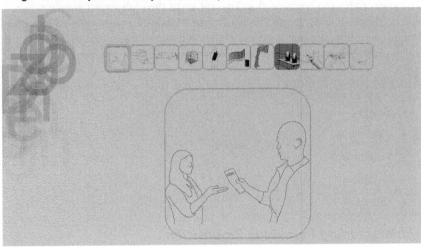

Image 5.23: Sample Final Step in Storyboard (Drishti [Vision] Project).[109]

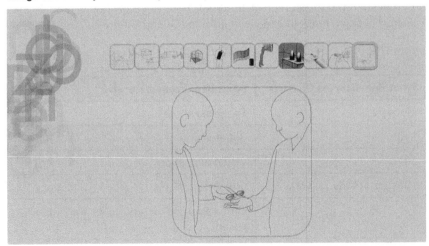

It is difficult to think of any detail being too much as far as these steps go. This exercise is somewhat akin to role-playing in that a number of steps that we may not stop to think about are explicated and factored into the design of the solution, the ecosystem, and the enterprise plan. One way to keep ourselves

---

[108] Ibid.

[109] Ibid.

honest is to refer to the storyboard as we develop various elements. This exercise also encourages bottom-up thinking in working through the steps the customer goes through.

The task, then, is to envision the different steps through which your product will go before it is used and finally disposed. The more comprehensive we are in doing this, the better off we will be in using this exercise to develop the value proposition and to communicate and deliver the value proposition.

Storyboarding Solution

- Supply
- Assembly
- Purchase
- Usage
- Disposal

Understanding Your Value Proposition

The value proposition articulates what end beneficiaries will give up and what they'll get in return (Anderson et al., 2006).[110] See the table below for how the value proposition looks to beneficiaries in the Drishti example.

What Beneficiaries Give Up and What They Receive

What Beneficiaries Give Up	What Beneficiaries Receive
Money	Eyeglasses
Time	Better vision
Effort	Vision education
The opportunity to work	Support
	Information on dietary issues that impact vision

You have to clearly articulate what end beneficiaries are getting and what they are giving up. Often, the tendency with concrete thinking and low income is to think purely in terms of money. This is also important because it provides the basis for later clearly communicating the value proposition to end beneficiaries.

---

[110] Anderson, J. C., J. A. Narus, and W. Van Rossum. "Customer Value Propositions in Business Markets." *Harvard Business Review* 84, no. 3 (2006): 90.

Exercise: Understand Your Value Proposition

- Write your value proposition to the subsistence user (what are they giving up and what are they getting?)
- Analyze and use as springboard toward designing the value proposition

Positioning Your Value Proposition

Once we have a value proposition, we need to position it with respect to the competition,[111] which could be a product that is on the market, people living in subsistence making the product themselves, or people doing without.

For example, in the positioning below (Image 5.24), the prototype is compared on independence from technology and spread of information, outperforming the competition on both dimensions.

Image 5.24: Sample Positioning Map (Sangam Project).[112]

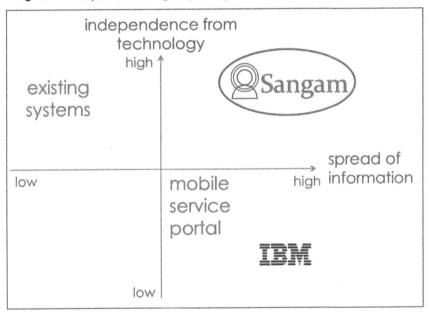

The key is to develop a solution that is better on some of these important dimensions rather than just imitating what is already out there. That is the

---

[111] Kotler, Philip, and Gary Armstrong. *Principles of Marketing.* Upper Saddle River, NJ: Pearson Prentice Hall, 2006.

[112] Sangam Project in the Web Portal: https://business.illinois.edu/subsistence/resources/resourcesmlp/. Use the password *subsistence* to access materials on the web portal.

challenge when serving a need. It has to be a compelling need, and we have to find a solution that is better than existing ones on some key dimensions.

Similarly, with IPT, the students compared themselves to their competitors on functionality, access, and network capabilities. And as you can see in the way they positioned themselves (Image 5.25), they were unique in terms of providing a network for people with amputations.

Image 5.25: Positioning (for IPT Compared to Other Prosthetic Options).[113]

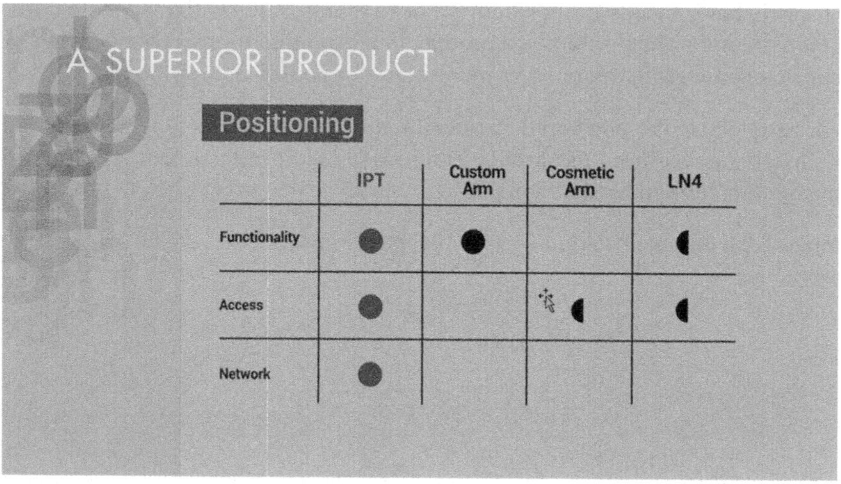

Exercise: Position Your Value Proposition Vis-à-Vis Competition

- Draw key dimensions.
- Locate your solution vis-à-vis competition.

Communicating Your Value Proposition

Next, to communicate the value proposition, consider how people think, feel, cope, and relate. We are not broadcasting a message to an audience that is waiting to hear it. We are entering a one-on-one world where people are constantly interacting with each other. To enter this world, communication should be concrete, local, and social. Communications have to be part of a social network, spread through word of mouth.[114]

---

[113] Image: Bob Dignan, Christina Tarn, Killivalavan Solai, and the Subsistence Marketplaces Initiative.

[114] Dichter, E. "How word-of-mouth advertising works." *Harvard Business Review* 44, no. 6 (1966): 147-160.

The value proposition needs to be clear in light of concrete thinking. What is the give, what is the get? How do these combine to provide a valuable solution? For our projects, we develop an example of a specific communication of your value proposition. This is very important. Rather than staying at a general level and talking about using advertisements and other means of traditional communications, it will force us to communicate in a way that a low-literate, low-income person can understand.

For example, the Drishti solution on vision used these tools and methods to communicate their value proposition:

- product brochures
- charts
- diagrams
- activities
- education

Note that education is often part of the communication. This is a part of the ecosystem, because people are deprived on multiple fronts. We have to educate people as it relates to the need that we are serving and the solution that we are designing. Image 5.26 shows some of the communication materials, keeping in mind the low-literate user.

Image 5.26: Sample Communication Materials (Created for IPT). [115]

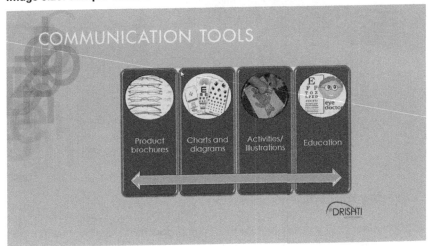

---

[115] Image: Bob Dignan, Christina Tarn, Killivalavan Solai, and the Subsistence Marketplaces Initiative.

The IPT team designed a brochure showing how the solution can be used in day-to-day life. The brochure depicted in Image 5.27 is pictographic and takes into account concrete thinking. It addresses how people can use the solution in the here and now, rather than some abstract information that they cannot relate to.

Exercise: Communicating the Value Proposition

- Consider how individuals think, feel, cope, and relate
- Concretize, localize, and socialize communication
- Make the value proposition clear in light of concrete thinking
  - o What is the give?
  - o What is the get?
  - o How do these combine to provide value?
- Develop an example of a specific communication of your value proposition

Image 5.27: Sample Brochure (for the IPT Prosthetic).[116]

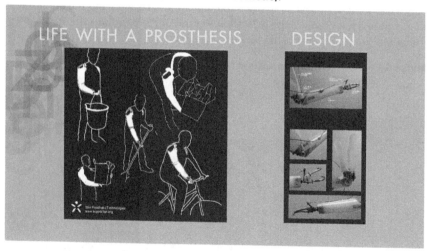

Delivering Your Value Proposition

Next, consider how you will deliver the value proposition. Again, consider the storyboard for your solution. Develop the value chain to deliver your value proposition. Perhaps there is a role for a local entrepreneur who understands the community and who can customize the product at purchase, and can

---

[116] Ibid.

engender trust as well. The local entrepreneur knows the community and understands how to customize the product and add value. In turn, how would you reach the local entrepreneur and so forth? How do you traverse the very last mile? The fact that you are in a village may not be sufficient if it still means distances from neighboring villages. Door-to-door may have many advantages, as people balance many competing needs.

Exercise: Delivering the Value Proposition

- Develop the value chain to deliver your value proposition

- Analyze and use as springboard toward delivering the value proposition

Developing an Exchange Model

One last aspect of the enterprise plan is to develop an exchange model. What are the exchanges happening, what are the entities involved in the exchanges? It is important to be clear with respect to all of these exchanges, using a detailed listing of entities and exchanges.

Think about a good versus a service. Sometimes, every household in a village cannot afford the good that you have in mind. Can it become a service? For example, you may not be able to provide water treatment for each household, but could that become a service, where there is a water treatment plant in a village that sells water in large cans? Can you piggyback on an existing distribution? Is it possible to align the way you charge for the product with the cash flow people have through their livelihoods? Can you think about livelihood opportunities for the poorest customers? Is education and skill a part of your value chain?

So, for example, for the product prototype in Image 5.20 (Almost Home Disaster Shelter), these are the entities involved:

- The social enterprise that provides the solution (Almost Home Disaster Shelter)

- A manufacturing company

- An NGO such as Red Cross

- The community

Image 5.28: Sample Exchange Model (Almost Home Disaster Shelter).[117]

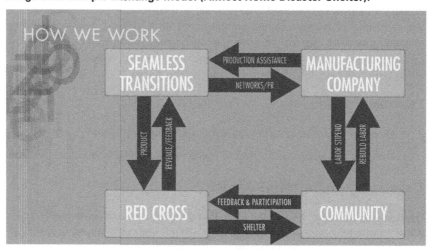

These are the principals involved in the different exchanges happening; all exchanges don't have to be about money. Many things are being exchanged. For example, the revenue that Seamless Transitions gets from their solution (Almost Home Disaster Shelter) is from a large NGO that is involved in disaster relief. This exchange model is important to chart out, because every entity is involved in an exchange – whether of money, or information flow, or support, or something else. When you chart this exchange model out, you get at economic sustainability as well. There are many innovative ways to generate revenue. And many things beyond money are being exchanged. This approach enables thinking about win-wins and trade-offs between different types of sustainability.

Related resources include frameworks to develop and refine the enterprise plan. You can use these frameworks as checklists or to stimulate thinking on the enterprise plan.[118]

Exercise: Exchange Models

Developing an exchange model involves:

• Clear listing of entities and exchanges

• Exchanges that each have "give and get" components, not necessarily financial

---

[117] Ibid. Seamless Transitions is the name of the hypothetical business.

[118] We have many examples as well of very detailed business plans and presentations, located at https://www.business.illinois.edu/subsistence/resources/resourcesmlp/. Use the password *subsistence* to access materials on the web portal.

Consider the following in designing the exchange model:

- Financing for customers as starting point avoidable
- Whether a good can become a service, and if the unit of analysis can be more than one household
- Piggy-backing of existing distribution, etc.
- Aligning pricing with cash flow/income flow
- Livelihood opportunities for poorer customers
- Education and skill development as part of value chain

Exercise: Costs

- Develop list of types of cost
  - o Use any categories you wish
- Consolidate categories
- Develop subcategories of costs and identify sources for each subcategory

Exercise: Implementation Phases

- What are the distinct phases of implementation?
- What is done in each phase?

Exercise: Financials

- Consider implementation phases
- Top-down
  - o Enumerate all expense items
  - o Enumerate all cost estimates
- Bottom-up
  - o In each phase
    - · Price
    - · Unit sold per area (villages)
    - · Number of villages
- Plan out financials (revenue and expenses) across implementation phases

Exercise: Performance

- From the web portal, use the business report entitled ASHA as an example for quantifying people-related metrics and the business report entitled Sunstuff for quantifying planet-related metrics.

- Develop objectives and measures for each dimension of performance.

Sustainable Business Plan Elements

Our business plan adapts previous business plans[119] and offers some new elements as well.

I. Executive Summary (synopsis and major aspects of the business plan)

II. Situation Analysis

    A. Internal Strengths and Weaknesses (including strengths and weaknesses in the arenas of sustainability and subsistence)

    B. External Opportunities and Threats (including ecological issues, such as depletion of natural resources, and challenges in subsistence marketplaces)

- Use field research and learning

- Macro environment

- Market (for product) – size and growth potential

- Competition

- Customer information – profile, benefits to customers, needs served, segments

III. Mission/Objectives in terms of Profits, People, and Planet

The parts above are about the organization not the product. Please make up the organization to give your creativity maximum leeway while reflecting some of the constraints of the real sponsor.

IV. Field Research and Product Development

    A. Discussion of learning from virtual immersion and emersion

    B. Description of idea generation and screening

- Discussion of process and outcomes and appendix of matrix

    C. Market Research

- Detailed discussion of planned market research method and findings

---

[119] Sahlman, William Andrews. *How to Write a Great Business Plan*. Boston, MA: Harvard Business School Press, 2008.

- Detailed appendix with field notes, images, and video

    D. Learning and Reflection from Field Research

- Discussion of broader insights about consumer behavior based on market research and learning
- Needs-Drivers-Context
- Bottom-up Problem Deconstruction
- Top-down Problem Deconstruction

    E. Concept generation and evaluation

- Focused generation of concepts
  - o Process
  - o Concepts
  - o Evaluation
  - o Discussion of Criteria and Rationale
  - o Discussion of Ranking
  - o Matrix of Concepts and Criteria
- Detailing of Chosen Concept
  - o Detailed Drawings
  - o Core Product and Core Process
  - o Packaging
- Augmented Solution
- Ecosystem and Process
- Storyboard

    F. Technical specifications and Detailed Drawings

- Customer Needs/Attributes –Technical Specifications (Metrics/Values) – Benchmarks

    G. Concept testing

    H. Prototype

    I. Preliminary Cost Analysis

V. Marketing Strategy

    A. Target Market Selection

- Rationale based on market research and consumer behavior

    B. Sustainable Marketing Mix (Sustainable Product design or redesign including life cycle analysis, Augmented product and ecosystem,

Sustainable value chain, Designing and communicating a sustainable value proposition)

VI. Action Plans

    A. Targeting and Positioning Statement Including Sustainability Issues

    B. Sustainable Product design

    C. Sustainable Value Chain

    D. Design of the Value Proposition

    E. Communication of the Value Proposition

    F. Manufacturing Plan, Product Forecast and Launch Schedule

    G. Financial Forecast

    H. Ecological (Planet) Impact Forecast

    I. Societal (People) Impact Forecast

VII. Implementation, Controls, and Evaluation

    A. Measures of performance – meeting triple bottom lines

    B. Monitoring and evaluating performance on multiple dimensions

The Logic of Our Business Plan

Part 1: Who we are, where we live, what we aim to do

- Who we are (take ownership of entity)
  - o Our strengths and weaknesses
- Our reality
  - o Opportunities and threats
    - · Use field research and learning
    - · Macro environment
    - · Market (for product) – Size and growth potential
    - · Competition
    - · Customer information – Profile, benefits to customers, needs served, segments
- Our goals in light of who we are and our reality
  - o Mission and objectives

Part 2: Our Journey to a Solution

- Virtual immersion and Idea Generation
  - o Discussion of learning from virtual immersion and emersion

- o Description of idea generation and screening
- o Discussion of process and outcomes and appendix of matrix
- Market Research
  - o Detailed discussion of planned market research method and findings
  - o Detailed appendix with field notes, images, and video
- Learning and Reflection from Field Research
- Discussion of Broader Insights About Consumer Behavior Based on Market Research and Learning from Fall
- Concept Generation and Evaluation
  - o Focused generation of concepts
  - o Evaluation
  - o Technical specifications and detailed drawings
  - o Prototype

Part 3: How We Develop an Enterprise Plan Around the Solution

- Storyboard, Ecosystem to Add on to Solution
- Marketing Strategy (whom is our solution for; how do we compare with existing solutions; how do we design, communicate, and deliver the value proposition)
  - o Segments considered
  - o Target market selection
  - o Rationale based on market research and consumer behavior
  - o Positioning
- Sustainable Marketing Mix (Sustainable Product design or redesign including life cycle analysis, Sustainable value chain, Designing and communicating a sustainable value proposition)
- Action Plans
  - o Targeting and positioning statement including sustainability issues
  - o Sustainable product design
  - o Sustainable value chain
  - o Design of the value proposition
  - o Communication of the value proposition
- Exchange Model (how to make the enterprise economically sustainable)

Part 4 – How We Implement the Enterprise Plan

- Manufacturing Plan, Product Forecast, and Launch Schedule
- Outcomes
  - o Financial forecast
  - o Ecological (planet) impact forecast
  - o Societal (people) impact forecast
- Implementation, Controls, and Evaluation
  - o Measures of performance – meeting triple bottom lines
  - o Monitoring and evaluating performance on multiple dimensions

Solution Prototypes

Following are some examples of bottom-up prototypes – one that we created, one created by an entrepreneur, and the others that students at the University of Illinois have developed to highlight some aspects of designing solutions. Over the years, we have designed many solutions, each distinctly geared to solve a specific problem in a specific locale for a specific community of people.

Note that our class projects are very detailed, with only a small proportion being translated to practice by our partner organizations, some indirectly through their learning. Moving from the outcomes of our projects to commercialization involves many more steps and champions that we are not equipped to pursue, although a small set of projects have influenced practice in different ways and we move to field testing on occasion. Nevertheless, the projects are based on intensive yearlong work, including field research, and have helped us develop insights on many aspects of understanding and designing solutions for subsistence marketplaces.

Marketplace Literacy Project

The Marketplace Literacy Project is a nonprofit organization that I founded in 2003 to enable marketplace literacy among low-literate, low-income people through educational programs and materials to improve the practices of businesses, governments, not-for-profit organizations, and educators. Our primary focus is on subsistence-level consumers and entrepreneurs.

But what, exactly, is *marketplace literacy*?

Marketplace literacy is not basic literacy; it is self-confidence, skills, and awareness of rights as a consumer and an entrepreneur. Imagine a poor woman who needs to survive. She learned how to cook growing up; that is the vocation or trade that she knows. So she decides to run a food shop to survive. But to run the shop, she needs know-how. She needs to know how to design menus, ensure raw material, and identify a good location. She also needs know-*why*, which is a deeper understanding of the marketplace.

For example, why should she be customer-oriented? Why not deliver to middle-class households? Why not supply to restaurants? Or why be in the food business at all? This kind of know-why is very important, because it is the poor with the least resources who have to keep adapting to changing circumstances.

People living in poverty need to have three major elements in place to participate in the marketplace:

- financial resources
- access to markets to buy and sell and get value in their exchanges (which is particularly relevant in rural settings)
- marketplace literacy

There are several levels of marketplace literacy. There is the vocation or trade level. There is the know-how level – how to design a product, how to communicate the benefits. And there is know-*why* level, which denotes a deeper understanding of the marketplace. Why choose an enterprise? Why strive to provide customer value?

The marketplace literacy approach begins with the know-*why* as a basis for the know-*how*. We don't focus on what people should buy or sell, but rather how, and, more importantly, why. We use social skills, which people possess irrespective of literacy levels. We use role-playing, picture sorting, and simulated shopping to teach people to be better consumers and entrepreneurs.

For many years, we provided a face-to-face program with numerous exercises. (We now provide video-based modules; more on that in a moment.) We began with general issues about the marketplace, such as what an exchange is, how exchanges add up to a value chain, what the different types of needs are, and so on.

For example, we would show people images of a farmer producing crops all the way through to a customer consuming the end product, as well as a picture of money. We ask people to place the images in concentric circles so that whatever is most important to run a business is at the center.

We found that people often pasted the picture of currency in the middle. Through discussion, they came to learn that it is the customer that is the most important, and if you cannot serve a customer need, you don't have a business.

Following these exercises on marketplace literacy in general, we conduct exercises on consumer literacy – for example, setting up shops and cheating people and showing them how they got cheated. We try to help people understand how to gain value as a customer so they can understand how to deliver value as an entrepreneur.

Over time, we have scaled this model by working with one of the largest microfinancing organizations in the world. This organization produced a movie as an emotional platform where we scripted in a variety of marketplace interactions for a woman who empowers herself through being an entrepreneur. We then created 14 video-based modules envisioning a program without a teacher physically present. Imagine perhaps 20 women in a room; they watch a DVD and take part in the exercises on the DVD, which are led by a teacher on the screen and a facilitator in person. The women learn about basic concepts from the DVD, and are given homework that involves applying the concepts to their own settings.

From this social initiative and other observations, we have learned that there are four different phases, at least, in developing a solution.

1. **Identify a need** that is not being served well.
2. **Design a solution.** In our case, the need was for marketplace literacy, and we designed an educational program as the solution.
3. **Use technology to maximize reach, deploy widely, or to scale your approach.** In our case, we use a video-based approach.
4. **Create an enterprise model.** Figure out why anybody would do what we think or believe they should do.

We've learned many intangibles from this social initiative. Here are just three of those intangibles. A subsequent part of the book elaborates on lessons learned in detail.

Three Intangibles Learned from the Marketplace Literacy Project

1. People and places are more important than money.
Most important – perhaps even more so than finding the financial resources – is to find the right people to implement the program. Find the best people, and a place to work in, and the resources will find a way to get there.

2. Implementation is everything.
Ideas are great, but it is really about implementation, about making things work at the ground level. That is why we need the people. It is important to start small, fail small, and fail quickly if possible. If you learn how to get to 20 people, you can then learn how to get to 100 people, and then learn how to get to thousands of people, and then beyond.

3. Keep your promises. If you are working in a village, the promise you make is like making a promise in a fishbowl. Only promise what you can deliver. Otherwise the word will get out, and soon you will lose trust. Not to mention that we should keep our promises, period.

Once again, think about your project in terms of the problem, the opportunity, the solution, the enterprise plan, and the sustainable outcomes. In our case, the problem was the lack of marketplace literacy, and our opportunity and our geography started out in South India and expanded to six countries. Our solution was the educational program, which we augmented in many ways. We also created an ecosystem by forming or reactivating self-help groups of women. Our enterprise plan was to take this value proposition to people and ask for their time and effort so we could teach them about marketplace literacy. And our outcomes, we hope, span social, environmental, and economic arenas.

Sun Oven

The need Sun Oven focuses on is energy for cooking. To that end, they have two products: a Villager Sun Oven, which is for the entire village and can be used to cook for large numbers of people in a community, and the Global Sun Oven, which can be used by a household.

Image 5.29: Family in Haiti Using a Sun Oven for Their Cooking Needs.[120]

---

[120] Photograph: Sun Oven.

Energy for cooking is a huge issue in developing countries, where people cannot afford the high cost of energy for cooking fuel. The drivers for these Sun Oven products are the cost of cooking fuel and lung ailments due to indoor smoke from using other methods of cooking. A key context element is deforestation due to the use of firewood.

In terms of the cultural challenges, one of the issues is in cooking the evening meal. The sun is out during the day when the women cook, but by the time the husbands come home in the evening, the food is cold.

Another challenge is taste. Food is such a culturally intensive aspect of life, and when you take somebody living in subsistence, for whom the central consumption event may be the evening meal, it is hard to sacrifice taste.

Moreover, cooking habits are hard to change. People are intuitive. Those who are low-literate or living in subsistence don't necessarily use a cookbook. They cook things intuitively, and having a new method of cooking is a big change to ask them to undertake.

It is also not easy to recognize the savings that are gained from using a solar oven. This has to be communicated in the value proposition as well. Moreover, people may value money and not value time, and end up spending a lot of time going out and getting firewood to save themselves the cost of buying a Sun Oven. These are just a few of the challenges that Sun Oven faces.

In terms of customers, Sun Oven uses a monthly installment plan and a revolving loan fund. As loans are paid off, the money is lent to others for purchase of additional ovens. Sun Oven finances women who have completed a solar cooking course.

In terms of business strategy, Sun Oven works with local entrepreneurs to create efficient business processes, and with NGOs to gain access to communities. They license private sector entrepreneurs to make and market the ovens. They establish an assembly plant and provide specifications to allow local manufacturing, with the exception of one gasket that is sold for a small royalty.

Sun Oven has taken a problem – the need for fuel for cooking – and created an opportunity in many places around the world. With their end user being the homemaker who cooks, Sun Oven has created a solution. And they have augmented it through education and through developing an ecosystem of women who are learning from each other.

In terms of alternatives, their solution is cheaper and much cleaner than the alternatives. Regarding their enterprise plan, they spell out their value proposition to the customers, communicating the savings gained and the reduced ailments due to indoor smoke. They communicate the value proposition in various ways and deliver it through their local partners. Indeed, their sustainable outcomes are beneficial socially, environmentally, and economically.

The Sun Oven Story

The following are statements from an interview with Paul Munsen, President of Sun Oven.

> My name is Paul Munsen, and I'm the president of Sun Ovens International. We are manufacturers of solar-powered cooking ovens. I didn't invent the sun oven, but one of my clients was a good friend of the inventor of the sun oven. Frankly, I knew nothing about cooking. I knew nothing about solar. I knew nothing about the developing world. But as I started to work with my friend on a pro bono basis, just to help him out, I saw the need for sun ovens in developing countries around the world.
>
> Because of that need, I just worked harder with it and can't say that I was any more successful than he is or was with it. It is just that our ability since 1997 to communicate around the world has changed totally. He'd wait an average of four to six weeks for letters to go back and forth to developing countries and trying to make a project work, or rely on faxes, not knowing if they went through or not. This morning I've communicated with people on three different continents already and don't think anything of it. People find our website everywhere and we can communicate.

The Need for Sun Ovens

> The need for sun ovens is that there are still 2.5 billion people in the world who cook with wood, charcoal, or animal dung as their primary method of cooking. And when a woman cooks over an open fire, she inhales the same amount of smoke as smoking three packs of cigarettes a day. Each year in the continent of Africa alone, 1.6 million children under the age of five die of respiratory diseases. In more than half of African countries, more children under the age of five die of respiratory diseases than they do of HIV/AIDS and malaria combined. And the primary cause of respiratory disease is when the mothers are cooking with the baby at their backs or their breasts and the babies are inhaling the smoke. So the effect it has on the health of women and children is just devastating. And in many of these countries there is a great abundance of sunshine. People being able to cook with the sun can have a huge effect on the health of women and children.

Also, the issue of deforestation is getting worse and worse around the world. As you look at countries like Ethiopia and Haiti – Haiti is almost 99 percent deforested, and prior to the 2010 earthquake a typical family spent more than half their total household income just buying charcoal to cook with. So, in places like Haiti that are blessed with an abundance of sunshine, we saw for people the potential to be able to use that sunshine rather than have to use wood or charcoal and then take money that was being spent for charcoal and use it for much more productive things.

Goal: To Create Self-Sustaining Businesses

Our goal has been to create a self-sustaining business, but also to create self-sustaining businesses in developing countries, rather than take a nonprofit approach. Unfortunately, many things with a nonprofit approach are totally contingent on grants, and finding funding becomes almost the mission more than the actual mission of the product.

What we've looked at when it comes to the culture is that women do not change cooking habits easily. People have cooked the same way for generations, and consequently if something that normally takes an hour to cook is going to take four or five hours, it is not something they are going to necessarily embrace.

So we've tried to look at the culture, but unfortunately, if you are going to make something that is high quality, it costs a lot of money. When your market is people who live on less than $2 a day, it is very challenging to have something that people can afford. But the reality is people who live on $2 a day cannot afford a $10 solar cooker any more than they can afford a $150 solar cooker, so consequently we developed programs where we use microfinancing. We use the Grameen Bank Model of microfinance, but instead of using it for income generation, we use it for cost savings.

Paying for the Oven Out of Savings

We develop programs where women can pay for the Sun Oven out of the savings. So to create an economic incentive, and the reason to use the oven, we make the payment about 60 percent of what they save, which comes out to about $4.20 US a month, or about a dollar a week. We form groups of women and collect a dollar from each person, so for groups of 15 to 20 women, the payment of $15 or $20 was collected using the Grameen model.

The women could guarantee each other's loans and they wind up then being able to support each other, and there is a lot of peer pressure and peer support in changing cooking habits. If one woman says, "Well, I stopped using my sun oven because the goats took it over," the other says, "Well, I place brackets next to the oven so the goats won't kick it over." These are simple things, but they are important.

The Women Become Self-Sufficient

As the money is paid, another oven can be made, and money can be rotated and they can become self-sufficient. We take an entrepreneurial approach, so what we attempt to do is wait in essence for entrepreneurs to come to us, entrepreneurs who see the need, understand the product, and understand their culture. So we have a program where initially we start in developing countries by licensing an entrepreneur who makes the ovens originally from parts that are shipped from the US. After the first 1,000 ovens have been made with US-shipped parts, we provide all of the specifications, all of the drawings, the CAD drawings, so that they could find local job shops that can make the component parts.

There is one gasket in the Sun Oven that is proprietary, and that gasket is why a Sun Oven will get considerably hotter and hold the heat more than any other type of solar cooker. And we sell the gasket with a small royalty, but that then allows the price to be reduced even further by making it in the country it is going to be used. And then using the microfinance system enables women to pay for it.

Spoken English Tutorial

Here is an example that my students came up with for a spoken English tutorial. Noteworthy here is that this need was first identified during actual immersion. It involves using a cell phone to call into a number and sign up for this program. This would help children who are not proficient in English even if they learned written English in school. Another problem is that their parents don't speak English – so the children will learn from each other and teach their parents as well. Children use the cellphone to call into a service, where they are matched with other children of similar skills. They see programs on television with the characters speaking in English, and sometimes themselves provide a voiceover for animated characters on the program. The children learn together and become part of a community to improve their English skills.

Image 5.30: Spoken English Program Prototype.[121]

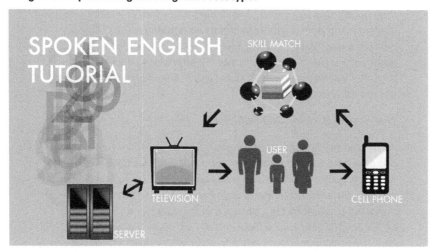

This particular need and its solution involves many issues. First, the solution addresses an aspirational need, because parents aspire to have their children learn spoken English. It provides them with a way out of poverty. Second, this product is for low-literate users, so the interface has to be easy to operate. It must be easy to call in and become a member. And it needs to be easy to watch the program and interact with others and provide voiceovers. Third, the solution has to be culturally sensitive. And fourth, it has to leverage existing infrastructure (cell phones and televisions).

Mobile Energy Device

Another prototype that my students at the University of Illinois came up with is an energy device for mobile entrepreneurs. It is a solar panel to heat water on top of mobile carts for entrepreneurs who make and sell tea. It is designed for harsh usage conditions and multiple purposes. If I have very limited resources, and I need to buy a product, I want a product that can serve a number of purposes. For example, if it could heat food as well as water, that would make it more useful, although this aspect was not captured due to design challenges. In addition, the device should have a culturally sensitive design, and it has to be locally sustainable. This last issue is achieved through producing energy in an environmentally sustainable way.

---

[121] Image: Bob Dignan, Christina Tarn, Killivalavan Solai, and the Subsistence Marketplaces Initiative.

Image 5.31: Product Prototype for Solar Heating Device to Warm Water for Mobile Cart Vendors Selling Tea and Food.[122]

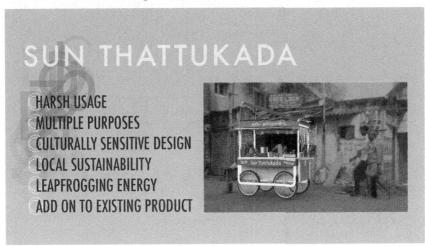

SUN THATTUKADA

- HARSH USAGE
- MULTIPLE PURPOSES
- CULTURALLY SENSITIVE DESIGN
- LOCAL SUSTAINABILITY
- LEAPFROGGING ENERGY
- ADD ON TO EXISTING PRODUCT

This product has the opportunity to leapfrog current alternatives. It uses solar power instead of the usual energy sources. Finally, it can be added on to an existing product, rather than be a standalone. It will be very expensive, likely not affordable, for an entrepreneur to buy the entire cart with the solar panel on it. So it is important that the solution adds on to what is already there. Concerns that arose during concept testing were unanticipated, as is often the case: will the device be stolen; will it attract attention from law enforcement?

Nutritional Product

Image 5.32 shows an example of a nutritional product. It is an additive that can be added to many staples. It taps into an aspirational need, as parents, particularly mothers, are willing to pay a premium if they can find a healthy alternative for their children.

---

[122] Ibid. Photograph: Subsistence Marketplaces Initiative.

Image 5.32: Prototype of Nutritional Additive (ActivEdge), Showing Packaging and User Instructions.[123]

This product serves multiple purposes and has numerous nutrients. It is locally sustainable and offers livelihood opportunities for local entrepreneurs who can add on to the product and customize it for different families that they know well. For example, certain additives could be used for the elderly, some for children, and so on, creating an entrepreneurship opportunity. Finally, its packaging can be used to educate people about nutrition.

Summarizing the Enterprise Plan

Let us go over the project details one more time. You need to cover:

- The problem
- The opportunity
- The solution
- The enterprise plan
- The sustainable outcomes

We earlier discussed how, at a product level, people face the lack of affordability, the immediacy of basic needs, and the decision to make, buy, or forgo.

To reiterate, products are about bettering life circumstances. What does that mean for you as an enterprise? It is critical to understand those life circumstances and to develop multifaceted product offerings to improve the

---

[123] Ibid. Original Image: Subsistence Marketplaces Initiative.

welfare of the individual and the community. This means you can't just think about the product alone; you have to think about things like how to educate people about the product and the need. The customer is not just deprived regarding that particular need; she lacks education about that need. The context includes lack of education, lack of educational opportunities, lack of access to knowledge, and so on.

In terms of relationships, resource constraints and interdependence are pervasive among people who live in a one-on-one interactional world with strong word of mouth while developing consumer skills as well. Fairness and trustworthiness and human aspects of the relationship are very important. Therefore, as an enterprise, emphasizing the welfare of the individual and the community is important. The key questions people may ask are:

- If you are an enterprise trying to provide me with a solution, can I trust you? Why should I trust you?
- A lot of enterprises have come and gone, will you be around?
- Will you be fair to me?

In terms of the market, we find resource constraints and lack of mobility and dependence on groups, and come across fragmented small markets that are geographically diverse. We encounter varied group influences as well. We cannot separate the social milieu from the marketplace. That means enterprises have to work with diverse groups, and one way to think about linking all these groups is to think about social good as the common denominator.

To summarize: products are about bettering life circumstances, relationships are about the human dimension, and markets are about the social milieu. For the enterprise, there are many ways to do well, meaning to be profitable, to be financially successful, and there are many ways to do good. Many companies do well, and they also do good through their products. But when it comes to subsistence marketplaces, it is difficult to separate the two. It may be essential to do good as it relates to your product in order to do well.

Image 5.33: Doing Good for Doing Well – Traditionally.[124]

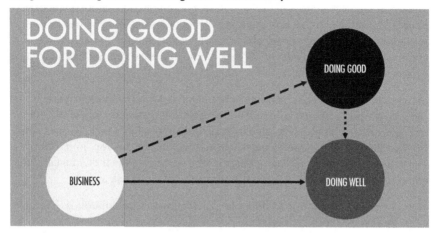

Image 5.34: Doing Good for Doing Well – in Subsistence Marketplaces.[125]

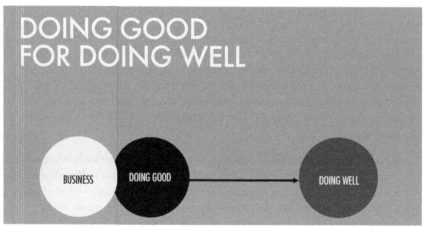

That does not mean that a business has to be a charitable organization. It means it is important to understand your product as it relates to individual and community welfare. It is important to understand that individual and community welfare may be essential for you to do well. So you have to think about how your product impacts the community and how you can incorporate doing good for the community as it relates to your product. This is based on our analysis at the individual or household and product level, the relationship level, and at the market level.

Products and betterment of life circumstances are blurred. Relationships and the human dimension are blurred. And markets and the social milieu are blurred.

---

[124] Ibid.

[125] Ibid.

What is good for the individual and community is blurred. The economic element is blurred with the human element. Your challenge as an enterprise is to merge doing good for the community with your product offering.

Three Phases with Commercial and Social Enterprise

The business case has three phases. The first phase is moving from sympathy to informed empathy through exercises such as virtual immersion. The second phase involves designing solutions for subsistence marketplaces. The third phase is designing solutions for advanced economies *from* subsistence marketplaces. For example, if you have a telemedicine solution that works in rural settings and subsistence marketplaces, this type of solution can also be used in advanced economies to provide health care.

The social enterprise case also has three phases. The first phase here also involves moving from sympathy to informed empathy. The second phase entails using understanding to help people in subsistence marketplaces. The third phase is designing solutions for advanced economies *from* subsistence marketplaces. In the third phase at a personal level, we realize that we are the most enriched in the process. Indeed, we do these things because we think we can help somebody else, but in the end, we enrich ourselves in the process in most fulfilling ways.

Image 5.35: Three Phases to Immersion-Innovation for Business and Social Enterprise.[126]

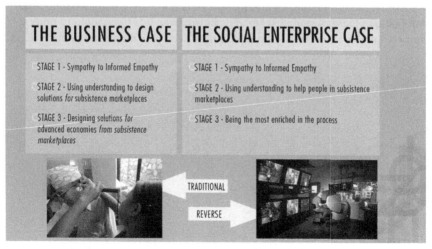

---

[126] Image: Bob Dignan, Christina Tarn, and Killivalavan Solai for the Subsistence Marketplaces Initiative. Photograph, Left: The Australian Department of Foreign Affairs and Trade. https://www.flickr.com/photos/dfataustralianaid/10659990954. Photograph, Right: Cornell Urology. https://en.wikipedia.org/wiki/File:Virtual_Reality_OR.jpg.

Are We Willing to Confront the Challenges?

We conclude this part of the book on designing solutions by showing some images, one of which you have seen before, where women are gathering wood for cooking. Now, from the perspective of those who live in an advanced economy such as the US, looking at this image, we might think that this is happening now, but it is happening far away to other people who are not like us, and it is probably not going to happen to us.

Image 5.36: Women Carrying Firewood in Nepal.[127]

The following is a picture that seems a bit closer. Now we may think it might happen in the future, but we are not sure. It is happening somewhat far away, but being in North America, it seems a little closer. It is happening to others somewhat like us, and we are not sure how likely it is that it will happen to us.

---

[127] Photograph: Engineering for Change. http://www.flickr.com/photos/44221799@N08/4521897946/%22Flickr%E2%80%9D.

Image 5.37: Polar Bears in the Arctic.[128]

Image 5.38: New Orleans, LA, August 30, 2005 – People Sit on a Roof in New Orleans, Waiting to Be Rescued After Hurricane Katrina.[129]

This is a picture of New Orleans after Hurricane Katrina.

---

[128] Photograph: The National Ocean Service. https://www.flickr.com/photos/40322276@N04/8290528613/.

[129] Photograph: Augustino, Jocelyn, and FEMA. "New Orleans Is Being Evacuated as a Result of Flooding Caused by Hurricane Katrina." https://commons.wikimedia.org/wiki/File:Katrina-14512.jpg.

Image 5.39: Oil Spill in the Gulf of Mexico, 2010.[130]

This is a picture after an oil spill. And now we may think that it is happening now, it is happening closer to home, it is happening to others like us, and we are quite certain that it happened.

So this leads to the ultimate conundrum. In subsistence marketplaces, people live their environment. Despite low literacy and low income, they have to envision the medium term to survive. In advanced marketplaces, a number of these problems seem to be far away. Yet we have the ability and the resources to envision the longer term and try to find solutions.

What we find is that in subsistence marketplaces people are unable to find the solutions – they lack the literacy and the resources – but they are willing. So the women we met earlier are willing to think about the medium term to conserve the environment. **In advanced marketplaces, the question we have to ask ourselves is, we are able, but are we willing to confront some of these challenges? Can we bridge these distances to create innovations that help subsistence marketplaces and help us all as well?**

---

[130] Photograph: NASA Goddard Space Flight Center. April 29th View, 2010. https://www. flickr.com/photos/24662369@N07/4563296541/.

Keys to Designing Solutions for Subsistence Marketplaces

We present the keys to designing solutions for a subsistence marketplace.

1. We need to design products that are sustainable and serve multiple purposes.

We should design products for harsh usage, for low-literate users, to be locally sustainable, to serve multiple purposes, and to be customizable. We should leverage existing infrastructure when developing products, add on to existing products, and develop product-relevant infrastructure.

2. We need to consider augmented solutions and ecosystems.

Designing a solution in a subsistence context requires deep understanding. We are fundamentally unfamiliar with this context, and we cannot take things for granted and just focus on the need and the product. We need to consider the core and the augmented solution and the ecosystem, and discern how they improve on current alternatives. We need an ecosystem because people are deprived on multiple fronts. Whether it is a network of farmers or a network of female entrepreneurs, the ecosystem is necessary to support the solution.

3. We need to clearly communicate the value proposition and deliver it to achieve outcomes on different dimensions of sustainability.

We need to clearly communicate and deliver the value proposition, along with sustainable social, environmental, and economic outcomes. We need an enterprise plan that addresses many different elements in terms of the value proposition, how it is communicated and how it is delivered, and so on.

4. Doing good and doing well can be intertwined in subsistence marketplaces.

The need/product level is really about bettering people's life circumstances. That means we have to understand their life circumstances and think about how we can better them. At the relationship level, we emphasize the human dimension, valuing characteristics such as friendliness and trust, and focusing on individual and community welfare. At the market level, we find that the complex social milieu is blurred with the marketplaces, and negotiating this milieu is central. We work with very different groups and use social good as the common denominator.

Enterprise-level processes should incorporate products being blurred with betterment of life circumstances, relationships being blurred with the human dimension, and markets being blurred with a social milieu. Doing good as it relates to your product offering is critical in order to do well.[131]

---

[131] Noteworthy here is that there are, of course, many ways of doing well financially. In fact, much of the history of the world proves how well exploitative approaches do that. Adding to the list are extremely harmful products. I am suggesting that, with the bottom-up approach, there is different path. It may be essential to do good in order to do well in the context of today's world, subsistence and otherwise. We are unique and interconnected; hybrid organizations combine social missions with economic sustainability; companies combine social with economic in stated missions; the Internet democratizes broadcast capability; and social media and the cell-phone enable one-on-one communications. Furthermore, I am speaking about businesses focused on adding value to the customer. In this context, others have argued that one could do good and do well. We are pushing this line of thinking further in terms of how it may be essential to do good in order to do well. There are no universals here and certainly not in subsistence marketplaces. These arguments should be viewed in context.

Part II: Lessons Learned

In this part of the book, we discuss lessons in envisioning and sustaining bottom-up enterprises drawing from our direct experience. This part moves the level of analysis to the enterprise, encompassing both the design of solutions and the leadership, management, and implementation involved at the level of an organization. Following a bottom-up sequence, we began with understanding subsistence marketplaces, then designing solutions and enterprise plans for them, and in this part, we discuss lessons in running a bottom-up enterprise, before moving on to applying the lessons in a variety of contexts.

At the outset, the scale of our work should be noted, whether in managing student projects or in our social enterprise. Also relevant is the nature of our work; we realize that there are much more complex problems in the world than the ones we confront. Nevertheless, these lessons have value in having emerged from our experiences. We should be careful, however, to not over-claim our direct experience in speaking to a variety of circumstances – quite a few of which relate to initiatives at a very large scale.

Our bottom-up experience also highlights arenas we do not have parallel experience in, especially at a more aggregate or macro-level. As with any approach, we have experienced and learned from our preferred vantage point, but we necessarily know much less firsthand about other vantage points. This is why we often match our bottom-up approach with a more traditional top-down process whenever relevant.

We also note that our lessons learned may translate to a broad range of contexts and domains. We discuss how these lessons might be applied in some detail and specificity in a subsequent part of the book.

Image 6.00: Overview of Lessons.

Charting a bottom-up journey	Implementing bottom-up enterprises	Sustaining bottom-up enterprises	Guiding values	Essence of the bottom-up approach
Chart a course	Set goals idealistically & pursue them pragmatically	Identity before branding	EQ: To get things done	The ultimate bottom-up principle – If all else fails, do it yourself
Define purpose	Implementation trumps "IP & killer app"	Being over strategizing	Do your best; accept the worst	
Inspire through purpose	Learn, try out, learn by trying out	Negotiate, articulate, re-evaluate value equation	Take the high road & stay there	
			Be thoughtful in adversity	
Determine purpose	Iterate many times rather than get it *right* away	Culture of mutual accountability	Go to the next level of understanding – Peel the onion	The ultimate bottom-up enterprise model – Do what it takes for each other
	Don't break promises – Break up promises	Blur the boundaries of organization	Get over yourself, see & experience	
Circumscribe purpose			What you do matters more than what you say, think, like, or want to do	
	Coevolve pathways to implementation	Different ways to thread the needle	If one relationship is dispensable, all are	
Delineate the domain of purpose	Create short-term yield	Principled flexibility	Intertwined destinies – Not replaceable parts	Be intensely practical & un-compromisingly idealistic
			Be aware of your power, & lack of it for those you work with	
Execute the domain of purpose	Complicate the revenue model	Activities before resources	View people by how far they have come	
	Fail small/scale through depth	Inspire & incentivize	Nurture leadership among those who have not had a chance	
Listen & learn – Bottom-up immersion	Experience & know the forest, trees, branches, leaves	Steps to social enterprise & enterprise plan	Avoid an "I cannot do this without you" & "You cannot do this without me" mentality	Bottom-up meets top-down

Chapter 6: Charting a Bottom-Up Journey

The first set of lessons relate to charting a bottom-up journey. We devote attention to the lessons we have learned about determining purpose – lessons that are not all original with us, by any means. Indeed, we are privileged to build on the shoulders of giants.

In charting a bottom-up journey, we cover the following topics:

- Chart a Course – Through Purpose, Passion, and Proficiency
- Define Purpose – Playing in Infinite-Sum, Not Zero-Sum, Games
- Inspire Through Purpose – Larger Purpose as the Engine
- Determine Purpose – Roads and Junctions – Walking Down Some Roads, Creating Paths
- Circumscribe Purpose – Addressing the Reality That is, Aiming for the Reality That Should Be
- Delineate the Domain of Purpose – What We Are Not
- Execute the Domain of Purpose – Finding People and Place – A Home or a Community Platform
- Listen and Learn – Bottom-Up Immersion

Image 6.01: Charting a Bottom-Up Journey.

Charting a bottom-up journey	Implementing bottom-up enterprises	Sustaining bottom-up enterprises	Guiding values	Essence of the bottom-up approach
Chart a course	Set goals idealistically & pursue them pragmatically	Identity before branding	EQ: To get things done	The ultimate bottom-up principle – If all else fails, do it yourself
Define purpose	Implementation trumps "IP & killer app"	Being over strategizing	Do your best; accept the worst	
			Take the high road & stay there	
Inspire through purpose	Learn, try out, learn by trying out	Negotiate, articulate, re-evaluate value equation	Be thoughtful in adversity	
			Go to the next level of understanding – Peel the onion	The ultimate bottom-up enterprise model – Do what it takes for each other
Determine purpose	Iterate many times rather than get it *right* away	Culture of mutual accountability	Get over yourself, see & experience	
			What you do matters more than what you say, think, like, or want to do	
Circumscribe purpose	Don't break promises – Break up promises	Blur the boundaries of organization	If one relationship is dispensable, all are	
	Coevolve pathways to implementation	Different ways to thread the needle	Intertwined destinies – Not replaceable parts	
Delineate the domain of purpose	Create short-term yield	Principled flexibility	Be aware of your power, & lack of it for those you work with	Be intensely practical & un-compromisingly idealistic
Execute the domain of purpose	Complicate the revenue model	Activities before resources	View people by how far they have come	
	Fail small/scale through depth	Inspire & incentivize	Nurture leadership among those who have not had a chance	
Listen & learn – Bottom-up immersion	Experience & know the forest, trees, branches, leaves	Steps to social enterprise & enterprise plan	Avoid an "I cannot do this without you" & "You cannot do this without me" mentality	Bottom-up meets top-down

Chart a Course – Through Passion, Purpose, and Proficiency

How do we go about charting a course in subsistence marketplaces? There is much to be done, and finding the intersection of passion, purpose, and proficiency is one way to think about what to focus on.[132] *Passion* is about what we love to do, *purpose* is about what we think we should do, and *proficiency* is about what we are good at doing. When these three meet, it is ideal. When trying out pathways for making an impact, not all of these may come together. But in due course, this is the desired state.

In our own experience, we have been very fortunate. Our proficiency is in research and education, our passion is to make a difference in subsistence marketplaces, and our larger purpose is to give those who have not had a chance a chance. This means junior scholars and practitioners willing to work in challenging settings, students who have not had a chance to be exposed to and learn about global challenges that they will face in their careers, and communities who have simply not had a chance in life.

In the arena of subsistence, purpose at a broad level is implicit, although it has to be further specified and delineated. There is much we can offer with our proficiencies – provided they are paired up with a mutual-learning mindset. Proficiency and passion need to go hand-in-hand to find the sweet spot that is personally rewarding and impactful to the community as well. In finding this intersection, we are able to make an impact in terms of what we love to do and are good at doing. This is an ideal, of course, but worth aspiring for, as it has the dual benefits of both realizing our potential and making an impact that is likely to be better than currently available alternatives.

Define Purpose – Playing in Infinite-Sum, Not Zero-Sum, Games

The potential to create an impact in subsistence marketplaces is endless. In fact, an enterprise with a long-term vision can often be all alone in providing solutions in the specific space they choose. From a business perspective, this is much different from competing for market share in a highly competitive arena with known entities. In subsistence marketplaces, there is rich scope for developing markets and products. Underlying this is the scope for developing relationships between the entity and communities. In many ways, competition is encountered through a variety of challenging factors, ranging from the lack of infrastructure in the larger context to lack of awareness and education about needs.

The personal parallel here is to compete with oneself (or one's organization) rather than with others (or other organizations) – the former representing

---

[132] Framing in terms of passion, purpose, and proficiency is another example of an insight derived from our experiences that many who have come before may have discussed in different terms. The fact that one derives an insight originally does not make it a new-to-the-world notion.

an infinite-sum game of realizing one's potential. This issue also ties back to one of identity and who we are and what we are in it for, issues that get accentuated in subsistence marketplaces (the usual markers in traditional markets are largely determined – e.g., market share, ROI, etc., whereas they have to be created in subsistence marketplaces). There is greater potential for the identity of the enterprise to evolve in a subsistence marketplace, rather than being a relatively static entity operating in known conditions.

For example, with our own approach of marketplace literacy, there is so much to be done in this arena. We are really not in competition with any specific entity, but rather with ourselves in furthering the idea into reality to have a positive impact on people. In our case, the potential here is infinite, our core offering being an idea that can educate people – the notion of enabling understanding of the marketplace, i.e., know-why.

Inspire Through Purpose – Larger Purpose as the Engine

The notion of a larger purpose represents an infinite-sum rather than a finite-sum game. It broadens the playing field and complicates the revenue model in the broadest sense, as it involves the larger social mission.

At the personal level as well, the notion of a larger purpose is most helpful. Again, it is not that this purpose does not evolve. It is that there is a broad purpose as well as specific pathways or means sorted out, relating to what will and what will not be part of the enterprise's activities. In other words, if the mission is broad, then the pathway to work toward that goal is important to delineate. With a larger purpose, traps of zero-sum thinking or "winning the rat race and still being a rat"[133] are avoided or decreased.

Larger purpose is a space that may draw people of similar motivation. It provides an arena to rally around for such people. There are nuances in why people do what they do, but larger purpose has the potential to inspire people to work with us.

Now, speaking about larger purpose is not the same as acting on it. So much of the notion of larger purpose is germane because of how we act. Rhetoric without actions is much too common in this arena. But when combined with action, it can indeed be an engine, a rallying intersection point for different people, and a guide through day-to-day decisions.

---

[133] As Lily Tomlin once said, "The trouble with the rat race is that even if you win, you're still a rat."
"Lily Tomlin Quote." BrainyQuote. Accessed April 19, 2016. http://www.brainyquote.com/quotes/quotes/l/lilytomlin100013.html.

Larger purpose clarifies why we do what we do. It provides for guidance in ethical day-to-day practices. For instance, if our larger purpose is to benefit communities, it begins with our employees and their development. It means that our priorities are clear – to safeguard the interests of those who trust us. Thus, if a hypothetical situation involves the best interests of a well-meaning employee versus perceptions about one's own organization, the choice is clear.

Determine Purpose – Roads and Junctions – Walking Down Some Roads, Creating Paths

How we choose our sustained pathways is akin to coming to junctions at roads. Each junction represents an evolution of our interests and abilities as well as the opportunities afforded to us. Determining the next path to take requires reviewing the roads and also going down a few, testing them, or creating new pathways. Going down a few paths helps us understand what they involve and learn by trial and error. Well-trodden paths also provide important lessons for creating our own paths. Returning to the junction, we can experiment with other paths before deciding on a longer journey and the next junction. When we create a sustained pathway, this, in turn, leads to other junctions where we make more choices.

In the end, looking back, a unique pathway emerges that represents ourselves and our identity, as well as, perhaps, a lifetime of work and a unique legacy. And we can create junctions just as we create pathways. Pathways and junctions become much more germane, as the terrain is so uncertain.

The ability to make these choices is itself a luxury, when considering the many who have no choices other than to survive as best they can. The people we meet in subsistence take many roads, out of urgency and the need to provide for their families. Despite the enormous constraints they face, many traverse a unique path and make an impact on other lives. This emphasizes even more the need to use our good fortune in tangible ways when afforded the opportunity.

Applied to ourselves for purposes of illustration, we examined consumers with low levels of literacy and income as a pathway that was motivated by our need to conduct research across literacy and resource barriers that could potentially be useful to the communities we studied. In turn, the next junction in the road led to the wider sweep of subsistence marketplaces. Hand-in-hand came the path of giving back to the communities we studied, leading to activities and creation of an enterprise.

This path soon led from developing programs to moving on to reaching a wider audience through innovative designs and partnerships and to developing our own community platforms, and more recently to diverse geographies. Teaching provided another pathway that came later, in turn leading to more paths relating to subsistence marketplaces, to environmental sustainability, and to international immersions, to courses for different levels, and to online courses as well. The pathways intersected or fed off each other, and the teaching led to a unique bottom-up innovation platform that we have written about.

Unique to subsistence is the need to iterate through trial, meaning to traverse several existing and possible paths before we judge their viability. In uncertain terrain with limited resources, the next roadblock may be difficult to anticipate, and a seemingly smooth journey may suddenly run into impossible obstacles. Taking diversions and deviating, creating pathways where none exist, and so forth, are essential. Closely related is the need to learn from walking down roads, and using trial as a central means to learn and chart future pathways. Persistence in moving in the general direction despite deviations, walking around, and sometimes going backwards are other apt metaphors here.

Circumscribe Purpose – Addressing the Reality That Is, Aiming for the Reality That Should Be

Solutions have to address the urgent problems of those we meet while hopefully steering a pathway to a different reality for them. Here, either-or arguments about one approach versus another at a macro-level are not as relevant as solutions that work at the ground level. This does not mean that we accept the status quo, but rather that we traverse a pathway which addresses the immediate problems of people living in subsistence.

When we work in subsistence marketplaces, we must balance between dealing with the reality that is and the reality that we would like to see. Wishful thinking about potential opportunities and changes down the road are important, but the urgency of the immediate situation overwhelms. As a result, effecting change in the short term is important. So we need to have a clear understanding of the reality that is and focus on small changes that we can make. Yes, we can have wish lists of potential employment opportunities and changes in the larger context to work towards, but these are long-term goals. In the immediate term, we focus on what we can change for positive impact. In the medium term, we consider a broader array of alternatives. Getting the immediate term activities going is often a good basis to plan for the medium term.

Considering our own experience with marketplace literacy, much can be changed in terms of physical infrastructure to enable access to markets, education to enhance basic literacy, and so forth. Much can also be done in related areas such as health and nutrition. However, we focus the domain of our work on marketplace literacy, which we constantly renegotiate at the margins to consider aspects, say, such as sustainability literacy and specific livelihood training, while achieving impact and sustaining resources. Clearly, holistic approaches that cover every realm of life would be beneficial. But we have to temper our wishful thinking with the practical realities of an enterprise's constraints as well.

Delineate the Domain of Purpose – What We Are Not

The danger in larger purpose is in being too broad and, as a result, not achieving impact in any specific area. Therefore, our larger purpose must direct us down some pathways and steer us away from others. As a case in point, pursuing the larger purpose of alleviating poverty, many pathways are offered up, and they are often interrelated.

So where does one begin? **Perhaps we begin at the nodal point, where we hope to contribute something that is better than the alternatives out there and that builds off our unique strengths. In** this respect, this is no different than the commercial world in terms of being better. The pathway in our social enterprise is through marketplace literacy. But this realm of life intertwines with others, and can be overwhelmed with more urgent survival needs. Nevertheless, to be effective, we have to delineate what we will or will not do. That is both about shaping our identity to be effective and signaling who we are to the world.

Let me give you an example. I am reminded of an instance when, standing outside one of our rural offices, a woman with a disability started a conversation and asked for help, as her husband had a disability as well. I explained what we do and asked her to participate. I also explained that we would be unable to do anything if we are not focused. Later, it occurred to me that, in a village setting, there is a fishbowl-like environment where word gets around about what organizations do.

Therefore, it becomes all the more important to avoid deviating from our focus – we could easily be pulled from what our true purpose is. At the same time, life happens, and we need to be human beings first. So, don't neglect to treat people with respect and grace, but don't deviate from your enterprise mission, either. On rare occasion, yes, we have deviated when we could be of help. For instance, our facilities are used by workers nearby to rest during a hot day or access water. This is the very least we can do when we can be of help.

Execute the Domain of Purpose – Finding People and Place, a Home or a Community Platform

In charting a course, the most important elements of the enterprise are people. Again, while this is true in every context, it is accentuated in subsistence contexts. Next in importance is the place of engagement. Finding the right people who combine intent and initiative as well as places to work in provide two key elements. Resources are important, of course, but don't exceed in importance the need to find the right people and places. People and place provide a community platform – a home. From that point forward, finding a pathway and goals for the home and the resources to get there must follow.

A home or community platform is a great way to learn as well and confront issues as they arise. Often, this is a test of the resolve of both the local team members and the larger organization. Necessarily, one has to make some tough decisions on communities to choose to work in or continue efforts in. But working out issues in-depth provides the type of learning experience that informs these decisions and helps future expansion.

Having a home or community platform has many benefits, not the least of which is in providing an anchor or base from which to venture out. For instance, in India, currently, we have moved to additional clusters of villages from our base cluster after establishing a strong foundation. There is much we have learned here that helps us, as does our track record and the consequent reputation we have earned, and the opportunity to show who we are in actual practice to communities we seek to expand to.

Listen and Learn – Bottom-Up Immersion

Listening and learning from communities is central to delineate purpose and the first step. On one occasion, a well-meaning student asked me how much money to take to try to help. The answer is not to take money but rather listen and learn to start out. We have said much elsewhere about listening and learning. Suspending our preconceptions and beliefs going in, we often speak of immersion. Perhaps an inflated description but something to aspire for, the idea here is to truly absorb what we can with our many senses. Comparison and analysis can wait until it is time for reflection, to put things in perspective. Seeing for oneself how people live and work and play, and talking to people about their lives is the starting point.

As we move up through different units of analysis, such as from individual to household, to neighborhood, to community, and upward, we learn how the micro-level interacts with higher levels. From homemakers and breadwinners to the village-level leadership to other stakeholders, the immersion journey takes many turns. But the critical starting point is learning from those at the bottom of the power hierarchy.

Predetermined plans and methods only go so far with respect to learning about inter-linkages. They are necessary, but so is the ability to change paths and be nimble in the field. Degrees of separation for an organization present a large problem as deep understanding cannot be outsourced. Yet, it is often impractical for a large organization to itself be involved in deep immersion. Add to this that the nature of the organization might prevent access to those at the bottom, as the community leadership may want to convey a certain message and handpick interactions (e.g., a large development agency and a local community).

What can we do? Baseline qualitative and quantitative studies are useful, but perhaps too restrictive and filtered in terms of what we learn from them. Moreover, focus groups in these settings are very useful, but one-on-one in-depth interviews may bring out confidential issues. And research reports do not provide a sense of being there and seeing and listening for oneself.

This highlights the need for a field level representative of the organization who can translate between the community and the entity and educate the entity as well. Such a person would have access outside the parameters of preplanned research to have incidental encounters and interactions to learn from.

This is likely a many-layered process, to take our own example. I interact with my core team that is based in a city. In approaching a village, we can identify the political/governmental leaders, as well as community leaders in other respects, such as experienced teachers. In turn, the next levels are our field coordinators and then people in the community. While I have direct interaction with all levels and lines of communication with many, most of my interactions are with my core team. I note here that my role is far from full time; in fact, I have a full time job across the world. Therefore, this is much cause for optimism for those who can devote a large proportion of their time to running an enterprise.

To accelerate listening and learning, accessible qualitative data that people can view for themselves is also very useful. Here, we like the format of a day in the life video, as it provides the details of life at the ground level. It also provides a way for others not physically present to observe for themselves. Often, we may assume away many steps in the difficulties involved in day-to-day life and this format forces us to understand each step. Another facet is bottom-up training for members of the organization. Such training can combine virtual immersion across contexts with deep immersion in one setting. As discussed earlier, such depth of bottom-up immersion can lead to breadth of understanding.

To summarize, finding one's purpose in terms of its different dimensions is worthy of much effort and time as we live with these decisions for a long time. Here, we have articulated some of the important issues to consider, based on our own journey.

Chapter 7: Implementing Bottom-Up Enterprises

Image 7.01: Implementing Bottom-Up Enterprises.

Charting a bottom-up journey	Implementing bottom-up enterprises	Sustaining bottom-up enterprises	Guiding values	Essence of the bottom-up approach
Chart a course	Set goals idealistically & pursue them pragmatically	Identity before branding	EQ: To get things done	The ultimate bottom-up principle – If all else fails, do it yourself
Define purpose	Implementation trumps "IP & killer app"	Being over strategizing	Do your best; accept the worst	
			Take the high road & stay there	
Inspire through purpose	Learn, try out, learn by trying out	Negotiate, articulate, re-evaluate value equation	Be thoughtful in adversity	
			Go to the next level of understanding – Peel the onion	
Determine purpose	Iterate many times rather than get it *right* away	Culture of mutual accountability	Get over yourself, see & experience	The ultimate bottom-up enterprise model – Do what it takes for each other
Circumscribe purpose	Don't break promises – Break up promises	Blur the boundaries of organization	What you do matters more than what you say, think, like, or want to do	
	Coevolve pathways to implementation	Different ways to thread the needle	If one relationship is dispensable, all are	
Delineate the domain of purpose	Create short-term yield	Principled flexibility	Intertwined destinies – Not replaceable parts	Be intensely practical & un-compromisingly idealistic
Execute the domain of purpose	Complicate the revenue model	Activities before resources	Be aware of your power, & lack of it for those you work with	
	Fail small/scale through depth	Inspire & incentivize	View people by how far they have come	
			Nurture leadership among those who have not had a chance	
Listen & learn – Bottom-up immersion	Experience & know the forest, trees, branches, leaves	Steps to social enterprise & enterprise plan	Avoid an "I cannot do this without you" & "You cannot do this without me" mentality	Bottom-up meets top-down

In this chapter, we look at the factors that will help you successfully implement a bottom-up enterprise. Every enterprise is different, and every situation is different, but we discuss the common principles from our direct experience – including:

- Set Goals Idealistically and Pursue Them Pragmatically
- Implementation Trumps "IP and Killer App" Mentality
- Learn, Try Out, Learn By Trying Out
- Iterate Many Times Rather Than Get It *Right* Away
- Don't Break Promises – Break Up Promises or Take One Step at a Time in Uncertain Terrain
- Coevolve Pathways to Implementation
- Create Short-Term Yield
- Complicate the Revenue Model
- Fail Small / Scale Through Depth – Depth of Understanding Enables Breadth
- Experience and Know the Forest, Trees, Branches, Leaves

So let's get started.

Set Goals Idealistically and Pursue Them Pragmatically

"Think big, start small" is a quote that has been expressed in many forms. Being idealistic about broader aspects of one's enterprise is very important. However, being practical in execution is also very important in these contexts. Getting things done in a way that does no harm but has the potential to do good is central here. Despite best of intentions, sometimes we can do harm, but we aspire toward causing no harm at all. We need to be intensely practical because of the challenges that this context presents and because of the sharp contrast with idealistic goals. In fact, this contrast is a key lesson here; it is akin to the need for a soft heart and a tough mind.

It is a constant struggle to be intensely practical in getting things done at a day-to-day level while at the same time being uncompromisingly idealistic in the broader vision and identity. This is not about ends justifying the means in any sense, nor is it about being expedient at any cost. That is perhaps why it is a constant struggle. Being practical here is to emphasize the highest level of integrity as well as clear thinking and direction about what we can do and how we can do it.

As a case in point, for our marketplace literacy program, we strive to maintain the integrity of the education. At the same time, ground-level physical logistics such as the number of sessions to hold and when to hold them dictate what we ultimately do. Fewer transactions may be more practical but they reduce the opportunity for homework and applying learning. Getting people to attend and getting them to stay in light of all their daily struggles means that the logistical demands at the ground level are paramount in consideration. We rework what we can do to maintain the integrity of our program in light of this larger consideration. Going where the people are means adjusting to their many urgencies.

With a degree of separation where a partner implements our work, new issues arise requiring constant support and oversight. This is a delicate issue at times and also emphasizes the need to select partners and sustain the relationship, while maintaining the integrity of our solution.

Implementation Trumps "IP and Killer App" Mentality

An "IP and killer app" mentality has gained ascendancy, particularly since the Internet revolution. The notion here is that a new "invention," intellectually protected, is the road to success, often through a "killer app," and perhaps through an eventual buyout by a larger entity. But in a subsistence context, this is barely the beginning of the road, as so much is about implementation.

Many ideas fail simply because of the sheer challenges in initiating and sustaining implementation. What may be considered a few steps in implementing breaks into a few more in any context. They break into many more in a subsistence context. So much of implementation is about having the right people in myriad different contexts with subtle variations. Implementation occurs over a very uncertain and challenging terrain. Champions and sustained energy, involved teams on the ground, and the right people and the right place are all parts of the implementation puzzle.

Implicit in implementation is the need to implement in one context, to sustain it over time, and to spread to multiple contexts. Perhaps most important here as mentioned earlier are people and place – having a trusted local team in each context as well as choosing places to work in. This is akin to having a home or a community platform to work in to call one's own.

A related point is that there are, indeed, many ideas. The problem is often in how to implement them, and the key ingredient here is sweat equity. This is not to denigrate ideas, but to emphasize that follow-up and follow-through is where so much of the energy is needed. The notion of an idea in itself taking off may apply to non-subsistence, where we can make a variety of assumptions about common infrastructure, shared knowledge, and so forth.

But "implementation is everything" would not be too much of an overstatement in subsistence contexts. This includes the will to engage and the patient human capital to sustain endeavors. This often begins with a champion. On the other side though, people often do so much with so little, which includes the little that we are able to do for them.

Learn, Try Out, Learn by Trying Out

There are at least three ways of learning: observing and seeing for yourself; communicating through conversations and interviews and listening and asking; and trying things out for yourself.

The third is a valuable method, all the more so in subsistence marketplaces, where unfamiliarity combines with uncertainty and a myriad of differences across contexts to challenge what works on paper or in theory with what happens in practice. Trying out is particularly important here in forcing detailed planning and action and, in turn, realizing the many steps involved and the many variables that emerge.

Again, trial is important in any setting, but it is critically important in subsistence marketplaces. Trying out also forces a small promise and a deeper understanding of what implementation takes, even if in circumscribed settings. It leads to the much-needed sorting of various issues that come about in delivering solutions, given the nuances in each context. It also forces a pathway from discussion to action.

Ideally, this first effort should involve the highest levels of the enterprise as a way for the leadership to gain deeper understanding and appreciation. With our educational program, we find it extremely important for someone in a leadership role to actually conduct the educational sessions. For me, personally, this experience is essential to calibrate for the audience in close proximity.

Beyond such learning, trying out actual activities in different contexts leads to much learning, and the many details of implementation and the follow-through of team members provides new insights. In a sense, it is learning under the stress of engaging in actions, which brings out hidden issues, including the will that local team members express, the obstacles to overcome in terms of access and transportation, competing alternatives and opportunity costs, community attitudes, and so forth.

Iterate Many Times Rather Than Get It *Right* Away

Certainty enables a comfort level with planning, based on reasonable assumptions about the future and implementation. I recall a woman in a village whom I asked if she plans. She asked why she should plan when she has so little. This is in direct contrast to the certainty-based plan and implementation approach that is fundamentally top-down. Rather, uncertainty demands a more iterative approach of enacting and learning and evolving pathways.

This notion of sequential planning and implementation creeps in through many ways. The act of putting together an enterprise plan is a necessary exercise. But also essential is the mindset that planning only takes us a portion of the way; the need to throw out the plan and change with new circumstances is critical. However, detailed planning is essential to begin with, so long as we are ready to change on a dime if needed. "Changing on a dime" implies that we have something to change *from*– and that something is our original plan, which has to be very detailed to reflect thinking through issues to the extent possible beforehand.

This comes home in international immersion experiences as well, where detailed planning considering a host of constraints and variables is essential – but we must be able to throw out the plan when needed due to unanticipated circumstances. Such international immersion is just a microcosm of sustained implementation on the ground. And implementation in turn is a microcosm of the lives of those living in subsistence.

Iteration is also an important means of learning, say, about the steps involved in implementation. As noted, each step breaks into several mini-steps in these settings, and as such, forces a level of detailed thinking that leads to deeper insights for the next iteration. Being iterative is about learning by doing as well.

Don't Break Promises – Break Up Promises or Take One Step at a Time in Uncertain Terrain

In a context of uncertainty for those who live in it and for those from the outside who engage in it, breaking up promises is an important way to move forward. **Being transparent and making small promises that we can keep, rather than breaking larger promises, is important. Instead of breaking promises, break them up into smaller promises that you can keep.** The reality is that a variety of factors may prevent a sustained effort – lack of funding from the viewpoint of the entity or unanticipated adverse local circumstances that overwhelm intended efforts. For example, acute water shortage in the face of efforts to promote marketplace literacy would suggest a different set of priorities for the communities struggling to survive, as we learned in East Africa.

Given the complexity of the subsistence contexts and the many steps that seemingly simple tasks break up into, a corresponding breaking up of larger promises into smaller ones is an honest approach. In fact, larger promises are best conveyed as a desired path and broken into smaller promises. In this regard, what the enterprise will *not* do is as important as what it *will* do and we need to clearly communicate the enterprise's identity. Skepticism about entities is a natural state of mind in subsistence communities that have often seen people and entities come and go and promises made and broken.

Breaking up promises is also consistent with iterating often and using the learning to chart a new course. It is consistent with learning by trying out. And it is consistent with the notion of implementation breaking up into many more steps than anticipated. Breaking up promises is practical, as it enables enterprises to get doable things done. Breaking up promises also builds trust incrementally, based on actual activities rather than hyped claims.

For instance, if initial discussions lead to one partner suggesting a huge media event and potential mistrust in terms of publicity being used to raise funds without true intentions, then a track record of fulfilling small promises allows for postponement of such practices. Keeping small promises engenders the trust we need to publicize or seek funding and so forth.

Coevolve Pathways to Implementation

Related to the notion of breaking up promises is the need to coevolve pathways to design and implement solutions. Coevolving requires transparency to engage in honest discussions with communities about where the entity is and the different paths it can take. Unfamiliarity coming in, combined with uncertainty inherent in the context, arises from extreme resource constraints and limited ability to confront adverse events, and complex interplay between myriad variables that may range from the cultural to the environmental. It necessitates deep understanding of the context and sincere dialogue with stakeholders to identify pathways. Transparency is not only an ethical choice, but a practical choice - an essential element to achieve desired outcomes.

Whereas co-creating solutions is one way to phrase what is done, coevolving pathways represents a broader discussion of directions to pursue, wherein core solutions are often created by the enterprise. Co-creation of solutions often occurs between local champions and the higher level leadership, but not necessarily with the end-beneficiaries. In our case, our local champions in the US, India, Tanzania, Honduras, Uganda, and Argentina are creating an emergent educational experience as they meet with different audiences. There is a bottom-up and top-down exchange of ideas, the latter mostly based on bottom-up insights from other geographies. Nevertheless, the broader philosophy of know-why and bottom-up approaches to education applies across settings.

The potential for mutual learning is very important, but while pathways can be coevolved, it is important not to overemphasize the potential to actually co-create solutions. Often, this is not the urgent focus of those living in subsistence, and it is the role of the enterprise to learn from people in subsistence and then design solutions for them. **Coevolving pathways emphasizes how the journey is a product of the enterprise and the community.** Even here, the pragmatic reality is that a few stakeholders represent the larger community in providing input. Beyond such feedback, further insights are gained by trying out activities.

While equal partners in a number of senses, the initiative and the impetus come from the enterprise in terms of potential directions they consider. The enterprise is at the cusp of learning about the people, the community, and the problem so it can design a solution. The new initiatives and suggested directions mostly have to come from the enterprise. This is simply a practical matter of bottom-up insights that then require relatively top-down consideration for the locally grounded enterprise in carrying out its mission. It is a matter of having the best vantage point and the objective of considering specific solutions. Given the multiple urgencies that people face, deep and broad dialogue is foundational, but the burden of designing specific solutions has to be championed by the enterprise. Implementation, though, becomes more collaborative, as local logistics in light of what one has to offer involve more concrete issues and deeper involvement.

Create Short-Term Yield

People living in subsistence face immediate needs. Low income and low literacy combine to narrow the horizon. As such, having a short-term yield to our solutions is essential. In marketplace literacy, such yield comes from our consumer literacy program, which provides an immediate benefit in savings and better quality products. People cannot wait for the longer-term yield of being an entrepreneur, which has many obstacles along the way.

Our short-term yield approach is also more closely aligned with the cycle of people's day-to-day lives. The same could be said in many different arenas such as agriculture and health and so forth, although showing a short-term benefit can often be challenging in some realms such as nutrition.

An approach based on short-term yield builds trust by offering and delivering on small promises and by the ultimate test: people seeing for themselves if there is a benefit to what we are doing. This holds true when designing solutions as well – people will be engaged and persistent when they see the positive impact of a project in the immediate and short term. The experience of local people in each interaction can yield short-term benefits as well, emphasizing how an enterprise and its local teams engage people in subsistence settings and value their interactions. With our marketplace literacy education, the immediate benefit is in savings and better quality products as consumers. As entrepreneurs, starting enterprises may take longer, if it is indeed the appropriate path for individuals based on their specific circumstances, but as consumers, the benefit appears to be universal and immediate.

Complicate the Revenue Model

Much has been written about the potential for economic sustainability and profit in subsistence marketplaces. The reality is that the potential is there, but the road is challenging and requires sustained effort. And it's important to note that a revenue stream can leave out those who are most vulnerable and in greatest need. Overstating the potential for "monetizing" is just as unrealistic as eschewing monetary outcomes.

One realistic approach is to complicate the revenue model, such as by combining social with financial outcomes in nuanced ways. Monetary revenue can also be complicated, using engagement in subsistence marketplaces for learning purposes, while breaking even and communicating about the larger entity and gaining a foothold in terms of exposure and credibility.

As an illustration, our own engagement has led to several outcomes, ranging from research to education for our students, to community service, each being a separate purpose and not a means to another end. In doing so, relationships with stakeholders involve complex exchanges that include academic, educational, and community-based aspects with mutual development.

Complicating the revenue model works to sustain initiatives until they are able to stand on their own right. Motivations are complex and stakeholders diverse – a parallel complication of the revenue model where the enterprise, its leadership, and its local teams think more holistically and appeal to different needs and motivations is important.

Fail Small / Scaling Through Depth – Depth of Understanding Enables Breadth

Depth of experience in a few contexts is both efficient and effective. This is not to suggest that there are pervasive commonalities across subsistence contexts. But deep understanding as well as implementation enables us to sort out unanticipated issues that take us up the learning curve rapidly. Such understanding informs us about the dimensions or variables to seek out and manage, often unanticipated due to unfamiliarity and uniqueness. In fact, depth can then enable breadth.

Again, subsistence contexts do not share a common infrastructure and knowledge base, as do more advanced contexts. Therefore, depth in a few contexts is extraordinarily important, first and foremost, in learning. In turn, it is invaluable in understanding the complexity in terms of the types of variables and their interactions that play out in these settings. Such learning also shakes loose basic assumptions and opens our minds to a range of possibilities. Depth enables understanding of relationships at several levels, from individuals to communities and social structures, as well as the larger context.

Unfamiliarity in terms of lived experience and complexity in the types of variables that impact consumption are key factors that accentuate the need for deep understanding of a radically different context. Something as simple as understanding of spatial arrangements and physical distances can lead to deeper understanding.

Depth also applies to trying out solutions. Narrow but deep implementation of a solution, its ecosystem, and the enterprise in turn enables sorting out a host of issues in a circumscribed geographic setting, timeframe, and relationship (as in making promises with full transparency).

How does depth lead to breadth? At the level of understanding, cognitive thinking patterns may generalize across contexts but manifest in different ways. Buying the cheapest in the US may be equivalent to buying the largest with an isolated tribal community in Africa. Understanding of spatial and social constraints and unexpected usage conditions in India in terms of physical aspects of poverty may translate to a small dwelling in Latin America. Local environmental issues such as plastic in the landscape in subsistence settings may translate to issues such as blocked sewage in many different settings. Health and hygiene issues stemming from the poor quality of the local environment may translate as well. The ill effects of long-term drought as well as human adaptation also provide learning that may be useful across contexts. On the other hand, the most unique aspects of poverty and marketplaces are culturally intensive, relating to arenas such as food, traditional practices to mark life events, the role of women and men, and so forth. How marketplace interactions impinge on these unique elements is part of the in-depth learning we aim for.

At the level of designing solutions, depth enables us to fully understand various issues, not the least of which is that implementation steps often multiply. What is taken for granted in resource-rich settings may not hold in subsistence settings, from something as simple as completing a transaction to transporting a product and using it. Again, the combination of unfamiliarity for the outside entity and an intensely complex, uncertain, constrained, and distinctively different environment requires us to learn in-depth about how to implement our solution in the subsistence setting. Depth is also necessary as an efficient means to consider many different contexts by learning about a few in detail. A deep dive also enables us to develop a detailed method that can then be adapted to different settings.

This lesson has played out time and time again as our first foray into arenas has been with much depth – research through immersion in specific geographies, a detailed five-day face-to-face marketplace literacy program leading to other configurations, a yearlong course for university students leading to many different offerings, international immersion leading to variations, etc.

Experience and Know the Forest, Trees, Branches, Leaves

Many challenges in bottom-up innovation relate to working remotely with a local team. Foremost, it is very important for leaders to know the forest, groves, trees, branches, leaves, fruits, vegetables, and weeds firsthand. This level of grounding enables deep understanding of complex variables and interactions and, as a result, a mind frame for understanding issues and working with local teams. In turn, this also builds credibility and trust in the long run, as well as respect for people willing to immerse themselves and do what it takes to understand things at the ground level and stay informed as things change. (The opposite approach would, on the other hand, encourage posturing and misrepresentation.)

Frequent visits and very frequent interactions with local teams and communities are critical, providing opportunity for the one-on-one interaction we speak of. Things change, and people change, and leaders need the cognitive makeup to absorb evolving issues and make changes. Lack of rudimentary understanding when managing an enterprise, an initiative, or a project, is as detrimental as nuanced understanding is productive. Even if direct communications are not frequent, a line of communication and underlying relationships with various stakeholders is important. Much can be achieved virtually, when interspersed with actual visits and based on healthy relationships.

Such understanding leads to informed decision-making while keeping the fickle circumstances and adversities of the local team in mind. It leads to consideration of the many uncertain moving parts to an enterprise. As noted, invariably, implementation magnifies into many more steps than usually anticipated. Being properly grounded while working with your local team, you can evaluate insights from them and gauge when to push forward and when to hold back on new directions.

However, the point here is not to micromanage and interfere. This is counterproductive. And it is important to often be above the fray, so to speak. You need the knowledge and ability to manage and, yes, micromanage, but the latter only if needed.

Overcoming Challenges in Subsistence Marketplaces

Here are five keys – not all of the keys, by any means – to overcoming the many challenges we face in working in subsistence marketplaces:

1. ***Develop the right people in place.*** You are not going anywhere if you don't have a solid team together. And it is not about hiring the "right" person, it is about helping them develop into the right person.

2. ***Choose your location.*** You need to choose a location – a set of villages or a community platform, or perhaps an urban area – to work in.

3. ***Create a plan, and implement it.*** Most of the earlier chapters have focused on various aspects of understanding subsistence marketplaces and designing solutions for them. You can have wonderful ideas, but if you haven't thought through how to implement them, or get bogged down in implementing them, then they don't come to fruition. And *implementation is everything* is not too much of an overstatement.

4. ***Be patient.*** Patience is a key virtue for working in subsistence marketplaces. Remember what we said earlier: Start small, fail small, and fail as quickly as possible. Why? Because you learn from your failure, and you readjust, and you will be more successful in the end if you go this route.

5. ***Be committed.*** We certainly never want to give the impression that it is easy to design solutions and implement them for this context. It is very challenging. It takes not only patience, but will and commitment. You need to see the big perspective, be in it for the long haul, and not be deterred by roadblocks. Instead, be creative in finding ways around those roadblocks.

I tend not to call our work "projects," because we need to have a longer-term commitment than what a project typically entails or suggests. Sometimes these are communities we want to be engaged in for a lifetime.

In summary, this chapter discussed some lessons we have learned in implementing solutions in subsistence marketplaces while following a bottom-up approach.

Chapter 8: Sustaining Bottom-Up Enterprises

Image 8.01: Sustaining Bottom-Up Enterprises.

Charting a bottom-up journey	Implementing bottom-up enterprises	Sustaining bottom-up enterprises	Guiding values	Essence of the bottom-up approach
Chart a course	Set goals idealistically & pursue them pragmatically	Identity before branding	EQ: To get things done	The ultimate bottom-up principle – If all else fails, do it yourself
Define purpose	Implementation trumps "IP & killer app"	Being over strategizing	Do your best; accept the worst	
			Take the high road & stay there	
Inspire through purpose	Learn, try out, learn by trying out	Negotiate, articulate, re-evaluate value equation	Be thoughtful in adversity	
			Go to the next level of understanding – Peel the onion	
Determine purpose	Iterate many times rather than get it *right* away	Culture of mutual accountability	Get over yourself, see & experience	The ultimate bottom-up enterprise model – Do what it takes for each other
Circumscribe purpose	Don't break promises – Break up promises	Blur the boundaries of organization	What you do matters more than what you say, think, like, or want to do	
	Coevolve pathways to implementation	Different ways to thread the needle	If one relationship is dispensable, all are	
Delineate the domain of purpose			Intertwined destinies – Not replaceable parts	
	Create short-term yield	Principled flexibility	Be aware of your power, & lack of it for those you work with	Be intensely practical & un-compromisingly idealistic
Execute the domain of purpose	Complicate the revenue model	Activities before resources	View people by how far they have come	
	Fail small/scale through depth	Inspire & incentivize	Nurture leadership among those who have not had a chance	
Listen & learn – Bottom-up immersion	Experience & know the forest, trees, branches, leaves	Steps to social enterprise & enterprise plan	Avoid an "I cannot do this without you" & "You cannot do this without me" mentality	Bottom-up meets top-down

Sustaining bottom-up enterprises:

- Identity Before Branding
- *Being* Over Strategizing

- Negotiate, Articulate, and Re-Evaluate the Value Equation
- Culture of Mutual Accountability
- Blur the Boundaries of the Organization
- Different Ways to Thread the Needle
- Principled Flexibility
- Activities Before Resources
- Inspire and Incentivize
- Steps to Social Enterprise and the All-Important Enterprise Plan

In previous chapters, we have talked about the various issues related to considering, designing, and implementing bottom-up enterprises. But you can do all the thoughtful and insightful considering, designing, and implementing that you want; if you do not have the means and understanding to *sustain* your enterprise, then the potential for positive impact will not be fully realized.

Indeed, sustaining a bottom-up enterprise is often the biggest challenge. Many enterprises and experiments simply do not sustain. In this chapter, then, we will share some lessons learned in our attempts at sustaining an enterprise.

Identity Before Branding

So much of sustaining implementation in bottom-up innovation centers on who we are and on signaling this to stakeholders, who have seen people and entities come and go. Rather than work on shared assumptions about how marketplaces work and how institutional mechanisms are enforced, this is a context where such assumptions exist informally at the cultural level. Thus, why someone is in an enterprise and how long they might be in it become important considerations, as engendering trust is at a premium, rather than relying on contractual obligations.

Identity in this setting, then, takes on paramount importance. This is not to underestimate the importance of branding, but to emphasize how important it is to understand yourself in terms of your motivations and intentions and how long you plan to sustain your efforts. You need to go through this self-reflection at a deep level, and then be able to communicate who you are – branding your enterprise. This process is as much about educating yourself as it is about educating others.

Communicating who we are through branding is important, but identity evolves in conditions of high uncertainty. Through high stress, unexpected events, and financial pressures, the true identity of an enterprise or individual emerges. Here, the point about evolving our identity along with coevolving pathways is an accurate depiction under extreme resource constraints. In turn, consistent and sustained communication of identity becomes extremely important, with the brand being the vehicle for engendering trust, in some ways, perhaps even more starkly than in traditional settings.

Sustained signaling of the identity of the leadership and the enterprise are extremely important in a context where outsiders engage for a complex set of motivations. All this occurs in a setting where local teams are of much lower status and power, and many things happen without logic or reason, often to benefit powerful individuals. Thus, sustained engagement requires sustained reinforcement of the identity of the enterprise vis-à-vis other organizations and the larger context.

This does not mean that the leadership or an enterprise is static in identity; just that, as it evolves, there is constant communication about its identity and what it stands for. People working on local teams require this constancy in the face of myriad influences in a complex social milieu along with enterprises with a variety of motivations. How one behaves in various situations takes larger meaning, as local teams and the communities served gauge the relationship and what can be counted on in a context of uncertainty. In a top-down world, things can be assessed based on such factors as labor markets and hiring and so forth. Here, **a bottom-up approach calls for building identity from the ground up and engendering trust.**

Many examples come to mind in this regard, such as the emphasis on accurate accounting to the values imparted in how we treat people, and women in particular, how we spend scarce resources, and to what we are ultimately about in terms of our goals, which is perhaps the single most important signal.

One example we have confronted here relates to what we would give for those who take our marketplace literacy education or the entities who enable it. Our fundamental answer is that people give their time and we give them an education. Therefore, we do not like to provide a monetary incentive for people to attend, not to mention the resources needed to make this practice sustainable. This basic principle is modified as we consider difficulties in transportation, opportunity costs that we can verify, and costs such as electricity for the entity hosting us. Such issues are often a matter of the leadership signaling to the local team, which in turn signals to the community. It is negotiated like everything else, but based on a sound principle. The key is to keep the value equation in mind and think it through and articulate it.

All of this emphasizes means and processes and the need to adhere to them no matter where they may lead. If ends justified means, then this signaling of who we are changes, and the processes and means become murky.

Sustaining Bottom-Up Enterprises

Ultimately, we signal the need for the highest level of integrity in what we do. Choosing partners of the highest level of integrity is important, and we need to maintain the same high standards. Any good thing can be used in bad ways, and this is certainly true of partners, such as in using a partnership for media attention and funding without any good faith intentions of serving the community on the basis of the partnership.

In terms of relationship building, frequent visits as well as involvement through the digital medium are important in signaling identity. In the end, though, nothing speaks louder than sustained behavior, akin to the importance of a continuing commitment in the relationship between buyer and seller discussed earlier.

Protecting the independence and continuity of engagement for local teams is also a form of sustaining identity, such as in financial matters. Sustained identity is a way of reducing the high level of uncertainty under which the enterprise and the people involved operate. This often means that financial and other shocks and discontinuities need to be absorbed by the leadership in order to sustain the enterprise. In fact, such absorption is a signal in itself of what the enterprise stands for. What can be achieved with some certainty using personal resources, financial and otherwise, is one way to provide constancy.

Being Over Strategizing

When identity is emphasized and strong and evolving, then *being* takes precedence over strategizing. This is not to understate the importance of strategy. But who we are, thoroughly thought through, enables us to just *be* in different situations and act accordingly. Once again, this is an ideal and it is a deep understanding of an iteration between the broader values, the specific planning, and the enactment, all of which over time, lead to the formation and evolution of identity. At that point, *being* actually takes transactional costs away from calculating every decision.

Through such practices as breaking up promises and keeping them, being becomes a natural state in the blur of day-to-day activities. We draw from who we are in guiding us and avoid expediency and compromise that detracts from our identity. As an example on a matter of great significance, we treat our team members as family, make small promises, and provide soft landings or transitions, keeping in mind their well-being. We avoid being beholden by any single resource that can potentially compromise us. We are transparent in our internal and external communications. Strategizing is not neglected but does not take us over; it is within the confines of who we are. **Moreover, strategizing never enters into how we deal with people who work with us; rather, their well-being is central.**

Well being

Negotiate, Articulate, and Reevaluate the Value Equation

Perhaps there is no more important concept in a bottom-up enterprise or any enterprise than the value equation. Here, though, the vagueness and nonmonetary aspects or unanticipated monetary and in-kind aspects in subsistence contexts require particular attention and articulation.

values

Once again, uncertainty combined with unanticipated circumstances (including adversities that communities and local teams face) require a constant renegotiation of the value equation in terms of what is given and what is received. This is not about setting the give and the get in stone, but about constantly reevaluating as things progress. For instance, the equation for our own marketplace literacy program may be to give an education close to homes of participants in return for time and effort in an urban setting. But in a rural setting with difficult access and mobility, it may require support for transportation and lost wages.

trade-off

However, the broader appeal and encouragement may apply to the first part of our educational program on generic marketplace literacy and consumer literacy. We could potentially offer the second part of our program, on entrepreneurial literacy, without any incentive, as the value we add should now be evident and individuals in the community need to invest in themselves at this point.

Another aspect of value relates to one's own local teams and the adversities they face. Providing a cushion in such times is important to sustain their families and the work they do – providing some certainty and continuity is critical. Here again, open-ended guarantees of support should be tempered with a clear articulation of the give and get. This is not at all about bargaining in times of need. Rather, what is signaled then is the constancy of being there and the emphasis on issues related to well-being – not as a strategy, but as a human sentiment.

Such a response is also very important for local team members to be able to prioritize their own lives to emphasize their own well-being. At the same time, we need to articulate what is support based on emergencies and what is a loan with repayment in mind, and we need to apply the rationale to others until we are required to reevaluate a situation.

The components of what constitutes value also make this issue more difficult, emphasizing the need to articulate and reevaluate. Recruiting people, helping with arrangements, facilitating meetings, transporting people, and being there to help or as a presence are just some examples of the get component from people in the community. The give component could be in terms of money, use of facilities, help in times of need, access to resources, and so forth. Many nonmonetary aspects and unanticipated monetary and nonmonetary aspects arise, making contracts based on anticipated scenarios much more challenging.

In any event, much of what is done is through oral communications without formal institutional mechanisms. The further value is broadened beyond specific monetary arrangements and deliverables, the more important it is to think through and articulate. Similarly, deliverables from local teams and communities have to be reevaluated and renegotiated constantly as different issues arise. Again, the terrain is not smooth as compared to a setting where the destination is visible and reachable in methodical, preplanned steps.

Culture of Mutual Accountability

A notion related to renegotiating the value equation is simply one of mutual accountability. With the lack of clear-cut inputs and outputs, this intangible becomes very central. Such accountability should cut across levels of the organization in setting the tone. Thus, leadership in the organization should be open to being held accountable as well. Noteworthy here is that this too is an ideal, as local team members would need to overcome power differences to hold those at a higher level accountable. However, it is an ideal worth aspiring for in an environment filled with uncertainty and goals that are not easily quantified or reduced to monetary terms in terms of input and outcomes.

In a setting where the immediate dictates and local team members and community members do not have the access or the resources to seek new knowledge to address new circumstances, open discussion within teams and between stakeholders becomes very important. However, this has to occur in settings where norms may be quite different and where implicit power differentials dominate. Thus, the ideal of mutual accountability is worth striving for even if the path to it is filled with obstacles. Such accountability in a sense is the central corrective mechanism in a setting where goals, processes, and outcomes are all lacking in specificity and clarity.

Blur the Boundaries of the Organization

Local teams need to be as much part of the community as part of the enterprise. Ideally, this division of loyalty should not be germane. In reality, of course, limited resources mean tough choices. Local teams need to be viewed as being in it for the entire community and not displaying favoritism based on who they know as well as existing socio-political hierarchies. This means placing appropriate safeguards in running the enterprise to the extent possible.

Our core team has, from the beginning, been composed of myself and members from the very subsistence communities we serve. However, while this leads to a diverse makeup at an organizational level, field coordinators need to also be tied specifically to local communities and be known there. These local connections that we tap into with our core team of individuals who can relate across different geographies is very important. There is much by way of sweat equity in developing teams from subsistence communities, but there is much learning as well. Often, enterprises lack such local access, and even middle managers lack exposure at the local level. Having core team members who have the experience and understanding, and who are from the same communities that we serve are critical elements of the bottom-up enterprise. Even when being from the same communities, their ability (and humility) to work bottom-up in familiar settings is vital. Our field coordinators adopt this approach, being selected for showing leadership in serving the community as individuals, yet not being part of the political hierarchy, which may be detrimental in some ways.

Different Ways to Thread the Needle

Related to the issue we discussed earlier, of coevolving pathways for implementation, is the importance of finding different ways to achieve outcomes for sustaining the enterprise. Being open to different paths in moving forward in the face of uncertainty is particularly important here. There are, indeed, many paths rather than one straight one, akin to traveling in a forest where the variables are complex and no obvious pathways exist, as opposed to traveling on a well-charted road with maps available. Paths have unexpected obstacles to overcome, not well-constructed roads to follow.

Therefore, sustaining effort toward goals but also being realistic in reaching them are both important aspects. Looking at different ways to thread the needle also involves treating failures as learning opportunities to glean insights from. The notion of a learning enterprise takes on new light in these settings, where inability to launch or inability to scale or sustain can come from a variety of factors. Thus, we should view each experience in terms of accumulated learning in a long-term perspective.

As an example, it took us more than six years to launch a program in a state in India, but we did so to follow through on our learning as well. By launching, we demonstrated to ourselves that there are different ways of threading the needle in that context. If things were simply not viable, we would then seek a different setting while keeping our promises. This attitude needs to pervade the organization in a variety of ways from day-to-day activities to broader thinking. This is where our common larger purpose provides a guide or a compass in then finding different pathways which sometimes may seem like going sideways or backwards but eventually moves us forward toward the impact we seek.

Principled Flexibility

A key aspect of evolving an enterprise's identity and signaling it relates to what it stands for. This is not about the leadership knowing what is best or what the guiding principle is, but standing for certain abstract principles while finding a way to be flexible in an uncertain environment. For example, not paying people or recruiters for participation in our educational program is a principle communicated constantly to our teams and communities. But rather than assume a rigid posture, the reality is that this approach needs to be tempered with reality on the ground. When there are clear opportunity costs that people have or when there are transportation needs or even the expenses of using a venue such as a community hall, the principle has to be applied in spirit and not in a rule-based manner. This is also an example of the top-down meeting the bottom-up.

The point here is not that we are more principled than the people we meet or that we know what is right. Rather, the point is to adhere to certain broader principles that are consistent with why the endeavor exists to begin with, i.e., its identity, while allowing ground-level realities to lead to nuanced learning and adjustments. Practices that compromise integrity are categorically and absolutely outside the realm of consideration for many reasons, not the least being in contradiction with the spirit of the organization. In a sense, this lesson is about living within oneself and the organizational entity in terms of who we are. This foundation is very important in providing a secure base from which to work in uncertain circumstances.

Activities Before Resources

You need resources to get things done – this is no secret. But starting a conversation with resources needed is, in a sense, the reverse of the entrepreneurial route. What are the overall goals, and what activities on the ground will it take to get us there? This is a more specific and pertinent way toward mobilizing necessary resources. It also maintains the all-important value equation in terms of what is invested and what the outcomes are, rather than making vague and open-ended resource commitments.

Such value-based resource allocations are likely more sustainable in the long run as well. Such an approach also crystallizes the most important priorities in terms of achieving goals, and scales back less important aspects as needed, based on resource constraints. Emphasizing activities as a starting point also signals the identity of the enterprise in its way of thinking, helping to attract appropriate partners.

For our organization, this comes with the need to break activities up. Planning, design, delivery, and assessment is one way to think about what we do. Here, delivery, the intended final outcome, forces our hand in focusing on the impact we seek. There are times when remuneration has to be tied solely to delivery, and other times when the focus is on design and so forth. The ability to break up goals into smaller activities and tasks is critical here in constantly refocusing teams toward action. For us and our potential partners, this means that being in a perpetual state of discussion is not going to be viable.

Placing activities before resources also means avoiding the tyranny of budgets and the budget cart leading the activities/objectives horse. Too often, budgets, once accepted, are set in stone. They are also related to resources to be allocated to units and individuals. Somehow, there is little flexibility on the means, whereas there is detailed discussion on the ends – the actual value creation. Well, we need to be flexible on means, ends, and the means-ends connection. Rather than think in terms of releasing the budget, it is preferable to think in terms of worthwhile activities and ways to garner support for them.

Inspire and Incentivize

Monetary incentives are necessary and earned. There is no question here. But many who choose to work in these settings seek a larger purpose at least to start out. Sustaining that larger purpose requires inspiration. **To lead in these settings is to both incentivize and inspire.** People work for money but not money alone – not a profound or original insight, but this reality is accentuated in subsistence contexts. Finding the synergy between their passion and proficiency and the mutual larger purpose is central. Their own development and vision for themselves and the communities they serve is important.

The ability of the leadership to inspire is very important. To inspire others, we need to present a sustained identity of who we are, as demonstrated through our day-to-day and longer-term behaviors. What we stand for is the compass that people derive inspiration from. Similar to multiplying value through small transactions, we multiply our value through being in it for the longer term. For our local teams, the fact that we are serving their own community or communities similar to their own means a lot as well, as does their reputation built around helping their communities. We need to focus on a person's development in terms of rich experiences as well as credentials as they move forward. **If anything, our experience has been that inspired effort based on shared purpose is as powerful a motivator as any.**

Steps to Social Enterprise and the All-Important Enterprise Plan

We view our social enterprise in terms of five steps:

- Identifying a problem (need for marketplace literacy)
- Designing a unique solution (emphasizing know-why)
- Deploying a means to reach a wider audience (multimedia, teacher-less approach)
- Above all, developing an enterprise plan
- Assessing our impact and making adjustments

The enterprise plan addresses this simple question: Why should anybody do what you think they should do or want them to do? It relates to incentive. Each step in the enterprise plan needs to delineate how people and organizations involved are incentivized. What is in it for them, personally and professionally? This includes but is not restricted to monetary incentives. Monetary incentives need to be commensurate with the value being created and articulated and explained as such. This point relates to the earlier point about sustaining an identity. Beyond the monetary incentive, the enterprise plan is about incentive as well as inspiration.

The lessons in this chapter relate to sustaining an organization, extremely important in a context where there are many pilot efforts that do not sustain and grow.

Chapter 9: Guiding Values

Image 9.01: Guiding Values.

Charting a bottom-up journey	Implementing bottom-up enterprises	Sustaining bottom-up enterprises	**Guiding values**	Essence of the bottom-up approach
Chart a course	Set goals idealistically & pursue them pragmatically	Identity before branding	EQ: To get things done	The ultimate bottom-up principle – If all else fails, do it yourself
Define purpose	Implementation trumps "IP & killer app"	Being over strategizing	Do your best; accept the worst	
Inspire through purpose	Learn, try out, learn by trying out	Negotiate, articulate, re-evaluate value equation	Take the high road & stay there	
Determine purpose	Iterate many times rather than get it *right* away	Culture of mutual accountability	Be thoughtful in adversity	The ultimate bottom-up enterprise model – Do what it takes for each other
Circumscribe purpose	Don't break promises – Break up promises	Blur the boundaries of organization	Go to the next level of understanding – Peel the onion	
Delineate the domain of purpose	Coevolve pathways to implementation	Different ways to thread the needle	Get over yourself, see & experience	
Execute the domain of purpose	Create short-term yield	Principled flexibility	What you do matters more than what you say, think, like, or want to do	Be intensely practical & un-compromisingly idealistic
Listen & learn – Bottom-up immersion	Complicate the revenue model	Activities before resources	If one relationship is dispensable, all are	
	Fail small/scale through depth	Inspire & incentivize	Intertwined destinies – Not replaceable parts	
	Experience & know the forest, trees, branches, leaves	Steps to social enterprise & enterprise plan	Be aware of your power, & lack of it for those you work with	Bottom-up meets top-down
			View people by how far they have come	
			Nurture leadership among those who have not had a chance	
			Avoid an "I cannot do this without you" & "You cannot do this without me" mentality	

We have spent the last several chapters talking about the issues surrounding the successful design, launching, and sustaining of a bottom-up enterprise. In this chapter we'll reflect on many of the lessons that we have learned over the years in going through this process, and we will delineate the guiding values that have helped to keep us on course. We believe these values and lessons will be of significant importance to you as you go forth with your own enterprise.

Guiding values include:

- EQ: To Get Things Done
- Do Your Best; Accept the Worst – In Fact, the Two May Coexist
- Take the High Road and Stay There
- Be Thoughtful in Adversity – Others' and Ours
- Go to the Next Level of Understanding – Peel the Onion
- Get Over Yourself, So You Can See and Experience More
- What You Do Matters More Than What You Say You Will Do, Think, Like To Do, or Want to Do – Enact
- If One Relationship Is Dispensable, Then All Relationships Are Dispensable – Or Viewing Individuals Not as Resources but as People to Develop to Realize Their Potential
- Intertwined Destinies – Not Replaceable Parts
- Be Aware of Your Power, and Lack of It for Those You Work With
- View People Not Based On Where They Are In Life, But On How Far They Have Traveled And Through What Terrain Or Gauging How Far Someone Has Come In Life, Not Where They Are
- Nurture Leadership Among Those Who Have Not Had a Chance
- Avoid an "I Cannot Do This Without You" and "You Cannot Do This Without Me" Mentality

EQ: To Get Things Done

If IQ is about ideas and what to do, then arguably, EQ is about how to get them done. In a setting where institutional mechanisms are in place and rules are enforced, ideas have a relatively smoother translation to practice. In subsistence contexts where relationships rather than rules are in play, emotional quotient becomes critically important. Dealing with a range of emotions, working with people, showing patience and empathy and so forth, become the hallmark of individual and organizational identity.

The difference between EQ and IQ is often the difference between what to do and how to do it, or ideas versus their implementation. EQ includes sensing, listening, empathizing, communicating, and conducting oneself in different forums. Not politicizing, personalizing, posturing or being cynical are among the important elements here.

By *politicizing*, we mean using means other than the issues on their merit and straightforward communication to achieve goals. In a one-on-one interactional environment, our words mean a lot more. And the means we use are eventually privy to everyone. The common denominator that may cut across different stakeholders is a sustained identity in terms of how we go about achieving goals as well; we need to be consistent with what we are trying to accomplish and how. There is a social ethic that goes with trying to achieve social goals.

By *personalizing*, we mean taking criticisms and disagreements personally. A thick skin is a good prerequisite in this arena. There are many stressful situations where we need to get things done and worry about feelings later.

By *posturing*, we mean using power and position rather than the merit of the issues involved. This is particularly difficult, as there is a large power differential with local teams and communities, whether it be through resources, connections, or other bases, such as education and status.

And not *being cynical* is, of course, essential when faced with daunting challenges in subsistence contexts. If anything, the adversity that people face emphasizes the preciousness of the certainties that we have in our own lives.

Most (if not all) human beings have a sense of fairness, and when people are treated fairly, this engenders trust. An education or a literacy level is not required to gauge what is fair at a human level. Respecting people for their inherent dignity and empowering them matters here as it does anywhere. As noted earlier, even with nothing else and the need to survive, dignity matters a lot, and sustains people.

Why are these elements so important here? It relates to the need for a sustained identity that is built on a common denominator that people can perceive – one that is oriented toward an intuitive sense of fair play that appeals to the low-literate, low-income individual and community. Motivations will constantly be questioned; a sustained identity in how one conducts oneself is central here. In the ultimate analysis, in more ways than one, what we *do* matters most.

Actions are paramount here and how we conduct ourselves says a lot about our identity. There is little margin for error when it comes to identity, and emotional quotient is an important piece of such an identity. In our day-to-day operations, EQ through sensing and developing personnel and team dynamics and knowing when to step on the accelerator and so forth are specific examples.

EQ also manifests in our own flexibility – emotionally, physically, intellectually, and operationally. Such flexibility (to be nimble and run around obstacles) in addition to power (to run marathons) and speed (to sprint when needed) enables constant adaptation to changing circumstances. A related aspect of EQ is perspective – the ability to step back and see the big picture in addition to the task at hand and the immediate goal to be achieved. This constant stepping back and convergence is a critical resource, accentuated in its importance by bringing larger life circumstances that we do not experience directly into consideration while also having an unrelenting focus on actions and positive impact.

EQ is also about creating a culture. Economic incentives only go so far, important as they are. Creating a culture is important in any setting, and all the more so in settings where the economic and the human are so completely blurred. Arguably, aligning incentives in a vacuum is relatively less difficult than using sustained emotional quotient to create and communicate a culture of openness to learning and shared purpose. EQ goes beyond strategic thinking to who we are in every aspect of day-to-day activity.

Do Your Best; Accept the Worst – In Fact, the Two May Coexist

Sometimes, these two polar opposites coexist in the same endeavor. We must always do our best, but accept the worst when it comes (not necessarily expecting it). Let me explain.

Observing and learning from people living in subsistence remind us of the things we take for granted. When the odds are stacked against us, doing our best often coexists with getting the worst. This is a causal relationship, or lack thereof, that often escapes us, due to the certainties in relatively resource-rich settings that enable us to draw inferences of cause and effect between our effort and outcomes.

This is not to suggest that random events are absent in the lives of those who do not live in subsistence – uncertainties due to health or tragic accidents are examples where normal assumptions about cause and effect break down. But the notion of causality can be thrown asunder in contexts of uncertainty, with random factors affecting lives in fundamental ways.

A cause having a diametrically opposite effect than what is expected is one such manifestation. For example, empowering women through marketplace literacy education may create resentment among men. The best of efforts to help personnel may be overwhelmed by their personal adversities and circumstances. Larger shocks to the system – such as water shortage and political unrest – may dominate our initiatives in communities. So many things are beyond our control in these settings.

We have much to learn here from both an organizational and a personal perspective. The fortitude to take negative events in stride and learn from it is one lesson. The notion that the exact opposite of what one is often certain about can happen is another sobering lesson. Resilience and persistence in the face of disappointments is another – emphasizing the need for a long-term orientation, different ways to thread the needle, and so forth.

Doing your best and accepting the worst may also transpire in terms of working with and managing people, often as a result of a survival mindset leading to counterproductive short-term actions. This requires an additional level of understanding covered in subsequent elements below. Unless, of course, the situation is simply untenable and destructive, patience and humility in this regard is very essential in dealing with people who do not have the certainties that those in leadership positions are accustomed to, nor the resources such as reflective knowledge and counseling to draw on.

Take the High Road and Stay There

Many issues discussed here relate to developing and sustaining an identity. One such aspect is to take the high road in how we treat people, no matter the circumstances. While we do not have to work with anyone unless we want to, how we conduct ourselves is an integral part of our sustained identity. Our communications on who we are and what we do are straightforward. But we realize the naiveté in believing that such an approach would work anywhere.

Taking the high road is particularly important in working with people, as our actions speak loudest in terms of setting an example. No matter the degree of verbal communications and open access, factors such as personal adversity in the immediate term can lead to emotional interactions that negatively impact the professional setting. **Despite the challenging nature of such situations, there is only one road to take. In addition to reflecting who we are, in the long run, this is the road that leads to credibility and respect.**

Taking the high road is an important way to communicate our identity. Given who we are and the uncompromising nature of key principles, it becomes critically important to communicate our identity in the early stages of the process of identifying a home – choosing to work with people at places where we see a fit and a pathway. This means getting a sense of the community and the leadership. There is a sad reality here that is so true of this arena – that those greatest in need may not be reached as a result of a variety of factors. Indeed, in the end we pick our battles, given our own constraints and who we are. Things change over time as well to the point of threatening our ability to stay in a community and testing the promises we made. Here again, breaking up promises is very important to stay true to our word.

Taking the high road is not always easy. It requires digging deeper and constantly taking perspective. But it needs to become a way of life at some point that is in the realm of *being* rather than strategizing.

Be Thoughtful in Adversity – Others' and Ours

This is a lesson learned from observing people living in subsistence. Adversity is a constant reality both in the communities we work with, our team personnel, and our partners. Health, well-being, even death, seems so much more common, sometimes tragically due to preventable causes. How we treat out inner circle, our local teams, and our partners should indeed mirror the larger ideals of working in subsistence communities to begin with.

The grace and dignity that many show in the face of chronic adversity is something we can learn from and apply to our own personal and professional lives. This is certainly true of enterprises and people working for them in terms of how we face adversity while maintaining our relationships for their own sake. Our adversity is a reminder to treat those for whom adversity is a way of life even better than we normally would. Our adversity coupled with the resources to face them is also a reminder to not give up easily.

This is true at a personal and organizational level. Not to strategize a matter of identity, but there are deserving benefits from constancy in a variety of circumstances, whether through your own adversity or adversity for the local team. The latter, a much more common matter, requires principled flexibility, a topic covered earlier. In this regard, it is satisfying to note that several escalations of my own investment and commitment for the social enterprise happened when facing personal adversity, although not of the scale or scope that those living in subsistence face and with the scarce resources needed to face the circumstances. Understanding team member and community member behaviors in terms of their personal adversities is an important aspect here that leads to new insights. Behaviors that would seem out of place in settings we are used to may need to be understood in the larger context of the life circumstances and personal situation that individuals are going through.

Go to the Next Level of Understanding – Peel the Onion

Many things we see in subsistence challenge our assumptions. We often ask why and may well be frustrated with our own discomfort, physical or otherwise. But this is exactly the situation that requires going to the next level of understanding, peeling the next layer of the onion, so to speak. The next level of understanding goes beyond what is apparent to us as to the reasons why, the contextual factors, and so forth. The next level of understanding peels away the superficial to focus on a need or problem, its drivers, and the larger context elements. Our assumptions are based on the contexts we are used to, which, in turn, are based on historical realities in the short-, medium, and long-term. As we peel the onion in subsistence contexts, we gain a somewhat deeper understanding of why things are the way they are.

Why the cultural beliefs? Why the rituals? Why the traditions? Why the concrete thinking? Why the survival mentality? The lack of planning? The role of intensive relationships? Norms rather than laws? Why the lack of institutional mechanisms? The lack of infrastructure? Our notions of rationality only go so far. The next level of understanding is needed – the next level of the onion. Specific to our initiatives, why will people not attend our educational programs? Why is an incentive needed at times? What prevents them from applying their learning? What are people looking for? What are leaders looking for? What is each entity or individual in it for? What are we in it for as well?

Peeling the onion here leads to deeper understanding at both cognitive and emotional levels. As noted, interactions with negative impact with team and community members have to be understood in the context of their adverse life circumstances. This requires us to dig deeper emotionally as well, setting aside our natural emotional reactions for the longer-term good. Adding to the emotional heat of the moment may lead to irreversible courses of action. In a one-on-one interactional world, words from a respected source said in the presence of others carries so much more weight. This puts an even bigger responsibility on the leadership of an enterprise.

None of this is an argument for avoiding issues or not being firm. Rather, it is about going to the next level of perspective-taking and understanding. In this regard, the people who work for us have not had the benefit of a high-quality education or the opportunity to work on a variety of dimensions of their personality. They also may not have the time, the proclivity, the access, or the capacity to seek out appropriate knowledge to deal with situations, rather being in the immediate, physically and socially. Therefore, the onus is on those with such capacities to dig deeper and peel the next layer of understanding to provide emotional and other forms of support.

Get Over Yourself So You Can See and Experience More

Related to the notion of peeling the onion, this lesson focuses on our own ego and priors that we bring to subsistence contexts. If we are willing to shed our preferences and baggage, we can learn a lot. This is in many ways the emotional counterpart to peeling the onion, which focuses on the cognitive aspect. Getting over our own egos enables us to be grounded and to then be able to see things for what they are without interference from ourselves in some ways. We also see people beyond appearance, to substance, a very important facet of learning from these contexts. People cannot afford pretensions or focus necessarily on how they appear to different audiences, as these are luxuries for them, that are a part of life in relatively affluent settings. Seeing beyond our prior conceptions in these matters is important to avoid knee-jerk reactions to what we see.

Getting over ourselves also provides a level of commitment needed for accurate understanding of subsistence contexts, and it emphasizes getting things done that lead to positive impact. It also leads to more transparency and candid exchanges with people of much lower status, as empowering them to think independently is a large undertaking. In the final analysis, it establishes a leadership style that is fundamentally about others.

What You Do Matters More Than What You Say You Will Do, Think You Should Do, Like to Do, or Want to Do – *Enact*

In the final analysis, actions speak so much louder than words. What you actually *do* matters more than what you *say* you will do, what you *think* you should do, or what you would *like* or *want* to do.

Actions on a small scale spread in terms of reputation as well. Akin to the discussion of different types of commitment between subsistence entrepreneur and others, what matters most is what one does. **In a world with little cushion and a lot of uncertainty, what matters is the real rather than the rhetorical. There is little if any time to wait for the rhetorical to become real. Small actions provide the foundation to build on; beneficial interactions create the climate to sustain your enterprise.**

Actions are also a great way to learn about what it takes to achieve positive impact. This does not mean one dives into action without thought, as it also sets a precedent in a one-on-one interactional environment. But action clearly delineated as a trial, a pilot, is important as a way to learn and to communicate. Over time, actions engender trust and enable actions on a larger scale and positive impact. Going back to subsistence entrepreneurship discussed earlier, what matters most is commitment based on what people do, more than on what they like to do or even should do.

With our local teams as well, how we conduct ourselves in the face of different urgencies, how we act and how we enact, matters more than anything else. Not acting means losing valuable momentum that has been built up over time, and the opportunity lost may never come back. Leadership here is also about inspiring people to the larger purpose as well as focusing on their development. Doing good for a larger community begins with doing good for one's own team, which, in reality, belongs to both the organization and the community. Above all, a focus on developing people, rather than thinking of them as resources or means to get things done, is critical.

If One Relationship is Dispensable, Then All Relationships Are Dispensable – Or Viewing Individuals Not as Resources but as People to Develop to Realize Their Potential

Related to the point above is a personal and professional mindset of nurturing and valuing each relationship. Indeed, this goes to the heart of why we engage in subsistence marketplaces, as individuals and as entities. In a context where relationships are so vital, the way we conduct ourselves in relationships speaks to who we are in a human sense. Again, this is not just an issue of what works, but what is the right thing to do.

Assumptions of respect and inherent dignity that underlie much of the personal and professional interactions in advanced societies and among the middle class in emerging economies do not necessarily hold for those living in subsistence. But they are no less important in subsistence contexts, and arguably more important.

Viewing some relationships as being dispensable is a statement about ourselves and the enterprise, not just to the community at large, but to ourselves and to others in the enterprise. It undercuts the trust that local teams have in an enterprise by questioning what the enterprise is in it for and whether the same treatment awaits them. This is a one-on-one human interactional mindset of interpreting how someone who runs an enterprise conducts himself or herself. It does not mean that we cannot make tough decisions, but how we go about such decisions is very important.

I am reminded of a 10-pm call from my lead team member that, due to a cyclone, people from the village would find it dangerous to travel to see our students the next day. My spontaneous response, spoken from my heart, was that their well-being was most important and they should not travel. This is not something I relate proudly; in my view, it is the least I can do. Looking back, I wonder what a hesitation or a request to reconsider would have suggested. This is not to strategize but to learn from this situation. If I cared any less about people coming to visit our students, then what does that say about what I would do for my team in adversity? More recently, we rerouted an international immersion trip just a few weeks before it took place because of the devastating floods in some of the communities we work in, as much to protect our team members as for any other reason. We hope that, in a variety of situations, we spontaneously safeguard the well-being of individuals who have given us their sacred trust. In this regard, the reputation of our organization is as good as the way we treat every human being we come in contact with.

As implied above, rules and relationships are in a constant tension. Rules take us only so far and have to be revisited many times. Relationships, in a sense, are everything. Yet, rules take a more nebulous form such as in articulating the value equation in many different interactions. In other words, rules have to be constantly articulated not so much as being inflexible or written in stone, but as a way to evolve the identity of the organization, nurture relationships, and articulate two or more sides of the exchange and the mutual value being created. At a deeper level, this is about the synergies and tensions in viewing people as an end in themselves as they serve as means to reach our collective goals or ends for the larger community.

Intertwined Destinies – Not Replaceable Parts

Intertwined destinies is a term we use in describing subsistence entrepreneurship and the relationships between entrepreneurs and customers that is spatially bound in local communities. A visitor's observation of our team at work reinforced the need to articulate this lesson. He noted that our magic is in hiring good people, suggesting that we set goals and then find people.

However, we would argue the diametric opposite. In fact, this is where coevolving pathways becomes very important. Much of what we do is based on detailed discussion in determining the pathway jointly. Much of the certainty we provide is through treating the enterprise as a family, except that it is a family with financial transactions. This is different from a family business, which is, after all, a family. Yet, the emotional and financial support in our enterprise resembles that of a family in a number of ways.

One way to consider our team members is as those with intertwined destinies similar to a family rather than as replaceable parts. Times do come when people transition out, but our full intent is to work with people and be completely transparent about the near and distant future while providing a soft landing and transition when the need arises. Thus, we view negative interactions and actions with this lens, attempting to help people work through issues and better themselves.

Be Aware of Your Power, and Lack of It for Those You Work With

This is a related facet, where the implicit power and position we possess needs to be at the forefront in considering our interactions. What we say and do means so much more due to the asymmetry in power. Therefore, how we present ourselves is very important, always keeping in focus our common purpose and the development of personnel and communities, rather than our narrower egoistic or circumstantial urges. We need to use power in a positive way, and we need to translate this viewpoint among team members at various levels. The power dynamics among people living in subsistence and the dynamics between them and others warrant separate discussion.

We need to cultivate a culture of valuing people for their opinions and their contributions, while articulating these aspects repeatedly. Here, we may be attempting to have people unlearn a lifetime of interactions based on socio-political hierarchies. For example, people are often used to being scolded and ordered around. Having them realize the value of their opinions requires a persistent message. People at a somewhat higher status from the same communities as well as those from the middle and lower-middle class from the same cultural background may use power and status in interacting with team members. Here, it is important to clearly articulate who is in charge. Sadly, judgments based on one's status are made quickly based on appearance, demeanor, and command of the English language.

Cutting through this issue in terms of both interactions and day-to-day operations is a substantial challenge. It's very important to identify and develop people for leadership positions, people who have a passion for serving their communities across status lines. This desire to bring positive change by empowering people sustains enterprises in such settings. However, the signal has to be transmitted continuously from higher levels, of the need to break through status barriers and appreciate one another for surviving adversity and making contributions. And passion for serving the community has to be converted into action, as people who have the former trait may need to develop the latter.

View People Not Based on Where They Are in Life, but on How Far They Have Traveled and Through What Terrain or Gauging How Far Someone Has Come in Life, Not Where They Are

The lesson here is to view people not based on where they are in life, but on how far they have come, what they have traveled through to get to their current station, and the potential you see in them to continue to grow.

This is a lesson at both the personal level and the enterprise level. How do we build lasting relationships at the ground level? Local team members are often driven by basic survival needs and perceive themselves as being of low status in comparison with others. In working relationships, valuing people for their unique strengths and for how far they have come is very important. Often, people remain in survival mode and have been suppressed by others. As mentioned, they may expect to be scolded for doing the wrong thing. First and foremost, similar to the way we begin interviews, impressing upon local team members that the value they add is very important.

Over time, empowering them to make decisions and fail is another facet of the relationship. In some cases, encouraging team members to take leadership roles and providing them with autonomy is also important. Over time, having them empower others may be as big a challenge, as we address in a separate discussion. Along the way, many people may come and go who do not necessarily fit the enterprise. But the key here is a sustained identity for the enterprise as to how it conducts business and treats people. Once again, this is not so much a strategy as a mindset that people and entities evolve toward.

Nurture Leadership Among Those Who Have Not Had a Chance

Are leaders made or born? We don't aim to resolve this issue here, but a question like this provokes deeper reflection of our own experience. Many of our statements belie a middle- or upper-class world and related assumptions. Thus, we assume that people have access to education and opportunities and seek out their professions while investing in themselves. In this world, all other things being equal and with everyone at this higher minimum threshold in terms of standard of life and associated opportunities, we may make attributions to inherent talent and so forth.

But what if the threshold is much lower, sometimes non-existent? The self-selection that goes on with a minimum threshold of standard of life simply does not happen. So much of who someone becomes is a matter of chance, at least relatively speaking. Yes, leadership and other traits may be both made and born, but the *make* aspect becomes very critical when it comes to nurturing leadership. People are looking for an opportunity to survive – where they are at a point in time is much more a matter of chance and randomness borne out of uncertainty than in a middle- and upper-class world, and individual preferences and aptitudes play a lesser role in finding survival paths. In other words, the uncontrollable is overwhelming, not that individual effort and attitude is any less; in fact, it is likely more.

Thus, the make aspect of leadership becomes more important, and mentoring and nurturing take on special meaning, as do opportunities provided. There are, of course, parallels in other settings where opportunities provided shape people's pathways. The point being made here is relative, that in subsistence contexts, where opportunities have not been afforded or realized, chance plays a much greater role in where people are, and lack of nurturing and mentoring are facts of life.

Avoid an "I Cannot Do This Without You" and "You Cannot Do This Without Me" Mentality

A related issue is how leaders from subsistence contexts will often be treated by others as being of lower status. As a result, the higher level of an organization has to step in to make things happen. This is another facet and reality of subsistence marketplaces, socially imposed. One's status in life moves but there are sociocultural forces that work to keep things where they are as well.

Often, suppression of those with leadership potential can come from those immediately above, a sad reality in these contexts. This is a reality in this context as in any context, but plays out in different ways. **As an example, impressing on people that they are leaders is very important, as is following through and both convincing and empowering them. As big a challenge is to have them empower others. Germane issues include distinguishing between taking ownership and exerting control, and emphasizing both taking and giving ownership.**

Setting a tone for candor and transparency is also important, given the natural inclination to view situations from a survival lens. What is said has to be emphasized over who said it, as power dynamics rules the day and respect for inherent dignity and other such values can be luxuries. Often, cultural norms are the counterbalance to harsh realities in terms of survival, as the collective sentiments of the community play out over individual needs. On the other hand, as we well know, the collective sentiments are shaped by and tilted toward those in power to begin with.

We can take the notion of "I cannot do it without you" to the level of subservience in light of the uncertainties that those living in poverty face or carry over after moving to the next higher level of socioeconomic status. This is hard to do away with overnight. At the same time, we need to address it in building healthy relationships where the value that local team members bring is highlighted.

All this is with the background of using one's own certainty to create a working environment. This awareness is important in how communications and activities transpire. Saying or even doing something that is consistent with this message may not be sufficient, as people's interpretations are colored by their life experiences. Nevertheless, we need to push practices that provide for a healthy work environment, although with the awareness that words and actions over a long time may still not be sufficient in the face of a survival mindset.

The other side of the "I cannot do it without you" coin is the notion of "you cannot do it without me." This could occur at different levels, from community members on to the local team and the leadership. At any level, this is a notion that needs to be tempered with humility. When gaining and possessing power from their personal relationships in a one-on-one interactional world, people tend to take on this attitude. At the community level, it happens sometimes when someone is sought out a second or third time to help. At the team level, this can happen with local leadership.

Thus, abusing newly-acquired power is on the other side of the coin of being subservient, and both can occur in close proximity and sometimes for the same people. There is an element here of moving up in terms of power and then using it on those below (or sometimes on those above) in the power hierarchy. Perhaps this is an effect of newly acquired power and the need to maintain it by controlling those below. When used against those above, it may be done in concert with controlling those below.[134] Again, while true in all contexts, it plays out in unique ways in the subsistence context.

These dynamics are present in any setting, not just subsistence, but they take on a unique nature in these settings. Perhaps the gain in power in proportionate terms is a factor here, as is the degree to which power is tied to personal connections.[135] Therefore, controlling those below becomes an all-the-more important means to retain power. Given the spatially bounded world that people live in and the lack of access to knowledge-based and other resources as means to informed decision-making, a number of issues arise.

Important here is to avoid reacting immediately and use a deeper understanding of the context to chart a productive path forward or at least try. This is all the more true when emotions run high and negative actions result. Bringing the temperature down by going back to what we do, akin to continuance commitment with subsistence entrepreneurs and also to the centrality of enactment, is very helpful here. When the time is right, communications need to be made firmly and actions taken decisively. However, we have to seek deeper understanding rather than interpret actions from a lens and mindset that one is accustomed to in relatively affluent settings. Deeper understanding does not mean the lack of appropriate decisive action; it just means a fuller basis from which to decide the course of action and a deeper search for emotional fortitude.

This chapter summarizes our guiding values and lessons learned in carrying out a bottom-up approach.

---

[134] Vredenburgh, D., & Brender, Y. (1998). The hierarchical abuse of power in work organizations. *Journal of Business Ethics*, 17(12), 1337-1347.

[135] Portes, A. (2000). Social capital: Its origins and applications in modern sociology. LESSER, Eric L. *Knowledge and Social Capital*. Boston: Butterworth-Heinemann, 43-67.

Chapter 10: The Essence of the Bottom-Up Approach

Image 10.01: The Essence of the Bottom-Up Approach.

Charting a bottom-up journey	Implementing bottom-up enterprises	Sustaining bottom-up enterprises	Guiding values	Essence of the bottom-up approach
Chart a course	Set goals idealistically & pursue them pragmatically	Identity before branding	EQ: To get things done	The ultimate bottom-up principle – If all else fails, do it yourself
Define purpose	Implementation trumps "IP & killer app"	Being over strategizing	Do your best; accept the worst	
		Negotiate, articulate, re-evaluate value equation	Take the high road & stay there	
Inspire through purpose	Learn, try out, learn by trying out		Be thoughtful in adversity	
			Go to the next level of understanding – Peel the onion	The ultimate bottom-up enterprise model – Do what it takes for each other
Determine purpose	Iterate many times rather than get it *right* away	Culture of mutual accountability	Get over yourself, see & experience	
	Don't break promises – Break up promises	Blur the boundaries of organization	What you do matters more than what you say, think, like, or want to do	
Circumscribe purpose			If one relationship is dispensable, all are	
	Coevolve pathways to implementation	Different ways to thread the needle	Intertwined destinies – Not replaceable parts	
Delineate the domain of purpose				Be intensely practical & un-compromisingly idealistic
	Create short-term yield	Principled flexibility	Be aware of your power, & lack of it for those you work with	
Execute the domain of purpose	Complicate the revenue model	Activities before resources	View people by how far they have come	
	Fail small/scale through depth	Inspire & incentivize	Nurture leadership among those who have not had a chance	
Listen & learn – Bottom-up immersion	Experience & know the forest, trees, branches, leaves	Steps to social enterprise & enterprise plan	Avoid an "I cannot do this without you" & "You cannot do this without me" mentality	Bottom-up meets top-down

We've talked about how to implement and sustain a bottom-up enterprise and noted many of the guiding values around envisioning, implementing, and sustaining an enterprise, using the bottom-up approach. In this section, we conclude with the very essence of the approach, delineating the principles that come into play and impact how successful you are in your endeavor.

The essence of the bottom-up approach includes:

- The Ultimate Bottom-Up Principle – If All Else Fails, Do It Yourself
- The Ultimate Bottom-Up Enterprise Model – Do What It Takes for Each Other
- Be Intensely Practical and Uncompromisingly Idealistic
- Bottom-Up Meets Top-Down

The Ultimate Bottom-Up Principle – If All Else Fails, Do It Yourself

The bottom-up approach in its essence suggests a high degree of grounding on the part of people who may be at different levels of the engaged enterprise. As noted, knowing the forest and the trees is merely a start. Knowing the branches and leaves and weeds and so forth is also extremely important. And it is not enough to merely know; you must experience these levels through listening, observing, and delivering solutions.

Those higher up in the enterprise should develop capabilities to deliver solutions on the ground. This is an attitude and a mindset of deep commitment to the purpose. While it may not come to it, this attitude also enables overcoming odds and uncertainties. In the bottom-up approach, there are many uncertainties and adversities on the ground that require flexibility and capacity. Although not always practical or necessary, the capacity to guide local personnel through transitions, to train new personnel, to deal with new adversities, to negotiate diverse stakeholder concerns, and so forth, is important. Such engagement may be necessitated by something as seemingly mundane as the behavior of an employee to sociocultural concerns raised by the community.

Such willingness to engage is also important in engendering trust in the community and strengthening the hands of community leaders who support the enterprise. Local concerns are a reality in these settings, and assurance from the highest levels of the enterprise of sustained engagement in the face of day-to-day challenges as well as the ability to both fully understand and confront such challenges is central. Again, with lives filled with uncertainty, including those of local personnel, this ability to interchange roles across what are usually perceived as vertical dimensions of an enterprise is critical. Another sense in which this personal commitment is important is in the lack of constancy of entities and funding. Ultimately, the promises made and kept are by people, fellow human beings – nothing more, nothing less.

I note that this lesson is getting increasingly difficult in practice as we work now in several countries. However, the capacity to do so is vital as it leads to other benefits as well – a deeper understanding of contexts, and a window into what our communities and partners on the ground face in terms of reality.

The Ultimate Bottom-Up Enterprise Model – Do What It Takes for Each Other

Adversity and uncertainty are a daily reality for local teams. The ability to support people through difficult times is both humane and essential for the enterprise. A way to articulate the enterprise model is the willingness to do anything to help as a mutually shared sentiment. This is a constant tightrope in that we need to be clear about our notions of value creation and related incentives, but we also need to understand that there are shocks to the lives of local teams, and they will need support.

Sometimes, such support will be misused, and so we will have to make tough decisions. The human element of being there for the people who work for an enterprise is critically important. Such a cushion is essential and is often rewarded with long-term loyalty, which, in turn, provides some level of certainty for the enterprise. This is the transference of the model of the marketplace that we have discussed for subsistence contexts, where relationships are central and blur the human and the economic.

Many insights discussed in this context that we gleaned from consumers and entrepreneurs apply to relationships with partners and employees. In fact, we can use much of what we learn from working with employees in designing aspects of the enterprise. The tension here is between responding to emergencies and other needs versus having some guiding principles for running the enterprise – akin to the need for constant customization with subsistence consumers. The same flexibility that is needed external to the enterprise is needed internally as well. The level of trust in a model of doing what it takes in a variety of situations provides the foundation for the situations that we will encounter in our enterprise.

As an example, "being there" during tough times, such as health emergencies, is important. This point is not communicated as a strategy as much as about who we are as human beings. Access to information and knowledge and counseling on various issues can be taken for granted in relatively affluent settings. This is again accentuated because of the constraints due to low literacy. Lacking basic education that we take for granted, certain dimensions that we assume away may not have developed due to lack of opportunity. In this regard, so much of what we communicate assumes those basic dimensions and a level of education. Constantly revisiting what is being understood (or misunderstood) is an important habit to develop. Providing monetary help, such as through loans, is often essential, although perpetual indebtedness is unhealthy, as is a lack of accountability or rationale for practices in a professional setting.

In this regard, it is important to keep the personal aspects of giving help separate from that of the enterprise, without making too much of the compartments here, as the reality is that they are blurred. As a result, there is a constant tussle between the professional and the personal. There is simply no easy way out here in both combining flexibility in relationships and codifying every aspect.

But it is important to think through some issues in terms of general principles (of humane behavior in times of adversity, for instance), and some guidelines to separate the professional from the personal and monetary losses or write-offs for the enterprise versus the individual in a leadership capacity acting as a friend. Ultimately, having a value equation in terms of the exchanges involved is important to understand, justify, and articulate, as it does not occur in clean, discrete, monetary terms, but in much more fluid ways in a climate of uncertainty and unanticipated events.

Be Intensely Practical and Uncompromisingly Idealistic

The bottom-up approach is intricately connected to the combination of a soft heart and a tough mind,[136] as alluded to earlier. It requires a deep coupling of sympathy, empathy, and larger purpose with the nuts and bolts and intense practicality of understanding subsistence contexts and enacting solutions.

This involves tensions, tradeoffs, and synergies, but not in the traditional sense of one versus the other. Rather, our approach requires high levels of both pragmatism and idealism in a constant dance with each other. If expediency is about getting things by cutting corners, the nature of pragmatism we speak of here is the opposite – and aims to sustain the idealistic identity and purpose that we work for to begin with.

This combination shows up in the way we structure processes and use resources. We are very focused on the impact on the ground and emphasize actual activities as a way of getting things started. This then shapes a variety of things we do and we are able to tie resources to activities and outcomes.

---

[136] The notion of a soft heart and a tough mind has been eloquently described by many who have come before – e.g., Dr. Martin Luther King, Jr.
"SERMON: A Tough Mind And A Tender Heart, by Martin Luther King, Jr." *The Value of Sparrows*. 2014. Accessed April 19, 2016. http://thevalueofsparrows.com/2014/05/04/sermon-a-tough-mind-and-a-tender-heart-by-martin-luther-king-jr/.

Meetings and planning precede but not endlessly. We would very much like to take the opportunity to engage and try out our education. An aspect of structuring activities and processes is to have dedicated or semi-dedicated staff. Particularly in developmental phases, we need this type of investment to move things forward. Purely variable incentives can often lead to activities not being a priority, as people seek some level of certainty in a context of uncertainty and lack of fallback options. In this regard, requiring extreme levels of entrepreneurial behavior and incentives closely tied to outcomes for those living in subsistence contradicts the certainty we seek for ourselves in relatively affluent settings. If anything, we find in subsistence contexts that providing some degree of continuity in terms of semi-dedicating time and earning proportionate income is important, while having continuous interaction on outcomes to achieve.

In terms of developing our personnel, we believe both in their well-being and investment in themselves as we do in initiating activities and achieving outcomes. On very rare occasions, we emphasize a soft landing for those whose aims and actions are not synergized with those of our organization. In terms of our impact, although no one metric is sacred, we think of both the absolute scale we want to aspire to as well as the monetary cost for reaching each person with our education. Typically, this cost after achieving current scale is about the level of savings that we find homemakers gain *as consumers* in a month or less as a result of our education.

Whereas ours is a nonprofit model, this is also the approximate cost borne by clients with our partner's self-sustaining model that has recently broken even. Once again, such metrics are an important piece of the puzzle. But speaking in terms of such specifics does not take into account the many years of development and patient human capital that preceded where we are now. Thus, when taking the long view and seeing the big picture, noteworthy here is to not understate the challenges and sustained effort that precede the timeframe when we can speak of self-sustaining models and cost per person reached.

Without passing judgment on individual preferences, we realize the need to push people with the right intentions toward action. This means speaking in terms of outcomes and resources as well as intermediary steps to get there. Open-ended relationships do not serve this purpose well, as there need to be specific goals and activities charted in specific time frames. It should be noted that, with a social enterprise and different sources of funding, this issue is even more accentuated.

The translation from intention to action is often extended in the social enterprise arena without sufficient oversight of resources being used to get there. In this regard, renegotiating the value equation is critical while nurturing the relationship. Tough questions have to be asked and decisions made about not moving forward with projects. This is another reason why making small promises and keeping them becomes very important in being true to communities. With degrees of separation from communities, the need for scrutiny and checks and balances becomes even more critical.

Bottom-Up Meets Top-Down

Many of the lessons enunciated here relate to the basic notion of the bottom-up meeting the top-down. Therefore, principled flexibility, learning and listening, learning by doing, renegotiating the value equation, and so forth, are important lessons. This interplay or dance is a constant and represents the essence of the bottom-up enterprise. As noted, this is not about being purely bottom-up. Any enterprise or individual who gathers information and then acts on it is, at some level, working top-down. Whether it be prior knowledge and planning at an individual or an enterprise level, decisions and subsequent actions are at some level top-down.

The notion of having some guiding principles is top-down, whereas bending it to circumstances is bottom-up. Responding to adversities and unanticipated situations is bottom-up, while articulating the value equation in response is top-down. It is this constant interplay between the top-down and the bottom-up that is at the heart of a bottom-up enterprise. Thinking that individuals living in subsistence need to be entrepreneurial in day-to-day activities is top-down – understanding that they need help in getting there is bottom-up. We acknowledge that all enterprises are top-down whether in terms of mental models or in terms of planning and finding efficiencies. The critical point is to allow the bottom-up to seep into the top-down and to respond and adjust the top-down with bottom-up learning. What was once bottom-up can become top-down and in need of fresh bottom-up insight and grounding.

We conclude where we began, with the irony in writing a book about being bottom-up. Writing about the bottom-up is, in a sense, top-down. And so goes the dance between the bottom-up and the top-down.

Part III: Applying the Lessons Learned

In this part of the book, we discuss and demonstrate how the lessons learned in bottom-up enterprises in subsistence marketplaces are, indeed, applicable in all settings. In order to be very specific, we focus on a recent assignment where I observed myself applying some of the lessons learned. A number of co-travelers in our journey share their observations, along with my own. Our aim here is to provide additional examples in different settings to both elaborate on the bottom-up approach and its application in creating more successful enterprises.

Chapter 11: Applying the Bottom-Up Approach in Non-Subsistence Contexts

Does our experience with subsistence marketplaces generalize to other contexts – and if so, how does it? After all, these contexts are radically different in many ways. We discuss this issue in this chapter.

Our Experience with Marketplace Literacy

Let us begin with some "data" we have directly been involved in – marketplace literacy in the US. By the time we offered marketplace literacy education in the US, we had offered it for a decade in India and had piloted it in Tanzania. The concept became reality in India in terms of addressing a large gap of know-why and know-how arising from our research insights both in the US and in India – and the realization that existing programs focused on the know-what. The actual educational program was created bottom-up for India with two of three team members being from the same communities.

But the notion translated and, over the years, we developed small lessons that would be appropriate in the US. In fact, parallel to the program in India was our work in the state of Illinois, with nutrition educational materials that were more user-friendly for low-literate audiences in the US. So what happened? The impetus to consider such a program in the US came from work that was triggered in more extreme settings. This is one way in which bottom-up experiences elsewhere translate back. It is simply that possibilities and opportunities to address a gap, serve a need, become apparent in such contexts and lead to the realization that they are needed at "home" as well.

Such an experience also led to the need to study the issue bottom-up by understanding the context in the state of Illinois through interviews. In turn, this led to the design of lessons that were piloted in very small scale – relating to consumer literacy for the most part. Some earlier work on nutrition education, mentioned above, was a useful starting point. But the biggest impetus came from making a commitment to teach a full program. This involved rethinking the approach while adhering to some deeper philosophical issues – i.e., focusing on the know-why and being bottom-up in design and delivery. However, the program itself, while motivated by our work elsewhere, developed to suit the context from the ground up. Thus, our approach broadened to consider the roles of customer, entrepreneur, citizen, employee, and so on. We also combined our approach of marketplace literacy with maker literacy and the forward-looking technology of 3D printing. We developed a number of educational materials which, in turn, influence our work elsewhere.

Thus, the iterative process of bottom-up understanding and design of solutions and development of enterprise plans, as well as implementation in one setting, then translates to other settings where, in turn, the bottom-up approach is needed, although there is prior learning that translates. The fact that we found this need to address in contexts of extreme constraints in turn led us to examine the need in contexts where poverty is not as extreme or widespread.

There has been a different type of diffusion as well – our experience with creating a teacherless multimedia approach as a way to overcome lack of resources and infrastructure in subsistence marketplaces has, in fact, influenced even the design of blended learning and online courses at the university. The process is another arena where our original innovation has borne fruit elsewhere.

So what is the bottom line? **Going to subsistence marketplaces opens up new avenues of thought and new ways of looking at things. Extreme contexts bring out needs starkly, needs that may also exist in non-subsistence contexts.** Trying to address needs in such contexts requires new ways of looking at things and new lenses (e.g., those of poverty alleviation and environmental sustainability). Such lenses can be applied in non-subsistence contexts as well. The translation of insights between contexts is iterative, but each context requires its own bottom-up orientation. Thus, our experience sheds light at the micro-level on how innovation *from* subsistence marketplaces (referred to elsewhere as reverse innovation[137]) happens.

Innovating *To* and Innovating *From* Subsistence Marketplaces

How do these insights transfer to other settings? *Reverse innovation* has been used to describe how innovations in developing contexts can find their way to advanced economies and to denote the opposite direction of the typical flow of innovation. The transfer with reverse innovation is to settings that have similarities, but connect more readily to infrastructure, institutional mechanisms, and an advanced marketplace. The subsistence context forces innovation under extreme constraints that, in turn, generalizes to contexts of poverty in advanced economies.

---

[137] Govindarajan, Vijay, and Chris Trimble. *Reverse Innovation: Create Far from Home, Win Everywhere*. Boston: Harvard Business Press, 2012.

Another level of transfer occurs in usage situations mimicking aspects of poverty. Natural disaster zones are an extreme example, as are war zones and refugee settlements, in terms of the extreme constraints and uncertainty that are inherent. Camping is a less extreme example involving usage situations that mimic a few aspects of poverty relating to living close to nature and away from infrastructure, as are very rural settings in advanced economies. Thus, transfer to specific usage situations that share elements with poverty accentuate the need for a bottom-up approach, and represent one level of analysis.

Another level of analysis with the potential for broad transfer is simply from the mindset of visualizing solutions in subsistence marketplaces. The notion of designing solar solutions at the household level as a distributed energy source in turn opens up the imagination in terms of transfer to non-subsistence settings. The notion of environmentally sustainable solutions is similar in this regard. Separate from subsistence contexts, applying new lenses helps to explain why some of the most efficient companies in the world to begin with, gained further efficiencies after adopting a sustainability lens.

Finally, similarities with other contexts at the broadest level present another level of analysis. A connected world through information and communication technology represents a different type of one-on-one interactional environment, with social media being inherently bottom-up in many ways. Uncertainties in the realm of climate, natural disasters, the environment, and natural resources present new challenges that are not so new for subsistence contexts where people live close to the environment.

The Bottom-Up Approach in Non-Subsistence Contexts

Our experience is one illustration that bottom-up innovation is relevant not only in subsistence contexts, but in non-subsistence contexts as well. It is applicable in similarly unfamiliar settings characterized by lack of infrastructure and resource constraints, such as for disaster relief or in poverty-stricken areas in developed economies. Radically unfamiliar settings also extend to resource-constrained situations in the future in advanced economies, arising from environmental degradation. Similarly, uncertain future scenarios in conditions of rapid technological changes represent another context, just as uncertainty is a central facet of resource-constrained contexts.

Our approach spells out how such innovation can happen and why. Innovation *from* subsistence marketplaces can take a number of forms: the direct form of product innovation typically covered in the literature, as well as the indirect form of reverse process innovation. Starting at a specific level, solutions designed for subsistence marketplaces can transfer to low-income settings in developed countries. Financial transactions through cellphones and telemedicine, innovations borne out of necessity, are two such examples.

The bottom-up innovation process we articulate here can ground managers in the lived experiences of customers in developed economies. Being top-down is efficient and customary for managers in organizations. Our bottom-up innovation process jars loose this comfort level and creates unique insights that expand top-down approaches and inform them in unanticipated ways.

Indeed, unique conditions make a bottom-up approach particularly relevant for subsistence marketplaces. Fundamentally different life circumstances than what a manager or designer is accustomed to, combined with unfamiliarity, make for this uniqueness. Moreover, variations across contexts are inherent in subsistence marketplaces due to lack of commonalities that come from development through infrastructure, institutional mechanisms, and education.

This is, of course, a continuum in terms of exposure to the old meeting the new. But the nature of this meeting has changed dramatically with time and with recent technological advances, particularly in the realm of information and communication. Maintaining aspects of the old while adapting to the new is an issue for all of us, but starkly accentuated for those living in subsistence marketplaces facing extreme resource constraints and who are now exposed to most recent developments through the media.

How Does the Bottom-Up Approach Apply to Non-Subsistence Contexts?

In this section, we examine how the bottom-up approach can apply to non-subsistence contexts. To apply this approach in such contexts, we must be tuned in to our customers or beneficiaries and the communities – both physical and virtual – that they live in. We explore how we can tune in, and we also look at how bottom-up insights can inform the design of our solutions and the development of our enterprise plans. Finally, we examine how, in order to apply the bottom-up approach in a non-subsistence context, that approach must impact how we manage our enterprise.

Being Tuned to the Bottom-Up

Let's consider the bottom-up approach at a number of levels in non-subsistence contexts. First, it is a challenge to truly understand the customer or beneficiary as well as the community (face-to-face and online) and larger context. We cannot overstate this. In fact, being from the same context may lead to complacency and a sense among managers and researchers that they know all the important issues. We need to develop new methods to be immersed in and learn, and we need to modify current methods. In fact, immersive experience can be part of required orientation for incoming employees. But just as importantly, it can be part of the continued learning and development for *all* employees. TV shows highlight the value of the highest level of management spending a day at the ground level (e.g., *Undercover Boss*). Such insights need to be a constant part of the learning process for many managers; these insights will then systematically inform decision-making. A day-in-the-life format enables managers to learn the fine-grained details and not assume them away or abridge them.

A very useful exercise here is to have higher-level management spend time directly with communities and beneficiaries or customers. At the least, such exposure refreshes learning and increases grounding. Beyond this, such exposure without filters or with minimal filters enables higher-level managers to cut through the layers and learn rapidly. Moreover, such an approach allows managers at higher levels exposure to the employees delivering the last mile at the boundaries of the organization.

Important here is seeing for oneself, talking to people in depth, and even trying out solutions. Templates and frameworks only go so far, as allowing insights and methods to emerge is an important facet of the bottom-up approach and mindset. This recommendation is particularly germane to highly reputed and resourced organizations (such as international development organizations), as who they speak to may be preselected by local organizations to present a certain agenda. A prelude to such ground-level experience is virtual immersion, which helps develop a plan for the actual immersion and in sensitizing the manager to key issues on the ground.

Akin to moving from sympathy to informed empathy, such a commitment to ground-level understanding flips the typical organization structure on its head and flattens it in terms of insights. This is a notion that has been emphasized in a variety of organizational studies;[138] however, we show how it works in a radically different context where being bottom-up is critically important and which, in turn, leads to practices on the ground that inform our insights.

Is it worth the time? We can reverse this question in terms of how other issues from the top-down can be worth the time when in fact the end customer or end beneficiaries and their environment are not experienced. As noted, the

---

[138] Simanis, Erik, Stuart Hart, and Duncan Duke. "The Base of the Pyramid Protocol: Beyond "Basic Needs" Business Strategies." *Innovations: Technology, Governance, Globalization* 3, no. 1 (2008): 57-84. doi:10.1162/itgg.2008.3.1.57.

Ritchie, R., & Sridharan, S. (2007). Marketing in subsistence markets: Innovation through decentralization and externalization. Product and Market Development for Subsistence Marketplaces: Consumption and Entrepreneurship Beyond Literacy and Resource Barriers.

top-down comes naturally from where we are and in terms of what we can do. **The bottom-up is counter intuitive. In this regard, working with local organizations does not make an entity bottom-up. The mindset of *learning from the micro-level and letting such learning permeate decision-making* makes it bottom-up. Bottom-up insights cannot be outsourced; they have to emerge from experience.**

Such exposure is required at regular intervals rather than as a one-time practice as continuous engagement can also lead to feedback on changes being made while keeping managers grounded. For us, immersion never stops, it is a parallel track throughout.

Letting Bottom-Up Insights Permeate the Design of Solutions and Development of Enterprise Plans

Often, in a phased approach, a subsequent approach such as the design of solutions does not sufficiently reflect the previous steps. Therefore, deliberate methods need to be incorporated to reflect bottom-up insights. Outlined earlier are some methods to stay true to bottom-up insights, thus moving beyond broader prescriptions to specific details. Such exercises are central to remaining grounded as we move to top-down approaches of design. To the extent that interdisciplinary teams experience the ground level together, greater appreciation for different perspectives can also emerge. In a sense, the bottom-up experience gets everyone out of their comfort zones. Trial and error or learning by trying out solutions is an important part of this learning experience as well.

In addition to product development, the design of enterprise plans also need to reflect bottom-up insights. Here as well, the grounded experience can include trying out solutions and role plays where managers, say, experiment with different messages. Ultimately, as noted, the dance between the bottom-up and the top-down needs to be deliberately incorporated, while allowing room for emergent insights that modify methods. This flexibility is a hallmark of the bottom-up approach as well. Templates and frameworks can quickly become top-down prescriptions that are uninformed by the micro-level.

Bottom-Up Management

Each of the categories of lessons we discuss here has application in non-subsistence contexts – charting a bottom-up journey, implementing and sustaining a bottom-up enterprise, guiding values and the essence of the bottom-up approach. Charting a bottom-up journey is critical for determining direction – the vision, mission, and broader strategy. What is the identity of the organization? How do bottom-up insights feed into this effort? As an example, listening and learning and bottom-up immersion can inform higher-level discussions of strategy.

In terms of implementing the bottom-up approach, the notion of implementation over intellectual property emphasizes the need to work things out in the marketplace – building an advantage in terms of identity and brand rather than having a predominant focus on intellectual property. This is not to understate the importance of the latter, but to highlight other facets as well.

Many recommendations about implementation relate to a mindset of trying out new things and learning from them:

- Rather than view each new direction exclusively in terms of top-down strategy or on current consensus-building, the approach here highlights the need for many experiments in *doing* that, then feed back into potential pathways. Again, this has been highlighted in a number of business contexts, but the radically different context of subsistence brings out many details as well as the rationale for when such an approach is appropriate.

- Related is the notion of being iterative and learning, rather than using a sequential approach of planning and implementation. Planning is very important, but so is throwing out the plans and turning on a dime.

- Also relevant in other contexts is complicating the revenue model – for instance, a business can consider a variety of goals such as learning about the marketplace, staying in tune with culture, trying out products and so forth, in pilot efforts that lead to iterative learning.

- The notion of scaling is also bottom-up, beginning with depth in a few locations and spreading radially outward, rather than top-down based on imposing scale based on common elements.

- And most importantly, the mindset at the higher levels should be to understand the different levels of the organization, which is not the same as interfering or micromanaging. Rather, bottom-up immersion enables higher-level executives to appreciate the importance of not micromanaging but rather empowering the local employees, while at the same time stepping in when needed as a result of being grounded.

In terms of sustaining the identity of the organization, the importance of identity under uncertainty and the sustained signaling that follows has lessons for other contexts. Branding is often emphasized and rightly so, but identity that underlies branding comes out in these settings. This is akin to character coming out in times of crises. Exercises in different scenarios capturing uncertainties and resource constraints can help evolve the identity of the organization. For social enterprises, such sustained signaling provides continuity and constancy in the face of a variety of uncertainties.

Similarly, considering the value equation both with external stakeholders and internal to an organization is another arena where learning from the bottom-up approach we outline is likely to be useful. This may be the case for both commercial and social enterprises in terms of understanding how activities are related to valued outcomes and in linking a broad set of outcomes to the larger mission. In commercial settings, activities that are not directly tied to monetary outcomes may not be valued when, in fact, their indirect effect is large or they provide the foundation for monetary outcomes. Such a discussion also provides the basis for mutual accountability and a strong focus on an informed and well-rounded set of metrics.

The notion that there are different ways to thread the needle is fundamentally a mindset that could potentially pervade all aspects of the organization. Such acculturation enables a sharp focus on value creation by the people in the organization. It is also associated with a culture that encourages failure and a perceptual learning mentality. The lesson of activities before resources is salient where budget reigns supreme and the source of funding dictates what is done. This is a reality for many organizations, public and private. However, a focus on activities helps clarify and place priorities where they belong in terms of why the organization exists.

In terms of the guiding values and the essence of the bottom-up approach, a number of lessons are central, such as through nurturing relationships and how an organization treats its employees, particularly during the tough times. The emphasis on how things are done reiterates the importance of process and not just outcomes, reflecting the identity of the organization.

Is it really practical for an organization, say a business, to embrace the bottom-up orientation that we have pursued it as a social enterprise? Even if such an orientation is not practical in its full sense, there are certainly lessons here worth learning and applying. In a sense, our journey has been instructive because of its extreme nature. Certainly, moving from a top-down approach toward the ideal balance with a bottom-up approach, there are benefits in gaining insights from a market research perspective, unique insights that would otherwise not be available. Such experiences are also useful from the point of view of developing employees with grounded experience.

A bottom-up approach is also worthwhile to experiment with through pilot programs as to what is generalizable or scalable. Moreover, such an orientation can help a business determine what aspects to seek to make more bottom-up, which may harder to imitate. For example, a bottom-up approach has much to offer a business seeking to move away from a distinctive advantage in terms of the core product offering, say a good, an aspect that can often be imitated, toward value-added in terms of service.

Why Engage in Subsistence Marketplaces?

We live in an era where certainty-based approaches that are inherently top-down – relying on planning and implementation – is outliving its relevance. However, a rhetorical stance in this regard or even surface level efforts in being bottom-up do not go far enough. In a sense, we have gone to the other extreme to learn just how valuable the bottom-up approach is.

In the time that it takes for a large organization in an advanced economy to gather people around the table and develop a plan, nimbler, smaller enterprises in emerging markets may have already tried out new solutions. This is not to discount the processes and mechanisms in place that slow things down with good reason. But we can learn lessons and make adjustments to have the best of both worlds – thoughtful processes *and* quick turnaround.

A certainty-based planning process permeates our mindset, as it has a long history and the immediate conditions around us encourage it. It is sometimes based on a zero-sum mentality, a risk-reward analysis. **A bottom-up immersion into radically different contexts can jar loose some of our assumptions and impress upon us the importance of a more emergent approach. In fact, an organization's identity is not just about what it does *but how it does it*. Being bottom-up, being nimble, are ways to define one's identity, one's brand as well. Is it worth failing at? Does failure put us on a path to developing ourselves or our organizations?** If the answer is yes, then a self-contained experiment is worthwhile. When communicated clearly as just that, we are keeping our promises as well. It takes a lot of effort to move in a new direction. But if the rationale is there to improve our capacities in light of where we see the future going, then such new paths are worth considering. The key here is to be alert to falling into the sequence of planning-implementation-assessment that is ingrained as a result of habit and immediate certainties.

We have come full circle. So why engage in subsistence marketplaces for its own sake? Here are four good reasons:

- To learn about culture
- To work with current partners, employees, suppliers
- To work with the future middle-class
- To innovate *from,* not only in terms of specific problems and solutions, but in terms of applying a very different lens to a very different context and then assessing its generalizability

But engaging in subsistence marketplaces is also worthwhile as a means to challenge traditional thinking in terms of understanding marketplaces as well as designing solutions and enterprise plans. This context is very useful from the perspective of an exercise, as many students, researchers and managers have related to us. We use this context to run a number of exercises – recently, we asked some entrepreneurial start-ups to consider this radically different context, understand it, design for it, and generalize the learning back.

Our journey is useful to those who do not necessarily engage directly in subsistence marketplaces. The lessons learned have wider application with appropriate caveats. Indeed, going to an extreme context often makes implicit assumptions and certainties more explicit and leads to new experiences and, in turn, lessons that translate back to contexts we are accustomed to. That has most certainly been our experience. We hope it is of benefit to you as well.

Chapter 12: Applying the Bottom-Up Approach in Higher Education

I have not been restricted to subsistence marketplaces in using the bottom-up approach in my larger purpose of enabling marketplace literacy for low-literate and low-income people. Indeed, I developed the marketplace literacy initiatives while working at a large public university in the United States. And I have also created curricular innovations for higher education at local and global levels, including international immersion, at my university. These initiatives are closely related to subsistence marketplaces and rely heavily on the bottom-up approach.

The yearlong course I developed emerged bottom-up, both as a course and in terms of the teaching methods in it, as described earlier. In turn, this effort led to a top-down opportunity to create a module for all our incoming undergraduate students in their first semester. This pathway was followed in terms of international immersion as well as bottom-up design and development of this learning experience, then influenced practice at the educational program and college levels.

For instance, our international immersions began about five years into being in the geography in terms of conducting research and about three years into offering educational programs there. The duration in itself is not of relevance as much as the listening and learning that happened during this time as well as the relationships we developed on the ground both with our local team members and with communities. Even in terms of the design and delivery of these learning experiences, learning emerged bottom-up, such as by trying out courses and international immersions. This approach has pitfalls as well in that bottom-up emergence has to be supported by top-down institutionalization in some ways.

So far, we have discussed our work revolving around subsistence marketplaces. In this chapter, I describe my involvement in launching a new worldwide online program – unrelated to subsistence marketplaces. The endeavors described so far originated with my own ideas; what I describe here is my role in guiding an innovative online higher education program conceived by others, a few months from launch to its next steps at a public university in the United States. By doing so, we derive lessons from the bottom-up approach at a more concrete, day-today level. The primary purpose here is to provide some data on how I apply the bottom-up approach in a very different setting. From a window into my instincts in such a context, we aim to provide additional insights into both the bottom-up approach and its application in a variety of settings.

Launching a Worldwide Online Education Program

Here I describe the bottom-up approach to the launch of a worldwide online educational program. This program was conceived by others and my role was to be a guinea pig in teaching on the worldwide platform three times before our offerings developed rapidly into a new online graduate degree program. What I describe is a situation that arose from introducing an educational innovation in a public university setting during a time of much transition with a metamorphosis of roles and entities.

We quickly went from experimentation with a single course (my own) to specializations and an entire online graduate-level program. Moreover, the design and delivery involved three additional entities at college, university, and worldwide enterprise partner levels, whereas the typical face-to-face course has minimal involvement of other entities in the design and delivery levels. Drawing inferences about what should or should not have happened before my involvement would be extremely inaccurate and misleading. If anything, the situation reflects on individuals doing the impossible. Any involvement I have had was purely in participating in a team effort with a large group of talented individuals working tirelessly.

Thanks to the people I reported to and worked with, my job definition was clear, and our goals helped guide the logical evolution of the course that I developed. What I describe below is not meant to suggest that we did everything perfectly or that this is the only way to go about it. Rather, the goal here is to reflect on my instincts when undertaking a responsibility, purely for purposes of explicating the bottom-up approach. What I cover here involves applying what I had learned elsewhere as well as some traits I bring into any situation, including subsistence marketplaces many years ago. To the extent possible, I connect the lessons here to the lessons discussed elsewhere in the book.

Processes and Issues Involved

To elaborate on the entities and people involved in this process, teaching online on a worldwide platform requires instructors (faculty/professors) and an online learning team consisting of people in different roles, such as instructional designers and videographers. It is a complex venture for faculty to master the media, and our online learning specialists help us get there and implement the technical aspects of the program. Additionally, at a large public university, such a venture requires a centralized unit at the university level that interfaces with our worldwide educational partner and the respective colleges such as ours, providing invaluable expertise. A college e-learning entity in turn is closest to the customer (student) and the instructor.

Bringing all this together is the program itself and the people responsible for running it. The units of analysis are quite diverse – faculty, college, university, and worldwide educational partner. The processes involved are diverse as well and uniquely intertwined – instruction, technology, and administration, beginning many months before actual teaching begins. This is in contrast to instructors working independently for the most part in teaching on campus; seeking support when needed in a classroom setting but having full control over all other aspects of the course.

To illustrate, let us make a simplistic comparison. I show up on the first day of class in a face-to-face course. If something does not work, I call someone and so it goes. Now let us compare it to what it takes to develop and deliver an online course in this educational program. I "show up for class" six months before class and work closely with three different entities at very different levels, at the college, university, and worldwide educational enterprise levels on everything from course objectives to slide preparations and videos to copyright. My instincts and what I am used to, on the other hand, are the exact opposite: to envision, articulate, and manage all aspects of the learning experiences I create.

This particular program is designed for both a worldwide audience and a specific admitted class of students, and requires students, faculty, and design teams to work on two different platforms. We work at the interface of educational content and delivery, administration, and technology – all evolving as we speak. And we do this in the context of a large public university – requiring a startup program mentality in a place geared for existing face-to-face programs. This means carefully designing processes that minimize touch points and identifying how we create value. Entities that work well within have to learn to work well with other entities, have clear and evolving role definitions, and come together to be program-centric just for this initiative.

Embedded in the discussion are numerous issues, such as how we move from offering a course to a specialization to an entire program. What does it mean for student support services? Networking? Experiential learning? For the virtual learning environment? What policies should be in place at the program level versus the course level? What are the new dimensions of performance in an online context? How do we know students are involved, focused, etc.? How does what we learn feed back into admission and design processes? Another issue spills over into our face-to face programs. How do we enhance value in all these programs? There is only one direction that the value we create goes: upward. What does the face-to-face classroom look like? What is our value equation for each of our programs? We are sorting that out as well.

On undertaking the assignment with about four-and-a-half months to go to launch, the first step for me was to listen and learn, where possible, in one-on-

one meetings. The latter approach allows free conversation although meeting with different entities as groups has additional benefits. Meeting with people at different levels of the hierarchy was another step. As noted, the entities in question were at individual faculty, college, university, and global educational enterprise levels. The listening also covered many different stakeholders. As the listening progressed and we developed solutions and action items, it was possible to sound them out as well. What we did is organized below as a free-flowing set of activities and also by stakeholder.

The What

Here is a quick rundown of the people and processes involved as we designed and created our course.

- Listening
- Process redesign
- Team -building workshops I and II and feedback
- Faculty engagement
- Faculty handbook
- Process handbook
- Metrics
- Program faculty committee
- Worldwide educational enterprise interaction
- Launch instructors scheduling
- Process observation
- Student committee
- Social media/branding committee
- Program schedule
- Course/specialization descriptions
- Onboarding planning
- Capstone instructor planning
- Admissions and guidelines
- Process for teaching assistant support
- Process adjustments
- "What the program can be"
- Process for recruiting potential faculty

- High-engagement workshop
- Labels and terminology
- Resource needs (e.g., personnel, equipment, and office space)
- Learning environment pathways
- Capstone proposals
- Iteration of course/capstone descriptions
- Launch and associated issues
- High-engagement course delivery issues
- Medium-term strategic issues
- Planning for scale
- Synergies across MBA programs
- Developing an academy for teaching assistants
- Fine-tuning grading policies and faculty compensation issues
- Learning from high engagement to make changes to policies
- Experimenting with the next generation of educational platform
- Reinstitutionalizing through documentation
- Reorganizing entities to sustain

We initiated the activities in rough sequence as listed above, with much overlap and iteration. Rapid listening led to process redesign and a workshop for college and university design teams to obtain feedback and initiate the notion of a single team building around the program.

A purpose here was to signal my role. Clear role definition enhanced my ability to work with people, thanks to full understanding and complete support from those I reported to. Initiating discussions on process design as well as documentation was another facet, which then provided the content from which to obtain feedback between workshops. Thus, the initial workshop served to bring everyone together, obtain feedback on the proposed process, and provide input to support immediate documentation in an internal process manual and a faculty handbook. In a second workshop soon afterward, the materials developed were fine-tuned and, at the same time, teams formed to address issues ranging from student support to communication.

In turn, faculty were another set of stakeholders to provide immediate follow-up to, whether the issue was minor with an ongoing course or broader in providing clarity and roadmaps. This involved aggressively following up on faculty requests, and perhaps most importantly, signaling that they had a representative to follow up on issues major and minor. Feedback from faculty was also obtained on the faculty handbook leading to responsive editing and finalization of the first version. A faculty committee was formed leading to a series of meetings discussing all aspects of the program.

Faculty teaching in the program were scheduled for the immediate and medium term to participate in the design process, taking multiple factors into consideration in terms of constraints. Extreme constraints on multiple sides had to be considered and the first step was to bring the people together. It was useful here to lay out the development process that was being documented and emerged from the process manual and faculty handbook.

Sitting in on meetings, I began at the outset to learn and subsequently to trace the new process and make rapid changes as needed in the intervening weeks. A schedule for the course offerings was vetted by all stakeholders and published, a very important step. Course descriptions and descriptions of specializations were vetted and the first version published, followed by subsequent versions. A student support committee was formed and students' perspectives brought into the mix. While listening and learning were ongoing, I devoted a week to more intense listening about a month and a half in, which led to process adjustments and discussions with a third workshop. Following workshops, I continued to follow the development process closely by sitting in on meetings and making adjustments or acting as the intermediary. The branding team was expanded to a communications and learning environments team to develop a plan, obtain immediate input, and begin implementation, again publishing as we went along.

Understanding the admissions process and getting it documented was another percolating issue, as was understanding the process developed for providing teaching assistant support and documenting it. Getting the design of the launch courses into some kind of momentum while resolving process issues was another aspect. In turn, the design of capstone offerings came to the surface. Developing communications and student support materials took on importance. We updated college faculty and staff in detail on what was happening, with all materials including workshop and committee activities shared. Conducting small-group meetings on what the program could be with a variety of college colleagues was a medium-term priority as well.

In turn, we developed and implemented a process of buy-in for recruiting potential faculty. The aim here was to delineate what it took before faculty decided to participate. We aimed for clarity of understanding and implicit sign-off before the final decision to participate was made, a way of building commitment and setting expectations on both sides and moving toward a smooth process during development.

We also addressed terminology that was slowly outliving its purpose. I learned of the resource needs from respective entities and communicated those needs to those I reported to. As well, we turned our attention to the design and implementation of the capstone and on the next iteration of course descriptions, based on feedback from our worldwide partners, through iterations with faculty in specific specializations. We began a discussion of the learning environment which evolved into developing capabilities for our virtual classroom and live sessions.

Next came the launch of the first courses accompanied by a host of issues that arrive with the scale of students enrolled. We explored and documented medium strategic issues such as synergies created between the online MBA program and other MBA programs. We came face-to-face with issues of the online medium and the scale of our program and learned and implemented changes to a variety of issues such as articulating course procedures and enforcing them. We addressed nuanced issues that arose, such as grading policy at the program level and grading issues to leave to the discretion of individual instructors.

The How

In this section I address the how, with emphasis on two topics: the workshops that I conducted for our design team and faculty, and the role the bottom-up approach played in these essential workshops.

Workshops for Design Team

Our first workshop for the design team, consisting of our college and university teams (instructional designers, videographers, etc.), was literally a week into my taking up this role as I had heard sufficiently from the learning to take the next steps. This is another aspect – a layering approach where we know enough to move forward and over time, the next set of issues can percolate or learning can happen to address the next layer, while maintaining a sense of priorities.

I introduced myself to the many people representing different entities and told them that I view the world in terms of a dance between the bottom-up and top-down, and that I will try to traverse the macro-/meso-/micro-levels as well as possible. I promised to listen and learn, and even when certain – that I would be willing to learn and change on a dime. Issues can be brought to me, and respect and relationships are of utmost importance to me, as is maintaining confidentiality. **The bottom-up approach is predicated on these individual relationships as the building block. It is also dependent on being there – period!** That means constant communication and the belief that, when the situation calls for it, there will be a quick response. I asked for constructive communication, restricting email for transactions and information, using me as buffer, and disagreeing with me directly as a way of taking trust to a different level.

I also explained the situation as I saw it. People had been doing the impossible with perhaps the most innovative idea for a new program in my 25 years at the college at a time of leadership transition while dealing with uncontrollable events. Entities had metamorphosed, leading to much more than growing pains, and all this was happening at a large public university – not the setting with the most nimbleness. As a startup program, we had to negotiate this setting with entities spanning individual, college, university, and external worldwide enterprise levels. This was not about blame or mistakes; it was simply the nature of what happens when innovating in uncertainty. This is quite easy to see in subsistence marketplaces but happens frequently elsewhere as well. Perhaps our senses are more keenly tuned as a result of our work in subsistence marketplaces, helping us to recognize and frame other situations as such.

I presented an entity map to highlight touch points and value creation, with students at the center followed by the program to which the entities were contributing while interacting with each other. Also part of the presentation was a detailed visual of a new process – essentially moving from everyone doing everything to some people doing some things, having distinct parts, different entities taking ownership of parts, building in lockdown periods to avoid last minute stresses, and so forth.

Image 12.01: Entity Map.

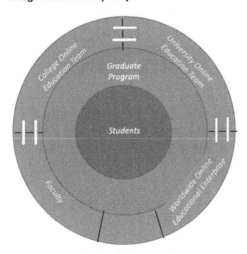

The primary task I gave the participants was to work back from launch and lay out the details in terms of course development, assuming the proposed new process. Such a task was as much for my learning as for everyone else. Peeling the onion, I can see how the assigned task at that stage could have been more nuanced. But that would have required understanding the next layer of the onion, which only occurs as understanding develops. **Second-**

guessing the precise nature of activities is not as important as moving forward with ways to learn and becoming more nuanced over time. I also used the workshop to clarify aspects of the proposed process. In turn, the workshop led to documentation of the process in a manual form, which I then distributed for feedback before the next workshop about two and a half weeks later. Between workshops, I obtained input and feedback on specific deliverables from specific individuals as well, setting the tone for rapid follow up.

In the second workshop, it was time to get more specific in fine-tuning the process. Framing the workshop were the following points: a clarification of my role in working with people; efficient, clear, and constructive communications; and the notion that we are on ONE team (an issue that we needed to clarify over time as well). We laid out a pathway for various issues in terms of discuss-debate-decide-delegate-deliver-debrief.

Warm-up exercises related to personal, professional, and organizational reasons people were involved. In getting there, we completed several exercises, such as a think aloud of possible pitfalls and follow-up required.

Specific exercises related to completing the following:

- If we are one team we will always (never) __
- If we are communicating clearly, efficiently, constructively, we will always (never) __
- The thing I don't understand with the new process is __
- We will fail with the new process if we do (don't) __

Noteworthy here is the micro-level and bottom-up nature of the exercises. Through small groups combining people from different units, another exercise we undertook was the direct fine-tuning of documents. We also used this workshop to form teams that interacted on specific initiatives such as student support services and branding/social media/communication. The teams formed here continued to work, moving forward.

The third workshop, about five weeks later, was preceded by an intense phase of listening. I put up what I had promised and what I had asked for from the first workshop about eight weeks ago and provided positive feedback on where we were. After presenting a timeline of what was accomplished, we discussed the following issues:

- How to bring our effort to fruition
- Put a hold on "what's wrong" and a go on "what's right"
- Put a hold on "we know better" and a go on "let's look for what to learn"
- Direct communication with me (preferably avoiding email)

During this third workshop, people completed the following exercises:

- Where were we eight weeks ago? Where are we now? Where would we like to be four to eight weeks hence?
- What are the pressures and constraints within which my counterpart (across entities within the university) is working?
- In light of where we are, how can I improve or what specific changes can I make?
- What will completion of the program mean to me?
- How will I create value five years from now? Or 10 years from now?
- What unique traits will I need to be successful?
- What traits would I have developed through this work?

These exercises provided some quiet time for thinking through how the work related back to people at personal and professional levels and how they could develop informed empathy for their counterparts working in a different unit on campus. Working in small groups with counterparts from the two entities or on specific teams such as communication, we also obtained input on how to get to launch and the timeline for specific actions.

Working with Faculty

Being very responsive to and engaging faculty was another important aspect of the process. Listening and being involved in responding and follow-up were some practices we implemented immediately. Creating clarity and roadmaps through a faculty handbook and other means was an important part of the process. We used faculty input to create such support materials and their feedback to modify it. Doing so with rapid response was very important to make sure interactions were efficient and effective while moving forward at a rapid pace. Perhaps as much as anything, aggressively scheduling faculty to longer schedules enabled a pathway of design and delivery that took into consideration the sometimes severe scheduling constraints on both sides. Something as seemingly simple as scheduling took on center stage here in a setting where everyone is doing so many things and we have to coordinate across different constraints.

Sitting through the design process with faculty was extremely important as it educated me on issues from both the faculty and the staff perspective that fed into various process and structural issues. Withdrawing from such meetings over time when I was getting in the way was just as important. Working through iterations of the course descriptions with faculty at multiple points in time was another aspect, often with small-group feedback related to their offerings. In this setting, I was able to translate and articulate in bridging the perspectives behind the interactions among different entities for instructional design. This was another form of continuous listening and learning.

Engaging faculty in a variety of issues was important as well. Developing a process for potential faculty to learn about the program and what it took to teach in it was another facet. This was a way of setting expectations and signing off on what it would take. Another form of interaction with faculty was through a committee to seek advice and support on various issues. Updating college faculty and staff on what was happening and sharing all materials including workshop and committee activities was another aspect. Faculty also had the opportunity to provide feedback through a series of small group discussions on what the program can be. As courses were launched, issues arose that required putting new policies in place. Again, sitting in on meetings at each step was very helpful.

Lessons

Throughout this process, we learned many lessons for implementing a bottom-up approach in a higher education setting. In this section you will see lessons grouped in these seven categories:

- Essentials
- Tasks and Processes
- Mindsets
- Traits
- People, Not Parts
- Bottom-Up, Top-Down Dance
- Pitfalls

Image 12.02: Applying Bottom-Up Lessons to Higher Education.

Essentials	Tasks & processes	Mindsets	Traits	People, not parts	Bottom-up, top-down dance	Pitfalls
Continuous listening, learning, & changing	Process follow-through & fine-tuning	Making promises, keeping promises	Recognition	Foundational emphasis: People!	Playing out bottom-up detail when making promises	Micro-managing to stepping back
One-on-one to group to one-on-one interactions	Start somewhere with many chicken-&-egg situations	Translating larger purpose to program & day-to-day	Energy		Bottom-up approach feeds into & modifies top-down plan	
Respon-siveness	Slice & re-slice tasks into 1.0 & 2.0 Publishing 1.0s			Changing the day-to-day	Prioritizing, reprioritizing, & percolating	Conversation to closure
Every detail may matter	Design, to do, do Switch from parallel to sequential to parallel processing	Startup mentally	Positive energy		Devil in the details	
Follow-up, follow-up, follow-up	Direct commun-ications	Truthfulness in the face of power hierarchy & decision-makers			Processes emerging bottom-up & not all preplanned	Avoiding overreaction (and over-reaction to
Buy-in, buy-in, buy-in	Top-of-mind commun-ications		Emotional fortitude	Helping people develop		overreaction)

Essentials

Let's start with the critical foundation: Listening, learning, adapting, paying attention to all details, following up in a timely manner on everything, and creating buy-in.

Continuous Listening, Learning, and Changing

As the listening evolves, it does not stop; it is not restricted to one phase. In fact, there are layers of understanding that develop and there are periods of more intense listening. Ultimately, the act of delving deeper is one of starting out top-down and letting the bottom-up learning unpack the next layer of understanding.

Like virtual immersion or re-grounding in the subsistence context, to be truly bottom-up, allowing continuous listening is very important. In fact, this is also true as solutions are designed and implemented, in terms of obtaining input and as adjustments are made to plans and implementations. For example, a process redesign was initiated which involved identifying discrete parts, sequencing of parts, ownership of parts, doing what an entity does best, and minimizing touch points. The process redesign, in a sense, aimed to reduce the stress, which had reached a breaking point from the workload and the rush to beat the deadline, addressing the need for a detailed bottom-up plan to match the top-down idea.

The problem with this description is that parts don't fall so easily into specific slots but get messy in the arena of instructional design and educational program development. Continuous observation, feedback, and adjustments were needed in this setting. Co-design and separate implementation had the gray area of "to do" plans and the "do" responsibilities. As noted, the aim was to move from an "everybody does everything all of the time" approach necessitated by metamorphosis and urgency to a "some people do some things some of the time" approach. The workshops allowed people to look through and critique what was proposed.

One-on-One to Group to One-on-One Interactions

In listening and creating buy-in, constant one-on-one or small-group discussions are required. One factor is of course sensitivity of issues discussed. Another is the sequence the discussions should take to receive input before going to small groups or publicizing more widely.

Responsiveness

Related to follow-up is responsiveness. Issues cannot linger without some direction. If nothing can be done about a situation, that can be communicated directly as well. Continuous flow of information is at the heart of the bottom-up approach.

Every Detail May Matter

At the micro-level, in a bottom-up approach, every detail may matter. How a top-down idea translates to implementation and how bottom-up insights modify ideas or lead to new ideas requires traversing details big and small. A technological constraint may end up affecting the ability to enact a strategy. Tasks and people responsible for them represent another level of detail in understanding how to move forward. People knowing that I follow every detail matters as much as anything; it is a signal of caring about all aspects of the enterprise, which, in turn, engenders a culture of doing what we do well and valuing what we do. And in terms of solutions, a seeming detail such as having people be in proximity in terms of office space may hold the key to solving larger issues.

Follow-Up, Follow-Up, Follow-Up

Plans and actions without follow-up really mean very little. Once again, this means a lot of energy to make things happen. Being highly detail-oriented and staying on task in driving the process is critical. Team members need to know that I mean what I say and will follow up as soon as possible.

Buy-In, Buy-In, Buy-In

With the bottom-up approach, buy-in from different participants is central and in a sense, inherent or built-in. People in enterprises talk of executing strategy, but this is often done by those at the bottom of the organization who deliver the last mile. Buy-in has to come from different quarters and stakeholders. For instance, we developed a process for potential faculty to learn fully about what is involved before committing to the program. In a university setting, the hard demarcation of issues under the purview of faculty even for discussion purposes can work against the ability to create productive teams consisting of people providing various types of expertise.

Tasks and Processes

The tasks and processes involved are not set in stone. Rather, they are fluid and in need of constant revisiting and fine-tuning.

Process Follow-Through and Fine-Tuning

Designing a process is only the starting point even if it is fully grounded in bottom-up understanding. What matters is implementing it through continuous adjustments. This requires continuous listening and learning and incorporating end-user perspectives into planning and implementation.

All stakeholders are end users in some aspect of the process: individuals such as students, designers, and instructors, and entities such as college and university teams, the worldwide online educational enterprise, and so forth. The bottom-up approach enables an understanding and balancing of needs; there are tradeoffs and win-wins to be identified here.

Start Somewhere with Many Chicken-and-Egg Situations

A key issue with many different tasks to juggle and many different priorities is to make a decision on where to start. Indeed, everything may be interrelated but it is important to start where there is immediate priority and the action makes sense in a way that divides up the task into components where progress can be made.

Slice and Re-Slice Tasks into 1.0 and 2.0

Dividing up tasks is another important aspect and related to this is sequencing sub-tasks. Is it better to assume one simple audience or should the complexity of different audiences be assumed from the outset? Perhaps the former provides a good starting point from which to complicate. This means prioritizing audiences, dividing up tasks, and sequencing them. This specific example is just an illustration of the broader point of how we approach, categorize, prioritize, and sequence tasks.

Publishing 1.0s

Getting output published rather than waiting for perfection is also another important aspect. Typically, what is published needs to have been vetted by various stakeholders but finer iterations can often wait. In our case, getting good communications out to different stakeholders was very important, with 2.0 versions following soon after.

Design, To Do, Do

Dividing up tasks between entities requires constantly revisiting where the division occurs. Multiple entities here are involved in the design and then in creating "to do" lists. But the responsibility for the implementation ideally belongs to one of the entities – the "do" part. When that part does not happen as planned, follow up is needed.

Switch from Parallel to Sequential to Parallel Processing

Another facet of what is needed is being sequential to bring closure to issues while being parallel all the time in one sense and in a more limited way when priorities dictate being sequential on some issues.

Direct Communications

Email is a medium that we are still learning to use. It works well for information, transactions, and updates, but often fails with deeper discussions, being asynchronous and sometimes polarizing. Therefore, direct communications are often important for deeper discussions. This is not easy and is often time-consuming; with sufficient trust, the email medium may work as well. This means avoiding or deescalating email-based discussions as they can feed off each other in negative or misleading ways.

Top-of-Mind Communications

As trust is developed, top-of-mind communications are useful in conveying issues that are germane or that need specific timelines. Describing where we are and where we are headed is another important aspect of the process. Placing it thematically provides a sense of progress and goals to achieve as well as a narrative, so to speak. This narrative has to be rooted in reality, and be positive, but should not paint a rosy picture.

Mindsets

To successfully use a bottom-up approach in higher education, it takes a mindset with certain characteristics, as enumerated here.

Making Promises, Keeping Promises

The bottom-up approach is ideally suited to bridging the gap between making and keeping promises. It involves playing out promises to their minute detail and therefore, what it will take to get there, and what can be promised to begin with. It also provides a realistic window into what is doable and when to focus exclusively on keeping promises.

Translating Larger Purpose to Program and Day-to-Day

Much of bringing people together is about the larger purpose and, in this case, its uniqueness and the nature of the innovation. This is a great motivator. But on the other hand, if the day-to-day reality is simply unsustainable, then the translation from larger purpose to actions on a daily basis has not happened. In fact, at that point, the larger purpose is a set of empty words that don't impact people directly. Thus, negotiating this process of translation all the way to the micro details is extremely important.

Startup Mentality

A startup mentality is an interesting proposition when working in a long-standing public institution with well-developed programs. Translating what this means is, again, ideally suited to the bottom-up approach. A startup mentality in a large public institution was essential to the subsistence marketplaces initiatives we describe elsewhere in the book. That mentality characterized my own approach as a professor.

In this case, though, the startup mentality had to percolate to many people in the institution. For instance, as a startup, the previous assumptions about what teaching is and what the roles of staff are has to be unlearned by faculty. Similarly, administration has to understand how to create a team dedicated by the common purpose from entities at different levels of the university. The word, startup, accurately describes what happens but understanding its implications for the minutest details is a very different story that requires a bottom-up perspective.

Truthfulness in the Face of Power Hierarchy and Decision-Makers

To be bottom-up involves building trust at different levels of the power hierarchy. This means honesty and transparency in upward relationships in conveying what is occurring at the different levels. An example of this issue is in bridging the gap between promises made at higher levels and promises kept through the implementing teams – an issue where being honest with all levels is critical. A byproduct of doing what we believe to be inherently right is the trust that it builds.

Traits

Similar to mindset, there are certain traits that will enable you to successfully launch an initiative using a bottom-up approach within higher education.

Recognition

Recognizing situations and providing what is needed and when it is needed is very important. This includes using energy smartly, providing as much of it as is needed, being decisive when it is called for, and so forth. It comes down to having a detailed grasp of the situation, which a bottom-up approach enables.

Energy

There is no substitute for the energy one brings into the situation. Rationing and providing bursts of energy when needed is very important. But this goes with recognition of when such energy is needed. Wasted energy is often a byproduct but cannot become a normal state of affairs, reinforcing the point about recognition above.

Positive Energy

Positive energy is invigorating and leads us out of vicious cycles as much as negative energy, even on rare occasion, leads us back in. Moreover, negative energy from someone in a leadership role need happen only once or twice to cause harm. It is sufficient for those with less power to anticipate and react. On the other hand, this does not preclude being spirited and up front and still receptive to ideas, all good things.

Emotional Fortitude

Drawing a parallel with subsistence marketplaces, the people I worked with had been doing so tirelessly, and deadline-based stresses lead to a focus on the immediate. Therefore, as the person with the perspective, I need to consider the mindset of those working day-to-day and focus on the immediate. Improvements in the big picture matter to the extent that they also translate to individuals. Emotional fortitude here means putting the burden on myself to find deeper understanding and perspective and supporting members of the team at every turn.

People, Not Parts

Facing significant challenges and monumental tasks can tempt us to focus on the issues and problems involved and not on the people who are at the heart of solving those problems. Developing and building a strong team and maintaining cohesion, and treating people with respect and placing them in positions to succeed are paramount to the initiative's success.

Foundational Emphasis: People!

The people who work on developing courses are at the heart of much of the efforts. They are the foundation and while tasks can be divided into parts, people completing the tasks need to be in constant focus. It is not an accident that a majority of our time was spent on our people.

Changing the Day-to-Day

Affecting people positively means improving what happens day-to-day. There is no substitute for this. Ultimately, the immediate matters. And it matters even more for those working tirelessly to reach deadlines.

Helping People Develop

Part of the process here is to help each person develop and gain the recognition she or he deserves. Again, this goes hand-in-hand with organizational goals. Mentoring and encouraging all the people we come in touch with and thinking of their paths in life is central to building strong relationships.

Bottom-up, Top-down Dance

I mentioned earlier the notion of a bottom-up top-down dance. That dance is ongoing; rarely is it only bottom-up, particularly in higher education. Here are a few lessons I learned along the way regarding this dance in higher education.

Playing out to Bottom-Up Detail When Making Promises

One of the advantages of the bottom-up approach is an eye to details. This is also the case when playing out the details of moving from idea to detailed plan to proposed implementation. Playing this out in great detail impacts strategy formulation as well and promising what is doable.

The Bottom-Up Approach Feeds into and Modifies the Top-Down Plan

The lesson about implementation applies here as well. Indeed, implementation modifies the idea to begin with. A large plan disassembles into meso- and micro-level plans and their respective implementation. At the meso- and micro-levels, there is a need to be strategic while being harmonious with higher-level strategy and ultimately the bigger vision. There are times when getting the things promised done take absolute precedence over more planning or more promises.

Prioritizing, Reprioritizing, and Percolating

When there are many priorities to address, being bottom-up enables recognition of issues as they percolate up, and an understanding of issues that could be postponed to address more immediate priorities. Being in the maze also means constantly prioritizing what to focus on. Clear thinking with respect to priorities is the single biggest trait with this type of immersion.

Devil in the Details

If there is anything that the bottom-up approach teaches us, it is that the devil is in the details. What can be seen from 30,000 feet is very different from what appears up close. For flying and landing the mission, both vantage points are important. So it is with innovative ideas and their implementation in real terms.

Processes Emerging Bottom-Up and Not All Preplanned

The pathway one takes in managing a variety of issues also emerges bottom-up. It is not that an action plan cannot be set in motion in the early stages. In fact, as the listening and learning is continuous and as actions have to be followed through, allowing for priorities and plans to emerge while being very proactive is another facet of the bottom-up approach.

Pitfalls

There are many pitfalls to avoid with the bottom-up approach in a higher-education setting. Here are a few I noticed as we went through the process of building and launching our program.

Micro-Managing to Stepping Back

Stepping away and entrusting people after micromanaging is one such arena. The bottom-up approach necessitates getting into the weeds, mostly to understand but sometimes to manage as well. But it is very important to have buy-in and trust in doing so and then stepping away. Clear role definitions are particularly important here. For instance, my purview of working *with* people provided a clear definition. This is not the case, of course, with my other initiatives where I cover a number of different responsibilities.

Conversation to Closure

There are many conversations happening in a bottom-up approach. It is very important that they go somewhere – whether it be in actions or in documentations and change. Otherwise, a pitfall is that one is completely lost in a maze of interactions, sometimes indistinguishable from background noise. The ability to step back and then converge on some relevant action is important.

Avoiding Overreaction (and Overreaction to Overreaction)

With a bottom-up approach, there is exposure to a lot of reaction and sometimes overreaction. In turn, for a number of reasons, we have a tendency to react more to overreaction. This leads to a cycle in itself that is best avoided. Keeping the noise out is important as well. Second-hand and third-hand information that could have been communicated directly are examples.

Lesson Summary

Here are lessons from subsistence marketplaces that directly resonate in this situation – in creating courses or initiatives in higher education. They are indicated in Image 12.03 below in italic.

Image 12.03: Lessons from Subsistence Marketplaces That Resonate in Higher Education.

Charting a bottom-up journey	Implementing bottom-up enterprises	Sustaining bottom-up enterprises	Guiding values	Essence of the bottom-up approach
Chart a course	Set goals idealistically & pursue them pragmatically	Identity before branding	*EQ: To get things done*	*The ultimate bottom-up principle – If all else fails, do it yourself*
Define purpose	*Implementation trumps "IP & killer app"*	Being over strategizing	Do your best; accept the worst	
			Take the high road & stay there	
Inspire through purpose	*Learn, try out, learn by trying out*	*Negotiate, articulate, re-evaluate value equation*	*Be thoughtful in adversity*	
			Go to the next level of understanding – Peel the onion	
Determine purpose	Iterate many times rather than get it *right* away	*Culture of mutual accountability*	Get over yourself, see & experience	The ultimate bottom-up enterprise model – Do what it takes for each other
	Don't break promises – Break up promises	Blur the boundaries of organization	*What you do matters more than what you say, think, like, or want to do*	
Circumscribe purpose			*If one relationship is dispensable, all are*	
Delineate the domain of purpose	*Coevolve pathways to implementation*	*Different ways to thread the needle*	.Intertwined destinies – Not replaceable parts	
	Create short-term yield	Principled flexibility	*Be aware of your power, & lack of it for those you work with*	Be intensely practical & un-compromisingly idealistic
Execute the domain of purpose	Complicate the revenue model	Activities before resources	View people by how far they have come	
	Fail small/scale through depth	Inspire & incentivize	Nurture leadership among those who have not had a chance	
Listen & learn – Bottom-up immersion	*Experience & know the forest, trees, branches, leaves*	Steps to social enterprise & enterprise plan	Avoid an "I cannot do this without you" & "You cannot do this without me" mentality	*Bottom-up meets top-down*

1. **The larger purpose is the engine and you must use this to inspire others.** In our case, our larger purpose was democratizing education through a one-of-a-kind program. This lesson needs to be accompanied by concrete evidence of improvements and advancements at a day-to-day level.

2. **Circumscribe your purpose and address the reality that is as you aim for the reality that should be.** Addressing immediate and practical

issues is as important as dreaming of a better medium-term as described above.

3. **Listen and learn through bottom-up immersion.** This lesson is at the heart of what is described above.

4. **Focus on implementing and executing.** You will constantly be adapting and coevolving pathways to implementation, working with people to figure out how to best move forward.

5. **Learn, try out, and learn by trying out.** Inherent in our approach is the need to try out new processes, follow them through, and make adjustments.

6. **Coevolve pathways to implementation.** Listening, learning, working with people to find solutions, and making changes based on additional feedback are all part of coevolving pathways to implementation.

7. **Create short-term yields.** Changes that people can experience in the immediate are very important. Complicating this possibility in our own initiative were previous commitments that were going through the process.

8. **Fail small and scale through depth. Depth of understanding enables breadth.** One illustration of this lesson is that deep understanding of individual course development processes enables the ability to redesign processes that apply to a larger set of courses.

9. **Experience and know the forest, the trees, the branches, the leaves.** You need knowledge and understanding at macro-, meso-, and micro-levels. This enables micromanaging and stepping back as described above.

10. **Negotiate, articulate, and reevaluate the value equation.** This is a constant pursuit in every interaction with people and entities. It gets compounded at the entity level in terms of who is doing what and why. A visual depiction and discussion of the entities and value creation at interfaces was almost always the first task that was done.

11. **Build a culture of mutual accountability.** Using our team-building activities and working with the dedicated people in our team enabled this culture of mutual accountability.

12. **Know there are different ways to thread the needle.** This is an attitude that serves us well in finding different ways to reach the destination.

13. **Use EQ in getting things done.** Again, this is a lesson that resonates with what is described above, and perhaps the most important quality that is needed.

14. **Take the high road, and stay there.** This requires emotional fortitude and can lead to positive cycles as opposed to adding negativity into the system, no matter how small.

15. **Be thoughtful in adversity, whether your own or others'.** It is incumbent on those in leadership positions to take this lesson to heart in working with people.

16. **Go to the next level of understanding; peel the onion.** Constantly improving our understanding rather than stopping at some level is another lesson reflected above.

17. **What you do matters most.** It matters more than what you say you will do, think you should do, like to do, or want to do.

18. **If one relationship is dispensable, then all relationships are dispensable.** The importance of striving for good relationships with everyone on the team and in other entities is highlighted by this lesson.

19. **Be aware of your position and power and the lack of it for those you work with.** This is a constant for those in leadership positions in building relationships and pursuing a bottom-up approach.

20. **The ultimate bottom-up principle is: If all else fails, do it yourself.** This lesson is more an attitude than a day-to-day reality and is reflected in the ability to participate at a detailed level if needed.

21. **The bottom-up meeting the top-down.** This lesson underlies everything that was done and described above.

Conclusion

The detailed example in this chapter represents an application of the bottom-up approach developed in a very different setting – higher education – than the more traditional setting of subsistence marketplaces, which I delineated in the rest of the book. As noted, the application is a mix of lessons learned from the bottom-up approach, inherent traits, and unique aspects of what the situation called for.

Nevertheless, it represents a very concrete and timely example of how the bottom-up approach learned in subsistence marketplaces transfers to other settings – in this case, higher education. Sometimes it is the mindset, sometimes the traits one has acquired, sometimes the transfer of a cognitive characteristic such as thinking in the immediate and so forth. But overall, there is much to be learned and applied as this example demonstrates.

Every situation is of course different. The fluidity of the bottom-up approach is well suited to meet your needs and an organization's or team's needs in a great variety of circumstances and settings. The bottom-up approach is just that: an approach, and not a recipe. When you are entrenched in the approach, when you thoroughly understand its nuances and idiosyncrasies and strengths, you are well on your way to effecting great change through your endeavor or initiative. The lessons we have covered stem from our experiences. If we sound too idealistic or too practical, it reflects the constant dance we have been engaged in. We emphasize that these lessons and our experience should not suggest somehow that ours is an enterprise that has arrived and is an exemplar. Far from it, ours is a continuous learning experience that we hope is useful to others. We fully realize that what we have today can crumble tomorrow, but we hope our insights, derived from experience on the ground, sustain.

At the heart of many of our lessons is identity – who we are. We do things because of who we are, for its own sake. But we are also strongly arguing here that it is an approach to sound leadership and management, to enterprise in all its forms.

There are numerous challenges in working in subsistence marketplaces, and it is critical to learn how to overcome some of those challenges. Each of you will find your own way to give back to these communities and to the larger society. **You will chart or are charting your own path. You will plan your own journey and travel forward. In doing that, it is useful to think about your larger purpose, your passion, and your proficiency.** In other words, what do you think you should do? What do you like to do? What are you good at doing?

Sometimes, these three aspects intersect – what you are good at, what you like to do, and what you think you should do. Sometimes a couple of these intersect; it may be the passion intersecting with the proficiency, and so on. In my case I can tell you that all three things intersect: my larger purpose, my passion for this arena, and what I am hopefully good at doing as well.

I wish you the very best in finding your own journey, and I hope it is at the intersection of your larger purpose, your passion, and your proficiency. As you move forward in life, I hope the lessons from our bottom-up approach serve you well and help you succeed in your endeavors.

A Final Note: My Own Path with the Bottom-Up Approach

Here is a (likely self-serving) account of how my personality and experiences may have shaped my perceptions, in the interest of full disclosure. I see myself as starting out quite soft-hearted but lacking in toughness of mind.

However, over time, I think I have become tougher but perhaps not tough enough.

I also do not have any appetite for personalizing things or having personal conflict. I note that I do not avoid personal matters but prefer to address directly and defuse potential conflict. In doing so, I am likely to put my own feelings aside, a tendency I learned due to a variety of life experiences. Where possible, I believe in being unconditional, using conditionality rarely if at all, and being sparing in telling people what to do. I also believe that **naiveté is both my strength and my weakness. And my errors tend to be those of commission rather than omission.**

I may not be able to explain my tendency for the bottom-up orientation fully. Perhaps, at a cognitive level, it comes from a need to figure things out for myself rather than be theory driven, often at the expense of educating myself on what is out there beforehand. I have noticed that this is how I do many things. The bottom-up is also stimulating at an intuitive level, particularly in the context of subsistence marketplaces. Each context is different and the challenges are ongoing in terms of adapting to each setting in terms of educational programs. Perhaps at a motivational level, it comes from a need to have direct impact even if it starts out small.

Much of what I describe here relates to providing a personal guarantee and certainty to the extent that I can. In a sense, more than specific resources, I view the commitments as an investment of oneself, myself. In turn, I have learned to find ways to sustain myself in terms of health and well-being, as this is the foundation and starting point for doing what I love to do, want to do, and think I should do.

Ultimately, these self-perceptions matter in the sense that what we do has to work for us, such as being within our comfort level on a variety of issues. We have to answer the question eventually, whether what we did "was worth it." I know that how I go about attempting to achieve goals is as important to me as anything. **In the final analysis, the biggest caveat here is that this is the approach that works for me.** Knowing my self-perceptions, I hope, is useful to you in discounting insights and lessons as needed.

Chapter 13: Observations from Co-Passengers in the Bottom-Up Journey

I have had the privilege to work and partner with a number of talented, hard-working, energetic, and brilliant people through my many years in bringing marketplace literacy to those who live in subsistence around the globe and bringing subsistence marketplaces into academic research and the classroom. Some of my co-passengers in this journey are from the United States; some are from India, some from Africa, some from South America. Though these people come from all over the world and represent a variety of cultures and experiences, what they share in common is a heart for helping people who live in subsistence achieve a better way of life. Together, they have immeasurably helped me in my work, and I am not only forever grateful to them; I learn much from them.

And I want you to be able to learn from their experiences as well. So in this chapter you will hear firsthand from them about their experiences with the bottom-up approach, how it impacts research and community service and education, how the approach has impacted their own lives, how it works with the top-down approach, and any advice they might have for organizations or individuals who want to adopt the bottom-up approach.

You will be hearing from:

- **Ramadhani Kupaza,** director and president of Oikos East Africa

- **Raj Echambadi,** senior associate dean of MBA Programs & Strategic Innovation and professor of business administration at the University of Illinois

- **Ron Duncan,** community and economic development educator, University of Illinois Extension Service

- **John Hedeman,** director of Business Leadership Program and Business Honors Program at the University of Kansas

- **Jason Brantley,** managing director, John Deere Sub Saharan Africa

- **Maria Jones,** extension program project specialist, Department of Agricultural and Consumer Economics, University of Illinois

- **Seth Faber,** subsistence marketing coordinator, international marketing department, Wahl Clipper

- **Srinivas Venugopal,** assistant professor of marketing, University of Vermont

- **Nagendra Rangavajla,** director of user experience process, Abbott Nutrition R&D
- **Sophy Cai,** PhD student in the College of Education, University of Illinois at Urbana-Champaign

The interviews were conducted by Tom Hanlon, who has helped me immensely with this book.

Ramadhani Kupaza

DIRECTOR AND PRESIDENT, OIKOS EAST AFRICA

For whom do you work and what do you do?

I am the director and president of Oikos East Africa. It is a conservation organization. We have recently been approaching conservation from the developmental perspective. So our idea is the philosophy that if you develop someone in terms of education, in terms of economy, then you have a better chance of convincing this person to conserve the environment, to conserve the wildlife. We have various community-based projects in terms of social enterprises, agriculture, and energy, and all of this is tied to developing people who live around areas that need conservation.

What is your experience with Madhu?

My experience with Madhu is basically what he is as a person, more than his professional teaching on the subject of marketplace literacy. He believes more in terms of the humane part of transformation of people rather than the traditional way of thinking, which is about the knowledge which we impart on the human beings.

How does the bottom-up approach impact research, community service, and education at the University of Illinois?

It's very important because our feelings are that there is so much knowledge in the field which has not been tapped yet, in terms of the people who live in a particular area. We believe to live in an area for 30, 40 years, you must have very rich knowledge about the area. So in terms of academics, I have a feeling that that has not been tapped yet, so if research and education is seen from those perspectives we can enrich the wealth so much in that sense. The academics are creating a world which is not existing, but it can be even a better world which they are working on in terms of research and academics if we open up to the knowledge which people have in terms of how they address the environment.

When did you first meet Madhu and what are you working on with him?

I first met Madhu accidentally in February of 2013. This time I was attending a water conference organized by the University of Illinois in the engineering department. In this particular meeting I first met Madhu without knowing he came to Tanzania. We discovered that we had a lot in common in terms of how people should be addressed in terms of knowledge and research. We left the conference and we organized transport and went to the field to meet people who we think we can start a program with. So I managed to organize some 15 or so Maasai youths who were able to speak to Madhu, and the program has continued up to now.

How has the bottom-up approach impacted or affected your work in terms of structure, processes, and attitudes?

It impacts my work in terms of patience. The work we do here, it's an NGO work and we have a donor who is expecting you to accomplish certain things which you have promised in a project proposal, but at the same time you have a community which has to understand and support the program for it to be sustainable.

The bottom-up approach adds an aspect of sustainability to a project in the sense that from the beginning you need to spend a lot of time with the people to understand and accept what you are bringing as an intervention. Otherwise, you can come up with a lot of infrastructure, then at the end of the project the people didn't understand it and accept it properly, then the program would not be sustainable.

So it is a conflict in the sense that on one hand you want to be very efficient because you want to impress the donor, but on the other hand you know that if it is your passion to help the people, you know that if you are just in a marathon to impress the donor, the project cannot be sustainable. So you're walking on a tightrope. This is a dimension that we have realized and it is very important, and in fact now we believe the results of a project are less important than the people.

So how do you balance wanting to impress a donor with wanting to create something that is sustainable?

I think one important thing we are learning is to get people to make the decisions. For example, if there is a conflict, instead of you coming with the solution, let the people come with the solution. So if there is a conflict – let's say with a boundary demarcation with a particular village or a particular property – it is better to assign the village community to resolve this problem before you come in with an intervention in terms of infrastructure. So you get them to do the more important part, which is conflict resolution, on their own.

Otherwise you can come with a lot of solutions, but at the end of the day, it won't work, because you probably come with the issues of contracts and arguments, and the important thing is for the members of the community to speak with each other and agree. It's not about the papers.

How does the bottom-up approach work with the top-down approach? Can those two approaches work together?

I believe it is possible. I think that the top-down shouldn't be imposed. It should be made aware that these opportunities exist. If you drop it on their heads, I think it's unfair and you can disrupt the lifestyle of a person or a community. I think this is where research and education comes in. Open up the opportunities and let people know there are these options and opportunities. That's where the top-down should come in, not to come in with programs that impose on the people.

Do you have advice for organizations or people to adopt a more bottom-up approach?

I would quote Madhu's thinking: First, respect the people as human beings. They are knowledgeable. The most important thing is this program which Madhu is getting up, which he calls immersion, where you go to a particular community to address a problem, and you assume that you don't have a solution at all. It's very important to listen, to respect, and then perhaps as you listen and you are living maybe with the people, you might have an opportunity to make a contribution.

But it shouldn't be these people have a problem, and I have a solution for them. It should be the other way around. You don't know anything. If someone is around for 30 years in the area, then they are definitely more knowledgeable than you. There shouldn't be an assumption that that person is ignorant. The person is knowledgeable and that's why he has survived in that particular environment.

So it is disruptive for organizations to come in with what they call solutions; the best would be to understand what's going on and then build on that. We can build a better world that way and spare the lives of the people who you have intended to help.

I know many organizations have a good intention. But if you approach it in a way that you disrupt what is going on in the moment then it becomes negative.

Is there anything else you would like to add?

The other aspect is to understand the dynamics. Every community has its own dynamics; for instance, there is the issue of gender in the community. You need to understand that – otherwise you might bring an intervention but if it's not fitting with the gender structure then you become disruptive instead of helpful. So if you bring an intervention which disrupts the social structure of a community or family, it's not worth it.

Raj Echambadi

SENIOR ASSOCIATE DEAN OF MBA PROGRAMS & STRATEGIC INNOVATION AND PROFESSOR OF BUSINESS ADMINISTRATION AT THE UNIVERSITY OF ILLINOIS

What is your experience with the bottom-up approach and Madhu?

I have to give you some context about my research. My research is about technology, entrepreneurship, and innovation. What I've always done is to look at entrepreneurship in high-technology industries and at a very philosophical level address issues of how small startups and large companies should compete. Traditionally I've focused on small startups, how they should focus, and I've talked about the various phases of the industry: Are you in a nascent industry, are you in an established industry, who has the dominant hand in your industry? That's what I've done in the last 15 years or so.

When Madhu came in and talked about his work, the big point of departure for me, compared to what I was doing, though we were both looking at entrepreneurship, I was looking at high-technology entrepreneurship and he was looking at subsistence entrepreneurship. But the major points of departure for me was that I was looking at it from a formal economy standpoint, I was looking at issues with uncertainty being defined in a very narrow context – uncertainty in terms of how the market is going to evolve, uncertainty in how the technology is going to evolve.

Uncertainty was there, but uncertainty in the subsistence phase is completely different. It is uncertainty in all spheres, uncertainty in life circumstances itself – which leads me to the next point, which is almost all the entrepreneurship that I had done had looked at it from opportunity entrepreneurship point of view. You see an opportunity, you seek that opportunity, and you go out and you do that. Whereas Madhu's subsistence opportunity was about survival entrepreneurship. You had to do that entrepreneurship because there were no other opportunities; therefore, you survived.

One of the most amazing things is the opportunity – subsistence is about informal economies, subsistence is about survival, subsistence is about many things, but one of the interesting things I found in talking with Madhu is that subsistence entrepreneurship really doesn't care about differentiation of product, which we care about in high technology entrepreneurship. My product, Apple, should be distinct from other products whereas in subsistence entrepreneurship you see people sitting next to each other selling the same set of bananas, if you will. So it is not differentiated. So the facets of entrepreneurship are very different. Subsistence entrepreneurship is extremely important, because it is about life, it is about survival, and I found out that subsistence entrepreneurship empowers people.

Madhu and I wrote a journal article last year which talked about the role of the community in subsistence entrepreneurship, which I never thought about in that way.

How does the bottom-up approach impact research, education at the University of Illinois, and community service?

To me, a university has three major functions. The University of Illinois is about the intellectual capital building; we are about dissemination of that capital through education; and we are about community building. This last part is often not emphasized.

I want to make two points here. One, the importance of original research has never been higher. And two, the universities of the future should start thinking about the footprint in their local and their global communities. For us, because we are a land grant university, and a renowned university around the world, I think it behooves us to have a global footprint, because we can influence people around the world. We need to move from a national land grant to a global land grant university.

How does Madhu's work fit in here? Madhu's work is top-notch. Madhu's work is one of the few things that the University of Illinois – if you ask about the University of Illinois College of Business, one thing that we are absolutely the pioneer of, that we are absolutely the leader in the field is in the area of subsistence entrepreneurship. We have developed sufficient capital, and we have been taking our students to various countries, so we are fantastic as far as the research and the capital-building missions. But one of the unique things that Madhu does is in the community-building aspect of it.

A lot of research doesn't lend itself to that, as his research does. So this is an enormous opportunity for the University of Illinois to capitalize on the great work that he is doing. I look at it at three different levels: at the Champaign and the state level, at the national level, and at a global level.

When you look at Madhu's work in India, in Honduras, in Argentina, in Tanzania, this is part of our global platform. When you have the majority of people at the bottom of the pyramid, which is what a lot of people would say, the prescription so far has always been, "How can Coca-Cola become a better player in India, and how can it capture the bottom of the pyramid consumers?"

But Madhu is the first person I know of who came out and said, Let's not look at it from that perspective. The focus before Madhu had always been, "How do we develop products for these consumers and engage in profit-taking?" Madhu is the first to come in and say, "What is in it for them? How do we use the notion of business and entrepreneurial literacy to actually empower these consumers so they can get out of poverty?"

So to that extent, this is not about the global footprint of Illinois, but about global wellbeing. That's how I think of his work. If we can find a way to scale and offer his entrepreneurial literacy to people around the world who are living in the bottom of the pyramid market, then we will be doing huge service by empowering people, by enabling people to get out of their circumstances and better their lives.

From a philosophical level, it is good for us, it is good for the welfare, but more importantly, when you have subsistence entrepreneurs catering to subsistence consumers, the life circumstances that they share actually makes them better in terms of offering something of unique value to subsistence consumers – value that a first-world country going into a third-world country for profit-taking cannot.

The bottom-up approach is phenomenal because it empowers consumers, it provides opportunities for subsistence entrepreneurs, and once they come out, they become better in terms of poverty circumstances, then their communities are enriched, which means the wellbeing of the nation is going to be better, which means globally we are all going to be better off. That to me is the chain in which Madhu's work operates.

How does the bottom-up approach translate to your own work?

Reverse innovation is basically developing products in the third world and bringing them back into the developed world, perhaps for marginalized markets. Innovation has always flowed from the developed to the developing world. It now has started flowing back from the developing to the developed world. I have always been impressed with the concept of reverse innovation, but what Madhu's work does is provide the building blocks for how to accomplish this. The actual steps are provided by Madhu. When he talks about the immersion process, and when he talks about the product development that he has undertaken in this rural world, that is very applicable. So I use those kinds of things in my classes right now.

From a research point of view, what I've started to think about is how these valuable innovations that come out of the university help a nation's welfare. So I started thinking about those issues. We can talk about subsistence entrepreneurship, but if you think about it very carefully, the entrepreneurship there is not very different from what you're going to see in Danville or

Carbondale. The situation of a subsistence entrepreneur in India or in Tanzania is very similar to what you would see in a place like Danville or Carbondale. So how do we transfer those experiences so that we could become entrepreneurially thriving communities here? I started thinking about those issues, which I had never before.

At a philosophical level, without Madhu's work, we would not be talking about community building in such a deep way. Because by his research and by setting up his NGO in India, he formed communities. And the moment I saw that, I thought this is a fabulous way of building communities. And it led me to think from an administrator's point of view: how do we build communities, how do we reach out to communities so that we empower them and we make an important contribution to enhancing their welfare? That's how I think about these issues.

Can the bottom-up approach work with the top-down approach?

It is not only possible, but it is imperative. I don't care what people say; top-down has never worked. And a pure bottom-up, to me, when I think about a business manager who is sitting in an organization, one of the jobs of the business manager is to get inputs from a variety of stakeholders. Bottom-up is nothing but getting and listening to your stakeholders and enabling them to grapple with the variables and arrive at a possible position.

Having said all this, bottom-up is fantastic for grassroots; it is beneficial in a lot of ways. But unless the bottom-up position meets with the top-down vision, I don't think we can move forward. To that extent, I think it is not only necessary, but it is imperative for everybody to have both. Because you need to set a vision, you need to approach it from a bottom-up point of view, gain various inputs, and come up with a potential position, and then drive along.

Top-down vision coupled with top-down direction doesn't work; bottom-up vision with bottom-up approach doesn't work, because you are going to have diffused ideas, you are going to have undercutting of your experts; the best scenario is a bottom-up approach to generating input and a top-down vision. They need to merge in an optimal way for you to move forward.

Do you have advice for individuals or organizations who would like to become more bottom-up?

To me, it's about diversity of ideas. Any manager who wants to do well has to think of the pipeline as a funnel. You need to have a lot of ideas, and when you have a lot of ideas, your decision-making is going to be better. How do you generate diversity of ideas? From an organizational point of view, you want multiple people who think differently.

But that still means that you are looking at the world through your organizational prism. **When you talk about bottom-up and you go to these consumers who are very different from who you are in every possible way, then it generates a diversity of ideas that you would have never gotten otherwise. And because of that diversity of ideas, you are going to be able to consider multiple perspectives, and therefore you are going to be able to arrive at a better decision than what you would have otherwise. It is a business imperative.**

What should an organization do? Enforce that you have diversity of ideas. Mandate that you go out and talk to consumers and listen to them and have formal mechanisms to capture their feedback. More importantly, it's one thing to mandate something, but it's another to implement it into your organizational DNA.

The people who are more likely to listen to bottom-up are people who are imperfect, who feel that the other side has a lot to offer and who have listening skills. So the same thing is true for organizations as well. One thing I tell organizations is you need to have organizational empathy. You need to build into you DNA that you listen to people, there is no prejudgment, but at the same time you derive all the information you can and then you arrive at your decision.

Ron Duncan

COMMUNITY AND ECONOMIC DEVELOPMENT EDUCATOR, UNIVERSITY OF ILLINOIS EXTENSION SERVICE

What do you do and how did that bring you into contact with Madhu?

I serve as the community and economic development educator for a unit of the University of Illinois Extension Service here in southernmost Illinois. My responsibilities span about five counties. Three of those five counties are some of the poorest counties in the state – there are very high unemployment rates and some other issues we are working with here.

That led me into working with the poverty simulation that the University of Illinois Extension provides as part of an educational tool. One of my coworkers at the time was familiar with Madhu, who was implementing that poverty simulation with some of his work on campus for business and engineering students.

I was invited to go along with a coworker to provide and provision that as a CDE educator. That was in 2013, in the Fall. I was very interested in what he was doing. So we struck up a friendship, and began communicating, and he was interested in some of the things I was thinking about, and lo and behold, the University of Illinois came up with a grant program that offered extension professionals and others in the extension community the opportunity to write a project for money that would increment a division of extension into a division of the College as a whole.

Over time, we created a project that would put the marketplace literacy project in line with the maker literacy project and allow us to deploy that in two places across the state.

I was interested to see if there was a way to adapt the very successful process that Madhu had developed over the years and see if we could apply it in a North American context.

So how is it going so far?

We have a good contextual handle on the curriculum now. It's taken about nine months to evolve the curriculum. There's a fairly significant offset to the curriculum, because we don't have as high a level of people living in subsistence in North America in comparison to what people face in India. But we have the same stressors and environmental conditions. So we had to find ways to implement the curriculum around that offset so that we could get at those key learnings that get people over the hump of understanding their capacities as consumers, of understanding their capacities as shoppers and participants in the marketplace as a whole. The challenge has been in trying to adapt the curriculum in ways that hold to those key tenets and still provide for this offset that we know is there. I think we've done that fairly successfully.

One problem is in modifying the language to express what we are about in different ways, because people don't want to identify themselves as low-literate. We also had to build a tiered approach to the curriculum overall. We have it divided into segments: we talk about the consumer, where we develop people's acumen about being a consumer, then we rotate that slightly to talk about the role of the consumer in a business setting, relating it to what the business owner would want or see.

I was blown away by how impactful a concept it is to start with the knowledge that an individual comes into the door with as the basis for building this acumen around developing good consumer habits and then evolving that into a good understanding of what a purveyor, a seller, or an employer would want or need, and then finally making that final leap as to what if you were the employer, what if you were the purveyor, what if you were the seller? How would you act, what would you do, how would you sell?

I was completely blown away by how powerful it is to start with where people are, building on what they know already, and putting labels and names on things they already know and understand.

Things might work differently in India and Tanzania compared to the US, but the key learning points are ubiquitous. They work in every audience I've worked with in North America, from juniors in high school through senior citizens.

How does the bottom-up approach impact research, community service, and education at the University of Illinois?

The College of Business, as well as other formal institutional structures within the University of Illinois, have come to the realization that there's three or four billion people out there whom they can reach in a new way. The idea of social entrepreneurism has always been there; it just hasn't had that name. The university has had an important outreach mission for a number of years. A lot of people have benefited from that, without question.

From the standpoint of the idea of raising folks' acumen and knowledge around their place in the market, their rights as consumers, what they need to do – that is something that is wholly new to the university arena in a lot of ways. From a business construct, that's been a very overlooked community. Now, the realization is there's four billion people out there that we'd like to market to if we knew how – who want to buy things. We have to figure out how to package those things and also find a way to put a little money in their pocket so they can buy more products. So that realization is getting a bit of groundswell from the community. We can do good and we can do well at the same time. Those things are in many ways no longer bifurcated, but they're together – it is possible to both do good and do well.

I think there's much more research to be done. The difficulty is trying to categorize people into buckets. I have variations from community to community here in Southern Illinois. It takes a ground-level view to understanding how these things work.

How does the bottom-up approach translate to your own work?

It's given me a place to pause. As an educator working in a given marketplace in rural economic development, we're always talking to the STPs – the Same Thirty People. They're the movers and shakers in the community. It's given me a place to think and pause to make sure that I'm adhering to those basic principles of whether I can start where people are, and whether I am sure that as I begin whatever it is I'm trying to do, I have the end in mind. Even though I have a broad audience, I can't ever assume what people's knowledge bases or capacities are.

So it's given me that pause to say I want to make sure we're covering all the bases and making sure we know where everyone's at, and then realizing that, based on my knowledge of the individuals I'm working with and what their stress levels are, I get a sense of the approach I'm going to have to use.

That has helped my understanding of the audience better. It's given me a few tricks up my sleeve to work with lower-resource audiences.

Can the bottom-up approach work with the top-down approach, and if so, how can those two approaches work together?

The bottom-up approach can work very successfully. But in order for that success to be realized, there has to be constraint removal, differentiated resources made available, and some of those more traditional small business opportunities brought down to that level. If someone using the top-down approach can devise a great gadget that makes a billion dollars, someone approaching from the bottom-up could have a fairly good idea about how to truck rice from point A to point B. He's got an idea. How can we learn, using top-down methodology, to evaluate that?

Let me give you an example: In the early part of the last century, Southern Illinois was a great place for fruits, nuts, and vegetables. We supplied a lot of the larger metro areas in Missouri, Illinois, and Tennessee with a lot of produce. After World War II that sort of waned, and then everybody found California and we were out of business.

But recently, in the last 30 years, we found that some of our soils were very well suited to growing grapes. There was a burgeoning wine industry that started. Thirty years ago, I can remember an acquaintance calling one of the local banks looking to borrow money to plant five different root stalks which would have ended up being about two acres of grapes in Alto Pass. And they looked at him like he was from Mars. They were clueless about how to do an economic evaluation on a vineyard. Today, we have more than 25 vineyards in our area, most of them in the black. We actually now have agricultural specialists in the bank who know how to evaluate vintner opportunities.

So there's an example of how a top-down approach can reach into an unknown and unexplored place and be successful – in fact, wildly successful. So if we – from the bottom-up approach – can raise people up to this standardized level of knowledge and acumen and understanding, and help to take the top-down approach, broaden their base and help them look for the right kind of opportunities, I think there is some sort of interface for them to meet each other, at least from an entrepreneurial standpoint. From a product standpoint, I think it's a little more difficult, because product development and product deployment in so many of these areas is so locally dependent that it's hard to get a broad scale indicator of how successful any one thing may or may not be.

Any advice to organizations or individuals who would like to become more bottom-up?

Number one, never assume anything about a participant, either positive or negative. They're there for a reason. They have some interest in what you're providing, in what you're doing. Test that, see why they're interested, and then work with them where they are. And no idea is a bad idea. Well, some ideas might be stinkers, but it sometimes takes four or five bad ideas to get a good one. And someone may have to go through four or five iterations of really stinky ideas before they build up enough confidence and enough peripheral vision from a subsistence marketplaces approach to understand what the capability may be, and then they have the opportunity to come up with the one really good idea that they can move forward with in their marketplace or in a larger marketplace.

The other thing is absolute patience. We are trying to get our assessment house in order. What are meaningful assessments? The real idea is patience. Sometimes it takes many years to develop enough foundational work before a project can take off. It takes time for people to get the courage or to get desperate enough to where they see an opportunity and can move to take that opportunity.

Never misjudge the people who are sitting in front of you. It doesn't matter what they look like or what they're wearing; they may have an idea about how to cure cancer.

Anything else?

These core tenets that work in a bottom-up approach are ubiquitous. But their successful application is going to depend on people realizing to what degree of offset they have to bring to that to make it realistic and applicable to the audience in front of them. That takes some skill sets on the part of the facilitator in knowing the appropriate levels of offset to bring to that and how to elevate the language, the conversation, the concepts, or how to demote them to the appropriate level for the audience. We find widely variable audiences under the same roof, at least here in North America.

John Hedeman

DIRECTOR OF BUSINESS LEADERSHIP PROGRAM AND BUSINESS HONORS PROGRAM AT THE UNIVERSITY OF KANSAS SCHOOL OF BUSINESS

How did you get involved with Madhu and the bottom-up approach?

I had always admired the work that Madhu was doing in the University of Illinois College of Business, where I was an assistant dean in the undergraduate office. I gained insight into Madhu's work when he and I were on the same group charged with introducing a new, unique introductory course for business school freshmen, Business 101: Introduction to Professional Responsibility. Madhu proposed that the course must have a global perspective on the challenge of professional responsibility. Madhu's module involved student teams that devised business solutions to poverty-based market opportunities. Madhu introduced the students to subsistence marketplaces through a poverty simulation, lectures, and virtual immersion exercises.

I had never seen anything so ambitious for a freshman course that introduced students to a level of society and a marketplace with which they had no experience. That experience on a working committee was when I got some insight into his thinking, his ideals, his view of creating an environment for people who live in poverty to help themselves and not to be subject to philanthropy, which often had only short-term benefit to their lives.

In the fall of 2007, Madhu was searching for a faculty leader for his January immersion program in India. Although I had never traveled to India, I volunteered to go because I had had much experience leading students on international programs and believed that I could learn more about what Madhu was trying to accomplish in his research and his teaching. I was thinking I knew what Madhu was doing, but, in fact, I did not really have a clue. So it wasn't until that first time I went with the students and had a chance to watch his team on the ground in Chennai, India, and talked with people who lived in that bare level of subsistence, that I really understood what he was trying to do for students and for the people he's trying to educate to be more self-sufficient and to be literate in the subsistence marketplace.

The experience was quite remarkable! Madhu recruits support from major corporations to support the India immersion program. Their interest is to make money. The students are interested in making the lives of people who live in poverty better. Madhu is hoping students come up with ideas that will help major corporations enter this huge marketplace with products that are going to make people's lives better but also make money. That's a real hefty challenge.

I learned that Madhu was trying to add real value and experience in this program to everyone involved. For the people being interviewed – the experience was a confidence boost for them, that someone would come from halfway around the world from a university and be interested in their stories. Over the seven years I've been involved, I've seen how their sense of self-worth has grown through their interactions with students. You add that to the lessons that Madhu is teaching through the marketplace literacy initiative, and I think that these experiences really are making a difference among people living at the subsistence level.

I know the experiences are making a difference on the students. They will be soon going out and becoming leaders in their professions. These students get an insight that allows them to develop a different lens for their professions. They learn that many people who live in poverty are smart, hard-working, energetic people who are trying to make better lives for themselves and, especially, for their children. To us living our privileged lives, the challenge seems almost impossible.

How does the bottom-up approach apply to research, to education, and to community service?

I'm going to pick education first. I think **students in professional schools are desperate for practical applications. Many students in business schools never see anything made. The bottom-up approach in many ways provides students with the basic human behavior that drives our society, be it consumerism, be it work, feeding a family, providing a shelter, creating a philosophy of life, all of those things which, when you are in poverty, become everyday decisions that have to be confronted.**

In a rich society like ours, we don't think about those things every day. We take out a credit card and buy groceries and don't even think about it. But when one faces people for whom every rupee counts, one develops a whole different perspective of what builds the marketplace that allows some to be privileged and that unfortunately creates situations where others live in poverty. That's the primary benefit for students, to see the human face behind the decision-making that's necessary to survive and then to think critically about what possibly could work to make lives better. That's what Madhu presents in his marketplace literacy project – a model for how things can change and how individuals can be involved in that change.

In research, I'm not a researcher, but some of the same lessons apply – seeing the bottom of the pyramid, hearing the stories and getting the insights of others who live through the experiences, obviously has to inform research in a positive way. I think about Madhu's students who are looking to make products that are low-cost enough to be able to help people in their lives. They are researching a solution, and if they were to just sit in the United States and read about people in poverty, that wouldn't be enough. To be there, see, talk, and experience makes the outcome of their product development much better. So there's a real value in informing research in that way.

And what about community service?

I would call it global service. It makes privileged people more aware of their responsibilities to the entire globe in terms of making sure that their decision making and leadership is in service to the welfare of the world that we live in. The insights that one gets through this experience, the ones I've gotten, have certainly changed my approach to decision-making. I think it has an enormous impact on the students. I'm hoping as they grow in their jobs and in their lives that they will be more globally responsible in their decision making.

How does the bottom-up approach translate to your own work?

The example I give to students, which is a trivial one, is I take much shorter showers. To see the value of clean water in a situation where there is no clean water and people essentially live their lives sick because there is no clean water... I came home after that first trip and said I can't take long showers anymore. That's a small thing.

But it has made me think more globally – the way I approach teaching leadership here in the business school at the University of Kansas, the way I approached teaching leadership at the University of Illinois, involved a lot more of the sense of responsibility to others as a result of the experiences I've had with Madhu. That's the biggest influence.

We do have an opportunity as individuals to make the world a better place, even if it's just one person at a time. I'd like to think that was a strong element of what I was doing before, but it has been reinforced and put in the forefront in terms of what I'm doing with the students in the business school.

How does the bottom-up approach work with the top-down approach?

Intellectually, I am not an extremist. I am very much a centrist. So, regarding the nature-versus-nurture approach, I believe in both of them. Top-down, bottom-up, I think that one has to look at things from multiple perspectives. So I think they're complementary – they're not situations where it's one or the other.

And I think this is the value of intellectual teamwork, getting people who work primarily bottom-up or who are primarily top-down, and seeing where there are ideals or practices in common that may be stronger as a result of looking at challenges from different perspectives. I'm not a disciple exclusively of bottom-up work and I'm not a disciple exclusively of top-down work. I think people find values in their approaches, but I think the mistake can be in saying this is the only way to do things.

Any advice to organizations or individuals who want to become more bottom-up?

My advice is to **get out in the field. Get in the factories. Talk to people. Every single community in this country has an opportunity for, at minimum, a bottom-up observation if not bottom-up involvement.** You don't need a lot of money or even a lot of time or resources in order to at least get some sort of bottom-up experience that's going to allow you to then develop that different lens of looking at our society and looking at the lives of people.

Jason Brantley

MANAGING DIRECTOR, JOHN DEERE SUB-SAHARAN AFRICA

How did you first get involved with Madhu and with the subsistence marketplaces initiative?

There was some luck involved. The John Deere Technology Innovation Center is located in the Research Park on campus at the University of Illinois. As a result of being there, our employees have a chance to be engaged with the university, and we became aware of Madhu and his marketplace literacy activities through the center. After a chat, he invited us to come speak to one of his classes about our experiences in emerging markets, and that was the start of our relationship.

John Deere has a successful global technology innovation network. It ends up being a nice touch point because we manage global projects for a variety of different businesses in Deere, and many of those are in emerging markets. We leverage resources across centers to bring both technology and business model innovation to opportunities and customer problems that we have around the world. By being at the University of Illinois and having that linkage with Madhu, we were able to link up some of our projects in emerging markets and leverage his team and his approach to put together solutions for some of these opportunities.

From your perspective, what are some unique aspects to the bottom-up approach?

Within our global technology innovation network, we apply marketing techniques to understand customer problems and work together with technologists and other people to innovate solutions to persistent problems that our customers have globally. When we learned about the bottom-up approach and had a chance to visit with Madhu and see how his students were approaching these problems, it lined up really well with how we believe you need to drive development for innovation within a company. It's all about truly understanding your customer, your customer's problems, and developing empathy for that customer.

Madhu's approach uses a lot of design thinking methodologies to really understand the problems and more broadly understand the value chains and the networks that these customers operate in, because that's the environment that these problems exist in and the solutions are going to have to function in. The thing that Madhu brings is so much experience in how to approach some of these emerging market challenges with unique tools and perspectives in order to be able to get the right type of insights to drive innovation.

What new insights have you gained from the bottom-up approach?

In India, we were challenged to figure out the best way to connect with customers in remote areas. We have a dealer network across India, but it is a very large country, and the rural areas are extensive, and you can go 60 to 100 kilometers sometimes to get to some of these customers in remote areas. We wanted to find a way to connect with them in a way that would resonate with them and help us provide solutions to them and build a relationship.

Madhu's team went to India, met with a number of our dealers, met with many of our customers in the villages, and prototyped different ideas for how to structure an environment for the right type of interaction in these remote areas. They came back with a proposal that ultimately became what we know as the Outpost Model. The Outpost is a designed environment, typically on a trailer, but it can also be in a knock-down form that has various types of touch points, information in local language, things that are pertinent to individuals in that market that we can take out, and have a hyper-local strategy for connecting with customers. We share information about farming, about mechanization, about agronomy, about how to maintain and repair their equipment, how to get the highest productivity out of it, and how to minimize their expenses. And we also connect them with other people in the industry who are working to solve problems in the farm ecosystem. And that's been quite successful.

How would you compare the bottom-up approach to other approaches?

I think it's pretty common in business to try to take things that you're good at and that you know work in different areas and bring them in to a new market with a few minor changes that you think are appropriate for that market. And that can certainly work sometimes. But the reality is that a customer-focused organization like John Deere has to find ways to take all the learning and knowledge that they have and the tools and resources that they have and put those together in ways that really target the specific needs of the customers they're trying to resonate with. The bottom-up approach gives you a framework to do that for customers at the bottom of the pyramid. I think that's where a lot of the power comes from.

Again, there's two sides to working with Madhu. One is this framework that helps businesses sit down and think about the problem we're trying to solve, and think about the tools and skills and resources we have to help solve those problems for customers and create new opportunities. But at the same time, he knows how to connect with these emerging customers. He knows the language and dialects and customs, the things you really need to get right if you're going to connect with the customers and get the best insights.

How does the bottom-up approach translate to your own work and to John Deere?

I mentioned the example around our Outpost, and that's a great one. The reality is, once you get people involved in these types of projects, they begin to take that thinking and those insights and apply them to many of the other products and services and activities that we have going on in markets. I think being sensitive to the bottom-up approach and recognizing that innovation has a place at all levels enables people to be much more effective in their day jobs.

How does the bottom-up approach work with the top-down approach?

I think they are very complementary. When you think about a company like John Deere, we've been fortunate to enjoy a lot of success in our core markets over the years. So we've built up a lot of resources. By resources, I mean people with a lot of experience in solving difficult problems, whether those problems are with a machine form or areas around the performance of machines, or complex man-machine systems. So you manage a lot of that through a top-down approach. That's the ecosystem a lot of those things need to thrive in. That's where you get the scale, that's where you get the critical mass to be able to maintain and grow those capabilities.

The bottom-up approach gives you a way to come into an emerging market and think about how to best deploy those resources in ways that are really going to make a difference for customers. And it's about what that customer needs in their particular production system, in their part of the world, with the problem they're trying to solve. And it becomes about that rather than trying to figure out how to sell something we already know how to do.

I think Deere's approach historically has been to go into markets and partner with local companies and others in those regional areas so we can appropriately scale innovations and solutions for those problems. Madhu's approach is very complementary to how Deere has expanded globally.

Do you have advice for organizations or individuals who want to become more bottom-up?

The biggest hurdle to get over sometimes is recognizing that what has worked so well for you in one market is not going to deliver the success for your customers and your business in the other market. And that's a hard thing sometimes to recognize. But it's important to realize it's the capabilities and skills and resources and knowledge that allow you to create that first solution, and those can all be reused. Even if you can't sell exactly the same solution, you can leverage those.

Anything else you would like to add?

Our experience has been that when you are able to really connect with customers and innovate appropriate solutions for the marketplaces that you're serving, it's tremendously rewarding. It really helps you build a sustainable business as you grow globally. One of the things at Deere that we've been fortunate in is we've always focused on truly being a global company that leverages its capabilities strategically, and Madhu's approach is very complementary to that and helps us zero in on some opportunities and innovate some unique solutions. So we very much appreciate the chances we've had to work with him.

Maria Jones

EXTENSION PROGRAM PROJECT SPECIALIST, DEPARTMENT OF AGRICULTURAL AND CONSUMER ECONOMICS, UNIVERSITY OF ILLINOIS

How did you initially get involved with Madhu and the subsistence marketplaces initiative?

It started when Professor Madhu was a guest speaker in one of my environmental engineering classes in the fall of 2011. We were working on projects in Champaign [Illinois]. My professor got me connected with Professor Madhu so I could get more of a business and social perspective on the problems we were trying to tackle as a class and in my independent study research project.

It led to doing an independent study where I was looking at poverty in the United States, specifically with youths to see if we could come up with an innovative solution to train the youths with business skills, specifically jobs related to the environment, what we call green jobs. We were working with low-income, underserved communities, and that's why Professor Madhu suggested that I could conduct research through his nonprofit Marketplace Literacy Program in India.

I had a chance to visit his nonprofit in India and talked to a lot of people in different circumstances over there, and that was how I first got involved with the work that Professor Madhu does. Coming back to the United States, Professor Madhu invited me to his MBA class and asked if I could bring the project that I was working on to his class, and I requested if I could take his class as a non-MBA student, and it worked out pretty well.

That's what led me to the MBA program, because I wanted to understand the business side of poverty, international development, and environmental sustainability with a business school perspective in mind. Getting into business school I was working with Professor Madhu and got involved in the work that he does, including taking his one-year-long class, and thanks to him and his initiative I was able to go to Tanzania and conduct marketplace literacy training on the behalf of Professor Madhu with a nonprofit in Tanzania called Oikos East Africa. It's been quite a journey!

What are some of the unique aspects of the bottom-up approach?

We treat the people we work with as humans. We treat them with respect. I find it's lacking in the development world. I've been working in my present job for a little more than a year, and this is a lot more top-down, much more dealing with donors and partners and NGOs across the world. I. The more I am here, the more I see the value of what Madhu does in terms of the bottom-up approach, because the approach is fundamentally focused on the people, not on the service that needs to get done, or the product that needs to go, or the particular tool that needs to go. It's focused on what the people need and desire and going straight to the point and helping people out.

If you ask me one main thing that I've learned from Madhu's work, it is this: Treat people with respect and give them what they really need. A lot of times I find what people really need are not what donors are ready to focus on, or what a lot of organizations have the capacity to do. It sounds simple, but it's not so simple in how things really work in the development world. So I find what he's doing is truly revolutionary.

And secondly, coming back to simply respecting people for who they are. Something that I walked away with is just put people first.

A lot of top-down organizations don't even understand the value of the bottom-up approach.

Exactly! And that surprises me. I feel like it should be common sense, to be honest with you. There's nothing magical or amazing about it. It's just common sense. But it's crazy to see how many organizations do not actually do that.

Do you sense that multinational or global organization are beginning to understand the bottom-up approach or will it continue to be a long struggle?

I would say there is hope. I was recently part of a conference, and a lot of the speakers who were coming in from around the world, consultants, people from different universities and organizations like NGOs, I sense that people are now starting to realize the importance of listening to people who they're trying to help. It is slow, but there's a glimmer of hope.

I feel that businesses realize this better than non-businesses, because if you want to sell a product, you have to understand the customer. Unfortunately, NGOs have not realized that as much.

***What are some of the insights you have gained from working with the
bottom-up approach?***

In addition to what I've mentioned about putting people first and listening
to what people want as opposed to my ideas about what *I think* people
want, that's definitely a huge thing. Another important thing I learned is
that marketplace literacy approach, is basically just empowering people. It
empowers people to think for themselves, to decide for themselves, what
is important in their lives. **There is a saying, give a man a fish and you feed
him for a day; teach a man how to fish and you feed him for a lifetime. The
marketplace literacy approach teaches a man how to fish.**

Enabling people to learn how to start their own businesses is different from
how the development world operates today. Training, for instance – there are
so many trainings by NGOs about teaching women how to sew, how to do
embroidery, how to do these beautiful exotic crafts that are sold around the
world at exorbitant prices. This is a great way of making money, but it falls
apart when people in the West are having problems and are not willing to buy
the crafts.

The example I'm referring to is when I was in Tanzania, in addition to training
people in marketplace literacy, I was doing a mini-consulting project with
a nonprofit organization that had a program that was training the Maasai
women there, using their traditional skills of beading, but giving them an
Italian design, making them look beautiful, making this truly beautiful jewelry
that they would then market across the world as coming from the Maasai
women in Tanzania. The interesting thing was, while the organization started
off on a good trajectory, when the recession hit the West, that organization fell
apart and affected the Maasai women because they were dependent on one
thing: getting money by making this beaded jewelry. Once the jewelry was
not being sold to its main customers, who were not in Tanzania, it pretty much
fell apart. So one of the things I realized was there are multiple problems with
that setup. It was set up with a very specific goal of training a community of
women to do one particular task, which is never a good way to go.

But training people with the marketplace literacy program enabled each
woman to do whatever she did, but better. Whether she sold corn, or whether
she sold livestock (which she probably didn't do because she was a woman)
or whether she was selling firewood, the woman just used whatever she
was doing and made it better, because of the training. So now no more of us
coming and saying "Here, let us teach you how to make jewelry with your
traditional skills. Why don't you do whatever you do – it could be jewelry, it
could be selling corn or beans and lentils and tobacco – you do what you do,
and we'll help you to do it better."

I trained people the summer of 2013 and I had a chance to come back six months later and realized that a lot of people who used that training were doing better for themselves. They were actually making more money, they were able to buy something as simple as a mattress, which to them is a huge deal. They were able to say that the minimal training they had received had already started making a difference in their lives. And that's why the marketplace literacy approach is very different from a lot of other approaches.

How does the bottom-up approach translate to your own work?

I would say currently with my position I don't have much of a chance to implement it, because my role doesn't let me choose or decide. But I try to use that approach in my personal life. I was teaching a class about a year ago. It was about enabling students to be much more creative and innovative in whatever they chose to do. we were given freedom in choosing how to teach the students. And I used a lot of these principles of the bottom-up approach, such as how to be the interviewer, how to focus on people whom we create products for, not just the product, and how to design solutions and procedures or services. I know the students really benefited from it.

How can the bottom-up approach work with the top-down approach?

I believe they can work together. What I see is the bottom-up approach is great; it's fantastic. But there are limitations in how much one can do. A bottom-up approach is more limited to smaller circles. It can almost be an ideology of how you do things. I feel that the top-down approach makes sense too sometimes. The key is to find that central meeting point between the two approaches. With a top-down approach you can access a lot of people – in fact with this approach you are technically supposed to impact people in the thousands – trainers and organizations and nonprofits and public sectors in multiple countries. The level of impact they are trying to achieve is huge. But they don't follow the bottom-up approach. Which is why I feel the bottom-up approach is like a methodology for the way you do things, but the top-down approach can reach a lot of different people. And the sweet spot would be right in between both of those.

Any advice to organizations or individuals who want to become more bottom-up?

I would just say listen – truly listen. Sometimes we listen with things going on in our head the entire time. Truly listening is definitely an art, and once we truly listen without any preconceived notions, it's amazing how much we learn.

I think if we have that respect for people, no matter their position in life, then we are much more likely to be able to truly listen to them.

Seth Faber

SUBSISTENCE MARKETING COORDINATOR, INTERNATIONAL MARKETING DEPARTMENT, WAHL CLIPPER

How did you get involved with the subsistence marketplaces initiative and with Madhu?

I got my MBA from the University of Illinois. During my second year I took Madhu's yearlong course in subsistence marketplaces. That course had a yearlong project, and my project was sponsored by Wahl Clipper. My work continues today from being hired by Wahl from that project; I've taken a role focusing on subsistence marketplaces for the company.

Did you go on a trip to India as a student? What did you learn there?

I did go to India. We did interviews with barbers and tried to learn about how they came into the business and what their challenges were and if we could provide a solution for them. The lessons I learned in that were we really do take a lot for granted, both in how you and I live in our day-to-day lives, but also in how businesses view the consumer. We had some assumptions as a group going into that trip, and just about every assumption was wrong. Without going there and asking people, you can't fathom it. There are things like electricity, access to clean water, transportation, and even just basic sanitation, in terms of hair cutting and beauty, that we take for granted. I think a company like Wahl Clipper that's had success in the United States, Canada, and Europe and a track record for almost 100 years now, just assume those exist. So there's a lesson for us in places where those things don't exist, and what that means for our business.

How does this approach impact how you work right now at Wahl?

There are a couple of projects we're doing right now. One way I view how we can meet these challenges is if we can innovate a product and make it more accessible. So an example of something like that would be if there's no electricity, can we get a product that's powered by an alternative energy source? That would be an example of innovating by product.

The other kind of approach is, which I've been spending a lot of my time on recently, is how do we innovate the business model? Some would call it service. One thing we've learned in India, for example, is the service structure that we take for granted here doesn't exist there. So we've done very well at leveraging the channels of our education to say "Here's how you not only cut hair but take care of the hair clipper and maintain it and service it." Those platforms don't exist there. So a lot of my time has been invested in helping to design a solution that has this impact but matches their context.

What percent of your job is involved with subsistence marketplaces?

Anywhere from 50 to 75 percent. It depends if you count the corporate social responsibility side; there is some overlap there. If you count the work I've been doing in trying to build our corporate social responsibility program and the CSR brand and bringing all that information in one place for the whole company, it would be about 75 percent.

What are some of the unique aspects of the bottom-up approach?

The most unique aspect is the consumer. It's how the consumer is different and why the consumer is different. We talked about things we take for granted: sanitation, electricity, clean water, etc. We know those are available here, but they aren't always available to people in subsistence marketplaces. One of the effects that happen because of that, and because they have these challenges, is they get very innovative and very resourceful. So we can learn a lot from the consumer. Beyond all the constraints that you generally put with the bottom of the pyramid, there's this mentality where they're very resourceful, and they tinker, and they find things out, they find their own solutions, which is different from consumers in America. Consumers here will tell you through social media and traditional marketing channels, hey, we have this need, there's something wrong with this product. That doesn't exist in the subsistence marketplace. It's much harder to gain access to a feedback system.

What are some of the insights you have gained over the years working with the bottom-up approach?

Some I've mentioned, but I think the main one is, companies can't just think, "Oh, it's low income, we need to make a really cheap product." It's a very easy connection to make [here in the US]. What we try to manage and deliver to the market is value. There's a lot of opportunities for that, because there are a lot of challenges in this market. So the biggest insight is with any sort of design, whether it's a product or a business model, it has to be human centered. These are people and they're going to want value. So that looks a lot different when you have all of these challenges – electricity and water and things like that.

The challenges and innovative nature of the subsistence consumers alone necessitate a bottom-up approach. To sum it up broadly, I would say that in the setting of business's traditional marketplaces, companies are able to make some basic assumptions about the consumer, and the feedback system for industry to listen to the market is already in place and fairly dependable. In the subsistence marketplace, assumptions are more likely to be wrong; it's necessary to go to the consumer in their own context to really understand their perspective and their pains.

How does Wahl Clipper work in a subsistence marketplace? How does Wahl help or serve its customers in subsistence marketplaces?

Sometimes it requires another partner. For instance, where there's no electricity, we needed to partner with a third party who knows about alternative energy. In some other places like India, we are looking at service. We learned a lot about what happens to hair clippers in certain conditions. We know they wear out a little faster, we know they are more likely to get informally repaired, maybe even in ways that, in terms of safety, we wouldn't want them to be repaired.

So in India we did set up some service centers to try to remedy some of that. Our office in India does a lot of education, but we don't reach subsistence markets with that effort, because it would be very top-down. So in my work we're trying to get more education and service platforms, more modular service, starting in rural parts of South India, and in doing so, build relationships with the consumer and learn more about a) what are they missing and b) how can we help, and at the same time, try to build that loyalty and that relationship.

Does Wahl have inroads in a lot of subsistence marketplaces?

Africa is probably the hardest one for us to reach. We're pretty developed in Latin America; there are different NGOs we're trying to work with in Latin America. The challenge there for me is communicating our intention and making sure it aligns with their goals. But at the same time that relationship doesn't end with "I've just given you a bunch of clippers." We want to build a relationship with the market, we want to learn about the market, we want to do good. Finding that intersection is very difficult, but it's also very rewarding.

I can say, for example, there are times when we've gone to Guatemala, where we've tried to get an inroad with an NGO or with a church mission, and we'd say we have this vision for our product being a platform for economic empowerment. What they need is the product and some education on how to use it and possibly some education on how to run a barbershop or a barbering business on the street corner so they can maintain it as a businessperson, and that idea is great and everyone loves the idea.

But when it comes down to partnering with an NGO and executing it, we come up short. Our hands are kind of tied. Maybe they think what we're doing is impractical or too big. There's something we're not giving them, and we're not getting the feedback on what's missing.

How does the bottom-up approach translate to your own work?

We view our product as a platform for entrepreneurship. That holds true in the United States and Europe and Canada, but it's much more formalized [in these places] – people who decide they want to be a stylist or a barber go to a school, and receive a certification, and those channels of education and certification we invest in. When we look at subsistence markets, those challenges that are there make this look very informal. In India, sons or nephews learn from their fathers or their uncles. There's no certification that goes with it; it's just passed down through generations. Our challenge is to bring what we bring to the formal channels in the developed parts of the world. We need to bring that same value but match the context for the subsistence consumer, and do it in a way that's appropriate for them and culturally sensitive to what they need. And the only way to do that is through the bottom-up approach – through being there and understanding them and how they live.

How can the bottom-up approach work with the top-down approach?

They definitely have to go together. We can build something on a small scale in South India and try to scale it and grow it, and the top-down approach in the company says let's build product and send it somewhere. Eventually there has to be that connection where what we're doing on a small scale connects to how things traditionally work as inputs and outputs of our headquarters, sales offices, warehouses, and factories. If I can make that connection, that's the secret sauce.

Any advice for organizations for people or organizations who would like to become more bottom-up?

I would say have humility. **Especially for us being nearly a 100-year-old company, the hardest thing to do is accept that the things that you've done, the frameworks that you've used, the best practices you've developed that made you successful, know that those won't translate perfectly in this context, and that you need to reinvent how you go about approaching the market and how you see the market.** That can be really hard to accept. The only way to overcome that in my opinion is humility. And not only that, but the humility to say: "I'm going to invest time into learning about this consumer and his daily life, which is clearly different from what I know." So there's a lot of acceptance and a lot of humility that goes into getting to that point. It's good advice to get from the beginning, because if you go without humility in the beginning, you're going to get it by how many times you fail.

Anything else you would like to add?

Just that unique idea where you can easily and quickly see that if you're successful in a marketplace like this, you can make a difference in the lives of people who really need it. So being successful in that context is a pretty cool reward, because you can do good by doing well. You can make an impact on humanity and also be profitable. Opportunities to do that aren't always apparent in the business world.

Srinivas Venugopal

DOCTORAL STUDENT, UNIVERSITY OF ILLINOIS

How did you come to be involved with Madhu and with subsistence marketplaces?

My background is in social entrepreneurship. Seven years before coming to the University of Illinois, I was running an education social venture in about 80 villages of South India. About eight years back when Madhu was running one of his field trips for students, ours was one of the organizations that they visited. I had the opportunity to talk to the students, and talk with John Hedeman, who was with the students, and that's how I came to know about Madhu's work in this area.

Some of the things Madhu was doing and writing about resonated with me a lot, because it was in line with what I was seeing on the ground. I was exposed to other literature in this area as well, but I found this to be a lot more rooted in the day-to-day reality I was working in. So I got interested and slowly started talking to Madhu and applied to come to the University of Illinois for an MBA.

While I was here I continued to work with Madhu on research and loved what I was doing so I decided to stay on here and work on a PhD studying pretty much the same phenomenon that I had exposure to as a practitioner, which is how do entrepreneurs who are poor themselves start and maintain their enterprise in the context of poverty, and I also studied how external organizations can be entrepreneurial in the context of poverty or subsistence marketplaces.

Over the last seven years I've been an integral part in almost all of the initiatives, including research, teaching, and some of the community-related activities.

As you have been involved these past seven years, tell me your thoughts on the unique aspects of this bottom-up approach.

There are two key aspects that I found very appealing in this approach to studying subsistence marketplaces in the context of poverty. One is in regard to gaining insight into or understanding these marketplaces. Typically, the way researchers go about it is they start with an extant understanding of marketplaces, mostly derived from studying contexts of affluence, and typically from a Western context as well. They use that to understand what's going on elsewhere. So the key aspect of the marketplaces initiative was its bottom-up orientation, which said that new knowledge or new understanding need not be anchored in past knowledge. It's about approaching these contexts from a fresh perspective, hoping to learn from them, hoping to learn from individuals and communities in these marketplaces, gaining knowledge that is informed by the realities of the field as well as the voices of the people who are living in poverty and telling us about their lives. **That is a key aspect, knowledge that is rooted in the realities of the field and the voices of the people living in this context as opposed to the prior knowledge and understanding that we might have in this discipline.**

On the second front, I think this has more to do with the political posturing that people might have. For example, there are scholars that go in from the prospect of what can businesses do in these contexts to make things better? There are people who go in thinking how can we design public policy that makes things better? The approach that subsistence marketplaces initiative takes is to first start with the interest of individuals and communities in these contexts. These are the people and the communities who are low in terms of power. Their voices are often not heard in discussions around businesses and policy issues. And that's an important component that needs to be brought to the table in discussions about macro issues like policy and businesses. So the idea was to privilege the voices of people living in subsistence contexts and make that a starting point instead of going in with the mindset of what businesses can we do or what policies can we design? Those two are the two factors I found very appealing about this line of thinking.

As you started working with this bottom-up approach, what new insights did you gain?

I've learned a lot of things. One thing I learned from my own research is that typically from the outside, there are these sweeping generalizations about poverty and how much people in these contexts are unable to do anything. A lot of people characterize them as either lazy or caught in a trap that disables them from taking any kind of action to make their lives better.

What I've found in my own research is that there is a tremendous amount of activity and action that people are already taking to make their lives better. To give you an example, most entrepreneurs in the context of poverty, more than a million of them, have started small enterprises in order to meet their basic needs. People are already engaged in the struggle to make their life circumstances better.

A lot of times people coming in from the outside will appoint themselves as the agents of change. We are going to go in and make things happen. We are going to make these products available or create this policy that is going to change everything. It's very easy to lose sight of what's going on there and how vibrant those contexts are.

In my view, what we can really benefit from is seeing how we can harness some of the energy that already exists in these contexts and combine that with well-meaning actors coming from the outside, be it policymakers or businesses. I think these two things coming together is what will make for a sustainable solution. A lot of times there is more emphasis on the outside actors, the big powerful organizations and the policymakers, and less emphasis on local people and local communities. That balance would really help in creating situations that would bring about sustainable solutions in these contexts.

How does the bottom-up approach translate to your own work?

I started off as a practitioner but now have become increasingly oriented to the academic understanding of these marketplaces. But something I've really benefited from is not just studying these contexts as an academic, but working in them at the field level, working in these communities. This approach doesn't make a distinction between if you're an academic you only create knowledge and understanding; you can work in the field, work in these communities. In fact, the view is that all of these ways of understanding enrich each other and spill over into each other.

For example, I continue to run a not-for-profit in a large urban low-income neighborhood in Chennai, focused on girls' education, helping them pass their tenth and twelfth grade examination so it would open up higher education opportunities for them and more employment opportunities. So what I've benefited from as I run this social enterprise is I learn quite a bit by being engaged in the communities, which really informs my research. And I'm also able to use the insights gained in order to run the social enterprise better. So this kind of synergy has really helped me as a scholar. Otherwise you close yourself off to other forms of information and understanding which comes from being a practitioner in this context. That's been extremely helpful to me.

Another thing I've been passionate about is accompanying students to these contexts so they can learn from firsthand experience as they talk to people in these environments. I've been able to do that across multiple countries, Tanzania, Argentina, and India multiple times, and I've derived a lot of satisfaction from being able to do that as well.

How does the bottom-up approach work with the top-down approach?

The key there is to dialogue with people who might come in with a top-down orientation. For example, I told you about the policymakers from big organizations, either local government officials or international NGOs, or even social enterprises that come from the outside. It's important to be able to talk to them and exchange notes on their own orientations and the insights that are coming from bottom-up studies.

What we are seeing now is the conversations are monopolized by these big actors, and there isn't sufficient representation or insights from subsistence contexts. Everybody is talking about the poor people living in subsistence contexts without there being proper representation of their voices. That's where I think a lot of contribution can be made, where we can capture these voices and bring them into the discussion forum so that initiatives and interventions are informed by what's happening at the ground level.

Eventually everybody will have to work together. Everybody has their own organizational goals that they have to meet, but it's a question of are we taking into account all sources of information to create a meaningful solution? That's in my view where bottom-up studies of subsistence marketplaces and people who are engaged in those kinds of approaches can have a big impact.

Any advice to individuals or organizations who want to be more bottom-up?

The key advice is to unlearn some of the existing preconceived notions you might have. The best way of not seeing what's going on in the field level is to have some preexisting hypotheses that you want to test when you're in these places. It's difficult to set aside preconceived notions that we might have, but it does us a disservice to go into these contexts trying to test a hypothesis we might have already generated before stepping into the context. So that is one.

A second important bit of advice would be working in these communities is difficult and it's a long-term thing. One has to generate goodwill over time and be engaged over an extended period of time so one can get an accurate picture of what's going on. So it's very difficult to do this as a top-down thing. If one is to do this as a top-down thing, one has to do it with someone who has been working in these communities for a long time so that they are able to give you access to the right kind of people who can provide you good insight.

The third thing I would say is to not just talk to high-powered actors in these contexts. Even in the context of poverty, there will be people within the local environment who are more powerful. It's easier to talk to them because they tend to be the most articulate voices in these contexts. But I would say that you would be well served to go a few levels down and talk to those people who are much lower on the power hierarchy within the local environment.

Nagendra Rangavajla

DIRECTOR OF USER EXPERIENCE PROCESS, ABBOTT NUTRITION R&D

How did you first get involved with Madhu and with the subsistence marketplaces initiative?

At Abbott, we believe that innovative, responsible, and sustainable business plays an important role in building a healthy, thriving society. We strive to foster economic, environmental, and social well-being through our operations and in our work with others. At Abbott Nutrition, we practice this through design and development of products that are intended to improve quality of life of a patient or consumer.

Further, we look for opportunities to leverage our knowledge and expertise in finding solutions for nutritional problems such as malnutrition around the world. In this context, we came across Madhu, and what attracted us to him was his expertise in problem-based immersion in various aspects of subsistence markets. We've been collaborating with him for five years now, consistently supporting his student teams in their subsistence market immersion program.

What is your level of involvement with Madhu and the subsistence marketplaces initiative?

We have a very high level of involvement. We actively engage the students so the immersion is not only a great experience for them, but also for Abbott to leverage their findings and insights. I am personally involved in facilitating the scope of the project and helping them engage broader Abbott teams for guidance or insights on their research methodology. At the end of the immersion, when the students are back in Champaign, an Abbott team meets with them to learn from their experiences.

Do you do direct work in subsistence marketplaces or is your work more removed from the marketplaces?

We have several initiatives underway in subsistence markets (such as Haiti), in addition to the immersion projects we have been working on with Madhu.

What are some unique aspects of the bottom-up approach?

I believe that the bottom-up approach is the best way to know deeper consumer needs and insights. What I really appreciate in working with Madhu is how he assembles the right multi-functional teams to get most insights during an immersion. For example, for one of our projects where the question was about assessing nutritional gaps in pregnant and lactating mothers, the team that did the immersion included a student with strong nutrition training, plus a design engineer, a business student, and a packaging engineer. This cross-sectional approach is key to identifying the needs and gaps that can be acted on.

The other aspect of the bottoms-up approach is the immersion where the team spends time with the consumers, caregivers, healthcare providers, retail channels, and other influencers in the subsistence market. This provides a better understanding of consumers' needs and insights. In summary, there are two aspects that make bottom-up approach more productive in a market such as this: multi-functional teams and the immersion.

What are some of the insights that you have gained from using the bottom-up approach?

A surprising insight for me is that consumers in subsistence markets prioritize nutritional needs of their children over their own and spend a higher portion of their disposable income on nourishing their children compared to the top-of-the-pyramid segment. It shows their resolve to make sure they are maximizing their kids' growth potential.

Can you compare the bottom-up approach to other approaches?

The top-down approach is a contrast to the bottom-up approach. In the rapidly changing consumer landscape and globalization, the bottom-up approach, such as the immersion that Madhu and his students do, is the best way to get right consumer insights and design the right concept.

How does the bottom-up approach impact your work and Abbott?

In our efforts to expand our reach to emerging markets, Abbott Nutrition has established regional R&Ds, manufacturing, and commercial operations so that the team is close to the consumer and designs the products to right consumer experience and expectations. Insights gained from these approaches helped us launch several new products that are closer to the consumer's culture and expectations. A key element of product design is to deliver value with a right balance of price and features.

When is it advantageous to a company to use a bottom-up approach?

In my view, this approach is particularly important for new category expansion, new markets, or in segments where there is rapid change in consumer expectations or needs.

Can the bottom-up approach work with the top-down approach?

Yes, for example, the bottom-up approach cannot happen in a vacuum; you still need the top-down vision and strategy that drives the purpose and sets the tone for the bottom-up approach. So I see integration, where the bottom-up approach validates top-down organizational vision and strategy.

Do you have any advice for organizations or individuals who want to become more bottom-up?

As I indicated earlier, with rapidly changing demographics and behaviors, the organizations that best understand the consumer would be more successful and sustainable.

Sophy Cai

PHD STUDENT, COLLEGE OF EDUCATION, UNIVERSITY OF ILLINOIS
AT URBANA-CHAMPAIGN

How did you get involved with Madhu and the bottom-up approach?

In November 2014, I was taking a class in education. This class invited guest speakers, and I was responsible for coordinating the talk by Madhu. Because I had to coordinate this talk, I tried to learn more about what he does through his websites. He gave his talk right before Thanksgiving break and it was very good. I kept in touch with him afterward and later he gifted me his e-book, *Enabling Consumer and Entrepreneurial Literacy in Subsistence Marketplaces*. Later, I went back to China for the winter break. My grandma was in the hospital and so I went home and saw the struggles of my uncles and aunts and my mom as they were trying to get her treated and how they were struggling to pay the bills. I am from rural, southeast China, Fujian province. So I saw the struggle of the poor very viscerally.

When I came back to Illinois in the spring of 2015, I felt what I had been doing at the University of Illinois was kind of disconnected from where I came from and the original motivation for me to come into education. I transferred from literature to education because of a course in social justice and equity in education, which for the first time gave me the language to understand the struggles that I witnessed. That course changed me; it was my original motivation to enter the field of education.

However, after I came to the University of Illinois, I was immersed in the world of theories and not really in touch with where I came from. It was at that time that I went back to Madhu's programs and his web portal and watched the interviews and videos he did with women in low-income, low-literacy communities around the world. I cried the whole time as I watched these videos because of how much they brought me back to where I came from. I got in touch with him and said I wanted to get more involved with his programs and that I wanted to study how he does that work. Every time I met him, he was always very supportive. By the time I told him that I would like to study his initiative for my dissertation, he said it was an honor and that he would do whatever he could to support me.

What are some of the unique aspects of the bottom-up approach?

In my study of the philosophy of education, one of the educators who impacted me a lot was Paulo Freire. He's from Brazil and he advocated a pedagogy that is very close to Madhu's idea about the bottom-up approach. When I watched the videos of Madhu and he emphasized bottom-up approaches, I felt very attached to the idea. After I got more involved with

Madhu's initiatives – I went to a couple of marketplace literacy training sessions in Southern Illinois, and later in India during the winter break – I focused more specifically on his teaching, especially his teaching at the university and how it relates to his work in local communities around the world. I understood how his idea about the bottom-up approach started from the bottom, in this case, teaching from the students' experiences. Let the students come to conclusions on their own. In education, most of the time, it is the teachers who are supposed to know and organize all the content and then give or deliver it to students. Madhu's approach is the opposite; he starts from the students. That's how I understand Madhu's bottom-up approach.

In classroom teaching, it's very simple to think of the students as being at the bottom. But then, students have different motivations and different experiences and are positioned in different social locations, which shape how they understand who they are and their perspectives.

So to have students come to conclusions on their own is a complicated process. It needs to unpeel a lot of assumptions that are shaped by social locations that students are situated in. It requires more of a facilitation by the educator and it requires a certain medium – videos, articles, or theories to discuss as a medium of reflection.

Bottom-up and top-down approaches do not follow one direction. There is always a mutually-influenced process that is multidirectional. It's complicated, but I just want to emphasize the bottom is multidimensional and the bottom shifts. When I think about Madhu's initiative and his teaching at the university, the bottom is not just his students, but also the people whom he teaches about, especially the women in low-income, low-literate communities. And so the key is to figure out how to facilitate from the "up" and to understand that the bottom shifts.

How does the bottom-up approach compare to other approaches?

The opposite of bottom-up very simplistically is the top-down approach. That latter approach is very prevalent in our education system. Teachers are supposed to know everything; they are supposed to teach and just deliver it into their students' minds in what is called the banking model of education. That's the top-down model. Madhu's approach is in the other direction – from the students to the teachers. And his research is bottom-up in that he takes a qualitative approach, which is not very popular in business or economic research. His research is to understand the women in these communities in their everyday lives. And also in his community training programs which I observed in India, it started from the lives of women in their circumstances.

One thing I have in mind is always our assumptions – the assumptions that a researcher carries into research, or that a teacher carries into teaching. We all bring our perspectives into anything we do or think about because of where we come from and our social locations. So no matter how much I try to understand what the students or research participants are trying to tell me, I am already wearing a lens in the questions I ask, in the analysis I am going to do. So it's never purely from them. I participate in shaping their narratives. That's one thing.

Another thing is from their perspective, it's never just what the students are saying. What they are thinking about is shaped by their backgrounds, their motivations, and their social locations, so it is not just simply what one student thinks about this issue. I really value the bottom-up approach but I am also aware of the assumptions I bring into the conversation either as a researcher or a teacher.

Any new insights that you have gained in working with the bottom-up approach?

I wrote in my PhD application that I come to graduate school trying to seek an education about the poor, for the poor, with the poor, by the poor, and it was just an aspiration I had coming into education here. But I didn't have a concrete picture of what that would look like. So it was not until I came into Madhu's program and tried to see the very complicated operation that he has in different aspects of his initiative that I got to see a picture on the ground how an education about the poor, for the poor, even by the poor, and with the poor was possible. That showed me the possibility of seeing what I was searching for.

It really takes a lot to make it happen. It is limited by a lot of institutional constraints. In my research, I am also trying to think from multiple perspectives how a very aspirational program would be limited by many institutional factors, but also taking that into perspective as part of the learning process and part of reflecting the point. I see how much it takes to facilitate an educational experience for these students coming out of the University of Illinois – who, just by the fact that they are coming from the University of Illinois, are relatively privileged – and how to facilitate the kind of experience that is for the students but also takes into consideration the benefits of the women and the villages derived from our visits and field research. It may be limited by institutional constraints, but those limitations are part of the learning experience itself, which deserves more reflection.

How does the bottom-up approach translate to your own work?

My work can be conceptualized as teaching, research, and my work in the College of Education. The bottom-up approach reinforced my teaching philosophy, to understand where the students are coming from and to help the students understand where they are coming from and also the assumptions that are built into their perspectives and their knowledge about the world and who they are. In terms of research, I do qualitative research. So that is challenging me to be aware of my own assumptions and values and try to understand the participants. But also I need to be aware of my own assumptions in the questions I ask and the analysis I conduct with the data I have.

In my office work at the College of Education, most of the time, I have helped with internationalization efforts such as study abroad programs or coordinating programs for teachers and students from China to come to the University of Illinois to learn about higher education. Most of the time, unfortunately, we are very top-down. We design whole programs and itineraries for visiting professors and students. Sometimes I try to understand their needs and where they are coming from and what they want to know about, but many times, they are just ready to come to get whatever we have designed for them. So in educational programming, there is not much space for a bottom-up approach, often due to considerations of efficiency, and also for what the other is thinking about.

If I could add one more insight, it's never easy to just be bottom-up in one's philosophy, because it depends on what the bottom is thinking. Sometimes the bottom, for example, the students, are used to, or conditioned to, just be given material and lectured to, and are not always ready to enjoy coming to conclusions on their own. It's a very challenging process.

How can the bottom-up approach and top-down approach work together?

I think these two approaches are two directions of the same process. It's never just purely bottom-up or top-down. My understanding is they have to work together. I think of it in multiple directions. It's not just one direction from the student to the teacher.

Do you have any advice for organizations or individuals who want to become more bottom-up?

The first thing I would say is, don't assume that it's just a purely bottom-up or one-direction approach. Be aware of the assumptions that we carry into the process, either at the bottom or at the top, and know that the assumptions require a lot of unpeeling and critical reflections. It's a never-ending learning process. Keep asking critical questions about our own assumptions in thinking about the other – for teachers, think about the students; for researchers, think about the participants.

Chapter 14: A Newcomer's Perspective of the Bottom-Up Approach

Note: This chapter was written by Tom Hanlon, who edited the rest of this book and who went to India in 2014 to experience firsthand what he had heretofore only read about.

– Madhu Viswanathan

Toto, I've a feeling we're not in Kansas anymore.

– Dorothy to her dog, Toto, in The Wizard of Oz

That was one of my many feelings upon finally arriving at Chennai International Airport in Chennai, India, at 3:30 am one early December morning in 2014. I am not a world traveler, and I had never been to India; I had envisioned a fairly quiet airport at that hour, with a few sleepy-eyed stragglers languidly rolling suitcases behind them in a relatively deserted concourse. What my wife Janet and I encountered was nothing like that. People, wide-eyed and moving briskly, streamed around us; it seemed like every square inch of the concourse was up for grabs. As we made our way to the exit, where we were to be picked up by Venkat, one of the three founders of Marketplace Literacy Communities in Chennai, we were amazed to see, through the window that ran the length of the concourse, hundreds of people standing outside, all watching for people they were to pick up. These people were waving, shouting, pumping signs with passengers' names in the air. **I felt a bit like the Beatles landing in America (understand I had gone more than a day without sleep, and if no one else in that concourse was groggy, I certainly was), or, to put it in today's terms, like Justin Bieber arriving at his next concert venue.**

I spotted Venkat (R. Venkatesan), whom I had met once before, at a conference in Champaign, Illinois. He was waving a sign with Janet's and my name on it. He broke into a huge grin when we made eye contact. We made our way outside, greeted each other, and we greeted Sudha (S. Sudhakar), and Viji (K. Vijayakumar), who are cofounders with Venkat of Marketplace Literacy Communities.

They were thrilled to meet us, they took our bags for us, they escorted us to their van, and they drove us to our hotel. Along the way it dawned on me that we were nearly two hours late. They had essentially been up all night, waiting to pick up a couple of blurry-eyed foreigners. And they looked as cheerful and fresh as if they were going to an outing at a beach.

"We're so sorry to make you miss so much sleep," I said as we started off from the airport.

"No worries," said Viji from the front seat. "We are fine. No worries at all."

On the way to the hotel, I was surprised to find that the traffic, even at that hour, was bumper to bumper, and the night was punctuated with the ever-present sound of beeps and honks and toots from vehicles of all shapes and sizes on the freeway (which, as I soon came to realize, might better be called a "free-for-all").

A New People, A New Culture

We got a few hours' sleep at the hotel, had breakfast in the hotel restaurant – we went with Indian food, not Western; we wanted the complete cultural experience – and we met Venkat, Viji, and Sudha in the lobby. They introduced us to Shanmugam, our interpreter for the duration. He was as warm and friendly as the other three, and he proved to be a walking encyclopedia of the history and culture of India, as well as a tour guide extraordinaire who knew fascinating details about everywhere we visited and drove by, and who could guide us in knowing what to do and not do, what to say and not say.

We piled into the van and entered the merry cacophony of traffic. There are about 7.4 million people in the Chennai metro area, and about 7.395 million seem to own motorbikes. There are far more motorbikes than autos in Chennai, at least in my experience, and most of them streamed by our van each day, like water bugs sluicing by. By this time Janet and I were getting used to the horns, which we learned were not blasted in so much of an American, "Get out of my way!" fashion as they were an ever-present, kindly Indian warning: "Coming up on your left!" "Passing on your right!" "Zigging left, zagging right!" As so many strange Indian customs proved to do, this one made sense after witnessing the alarming mishmash of traffic for a few days.

After our third day in Chennai, I wrote this in my journal regarding the traffic:

> Have been driven down narrow alleys with cars, motorbikes,
> and little three-wheel taxis streaming down them in haphazard
> fashion, each narrowly missing other vehicles and pedestrians by
> an inch or two, no one batting an eye. While the driving laws are
> like England, where you drive on the left side of the road, really in
> Chennai you just stream wherever. I would say you change lanes
> a lot, but there are no discernible lanes. We have passed cows
> and bullocks and goats on the road, and a million people, some
> walking, some standing, some sitting on the roadside, hands out,
> asking for money or food.

We drove probably half an hour to the Marketplace Literacy Communities office – a humble but clean whitewashed building with a main room, two side offices, and a back room that let out to an alley. We were led into an office where a large fan, running full blast, kept the room quite cool. (In December it was "only" mid-eighties Fahrenheit in Chennai. Our Indian friends laughed at how hot we thought it was. "Don't come here in April!" they cautioned. "You might melt!") Shanmugam pretty much stuck to us like glue for our ten-day venture in Chennai; he took his interpreting duties seriously. Venkat, Viji, and Sudha all spoke English quite well, so our conversations with them were really not hampered at all, and Shanmugam made sure our conversations with the people we interviewed were not hampered, either.

Suffice it to say we were treated like royalty at all times in Chennai. There were times when one or more of the four men would act almost as bodyguards, particularly when beggars would come up to us. And yes, impoverished people approached us, hands out. During our early days there, a festival was going on, and we visited a temple. Vendors and people filled the streets; it was all but impossible to park. (No amount of money could convince me to drive in Chennai.) This is my journal account regarding a portion of our festival experience:

> It is some festival time, I forget which; we heard fireworks last night - many people were out begging, and Janet and I stuck out like sore thumbs. We had two people in particular follow us, one a mother carrying a young child (Janet smiled at the child and the mother caught the smile and latched on to the hope of getting a handout from a compassionate woman), another a slightly older woman, the latter who followed us a block or two to our car, asking in a quiet voice for a handout, I assume; she was not speaking in English, of course. She knocked on our car window once we were inside and kept knocking until we went away. Stopped in traffic a mile later, another girl came up and knocked on our window and kept knocking until the driver told her to go away. It is sad and disturbing; it is not that we don't have compassion, but we don't have the capacity to help them in the way they need help, and if you help just one, dozens if not hundreds will flock to you.

It is apparent that the poverty in India is far greater than it is in America. This is not to say that impoverished people in America have it easy. It is to say that low-literate, low-income people in India face a level of poverty, a lack of the most basic and essential resources, that people in advanced economies do not face.[139]

It is in the midst of this great lack that Marketplace Literacy Communities (MLC), a partner organization of Marketplace Literacy Project, rose up. MLC offers marketplace literacy education, links to financial institutions, assistance in maintaining financial records, and ongoing support for running enterprises. It works with about 100 self-help groups of women, with each group numbering 15 to 20 women.

It was with one of these self-help groups that Janet and I met in MLC's main room on our first day of interviews.

Self-Help Groups

The women sat in chairs fanned out in a large semicircle. A few were young – at least one younger than 20 – and a few were a bit older, but most were in their 30s or early 40s. They were arrayed in brightly-colored, beautiful saris. Many wore jewelry. All wore smiles. Janet and I smiled back at them. We don't speak their language and they don't speak ours, but we felt welcomed and comfortable in their presence.

As Shanmugam translated, we talked with them about their group. One by one they spoke, sharing their stories both as individuals and as a group. We learned that they run several microbusinesses within the group, that they have a treasurer who is in charge of the money, that they pool their resources together and go to banks for loans to get their businesses started.

Some were more talkative than others. Many took great interest in us and wanted to know what life was like in the US. We swapped stories about our children. We showed them pictures of our children and we took pictures with them. They smiled incessantly throughout the hour-long interview; when it came time for a group picture, though, they all had poker faces for the camera. I guess the moral there is to capture what life is truly like in India, you must be there.

Parvati, 20 years old, sold saris as her business. Janet and I made an appointment to visit her the next day to buy a sari for Janet and for our daughter.

---

[139] The World Bank in May of 2014 defined the poverty line at $1.78 per day on a 2011 purchasing power parity basis for the US dollar. India has 179.6 million people below that line, representing 20.6 percent of the world's poor, though the country represents only 17.5 percent of the world's population. Nearly 22 percent of India's population lives on less than USD $1.78 per day.

The next morning, Janet badly sprained her ankle and had to stay back at the hotel. As I interviewed several of the women from the self-help group individually, the first question each had for me was "Where is Janet?" And when they heard she had hurt her ankle, they were dismayed and continued to ask about her. Parvati, hearing that Janet was stuck in the hotel, sent several saris back with me for her to choose from.

This is how I would describe the women that we met in the self-help groups: Strong. Supportive. Unified. Forward-thinking. Bright. Sweet. Kind. Resourceful. Confident. Brave. Enduring. Wise. Persistent. Tireless. Purposeful. Beautiful.

And empowered.

Marketplace Literacy Education

Many of those descriptors – resourceful, confident, supportive, and unified, among others – come at least in part from the women's participation in marketplace literacy education, which MLC offers in various sections of Chennai as well as several villages in the surrounding area.

The education includes picture sorting, group discussions, and role playing, and assumes that the participant cannot read or write. The women focus on the process of exchange, learn about the value chain from creation and production of products to consumption, and assume the role of consumers as they learn to identify common traps that illiterate consumers often fall prey to. They learn about the value of a product and the importance of being an informed consumer.

They then take on the role of entrepreneurs. They learn how to evaluate business opportunities based on how the opportunities meet consumers' needs, on the competition they would face, and on their own strengths and weaknesses.

In short, they learn how to operate in the marketplace – and how to create and run their own businesses. They learn to become self-sufficient or at least to contribute to family earnings. Understated but not lost in all of this is they learn to value themselves, to see their capabilities and possibilities, and to take the calculated risks they need to take to better their lives.

And that is exactly what Janet and I saw in Chennai: a group of women who were confident, who were taking charge of their lives, who were moving forward, who were asking the right questions, who had learned to become wise consumers and savvy entrepreneurs.

Amidst much of the bleak poverty that we also witnessed, it was a refreshing and heartening sight to behold.

We also journeyed two hours south of Chennai to a village called Uthiramerur Taluk in rural Tamil Nadu to observe the final module of a training for a group of women who were learning various facets of marketplace literacy. They watched a video showing the process that female entrepreneurs went through to successfully start their businesses. They then took part in a group discussion and an exercise. The group discussion was orderly but lively; women were eager to give their opinions and state what they learned and how they would apply it to their lives.

These women were of all ages – late teens to perhaps late fifties or sixties. A few had infants in their laps. One had a cane by her side. Some were reserved, some were outspoken. Their skin tones and their saris were of varying shades and hues. But this is what they all shared in common: a joy and a vibrancy in the learning together as a community. A hope for the future. A confidence in approaching it. A purpose in their lives; you could see it burning in their eyes. An energy and an eagerness to make a better tomorrow, for themselves and most importantly, for their children.

In a very real sense, we witnessed these women being equipped for battle. The battle is subtle but very real and challenging. In India, women who are low-literate and poor are seen as the dregs of society. They carry no value in the eyes of many who see them either as nuisances or, perhaps worse, who do not see them at all. To some, they are ghosts wandering around until one day they completely disappear.

But not these women. These women, through their marketplace literacy education, know their true worth. They do not hang their heads; they do not shrink back. They do not stand silently by, accepting their lot in life.

Their learning, in community with other women, opens a door for them. Right now you sense that the door, for some, is just cracked open, with a bit of light streaming through from the other side. But collectively, the women can push that door wide open. Collectively they can buy products wholesale; collectively they can obtain bank loans; collectively they can start and expand businesses.

One woman at the training stood and said, her eyes gleaming with pride, "It is not only me who is being educated; it is my entire family." Nods and murmurs of appreciation spread through the group.

Another woman, one holding an infant, stood and said, "I was in a shop the other day and the shopkeeper said, 'You are one of those women!' And I said, 'One of what women?' And he said, 'You are one of those women being trained in a self-help group! I know this because I see how you shop now. This is a good thing. And I am going to give you a good deal because of it.'"

A Newcomer's Perspective of the Bottom-Up Approach   **297**

The women around her burst into cheers and joyous laughter. The woman who gave this report beamed.

She looked down at her baby in her arms. That baby had no idea what was going on. But that baby's future is far brighter for the steps her mother is taking.

Tireless Work

All of these self-help groups are administered by Venkat, Viji, and Sudha, the aforementioned cofounders of MLC, a partner group of the Marketplace Literacy Project started by Madhu Viswanathan. As it is said that athletes reflect the personality of their coach, or that group members reflect the personality of their leader, so it is with the self-help groups, for Venkat, Viji, and Sudha are tireless, pragmatic, optimistic, and filled with a seemingly boundless energy that propels them forward each day. During our 10 days in Chennai, they seemed to work about 18 hours a day – cheerfully and joyfully. We encountered numerous wrinkles in our plans – each wrinkle smoothed out and handled with grace and aplomb, and a healthy dose of laughter. They are like three strands of a cord; together they exhibit amazing strength. Their minds are nimble, always assessing situations and thinking not just one, but two or three steps ahead. Watching them operate was like observing chess masters in action.

One reason they are so adept at running Marketplace Literacy Communities is that they – or at least Venkat; I'm not sure of the backgrounds of Viji and Sudha – embody the bottom-up approach that this book is about. Venkat knows poverty firsthand; he was immersed in it from his infancy. He lived in a one-room apartment with four siblings and his parents; they had no electricity until he was 15. They shared a common toilet with 10 other families. Their room was cramped and airless, and he had no shoes.

Venkat's father died while Venkat was in ninth grade. He had to quit school – which he liked and which he excelled in – to support his family. But a teacher saw his potential and, a few years later, funded his studies to prepare for his twelfth-grade exams. He failed at first, but passed on a second attempt. (And even there is a lesson: you don't quit. If you give up on yourself, you allow other people the opportunity to give up on you.)

In 2001, Viswanathan asked Venkat's project manager to recommend someone to help him with a research project for the Marketplace Literacy Project. The manager suggested Venkat. Venkat began working for Viswanathan that year, and began full-time in 2003.

The boy who grew up without electricity or shoes turned into a man who directs an organization that has impacted thousands of women. As he looked to better himself, as he believed in himself, as he was given a hand up, so he is part of the triumvirate at MLC that helps women in the same way.

And that is the bottom-up approach in action.

East Meets West

The flow of life and work in Chennai – at least certainly within MLC – is different from what I am accustomed to. In the West, it seems that people are consumed with the future. Where are they going, how will they get there, what will they do when they get there? These thoughts are at least in the backs of the minds of most Westerners.

In the East, from my brief observations, people live more in the present. They are not so consumed with tomorrow. They face enough troubles for the day; better to focus on what is in front of them.

As a result, it seems that Indians are better equipped to adjust on the fly, to handle change with an even-minded thoughtfulness, to find immediate solutions to the problems and challenges of the day. And so, the road to their future is plotted with switchbacks and detours, but those who approach life like Venkat, Viji, and Sudha – and the women in the self-help groups that they administrate – are ready to take on the challenges of life head-on, with equanimity and a cool confidence.

Marketplace literacy education, at least as played out in India, seems to be an amalgam of East meets West: you take the best of both trains of thought, both approaches to life, and you combine them, with the result being people who are ready to seize the day while creating a better future for themselves and the generations behind them.

House Visits

We made several house visits during our stay in Chennai. These dwellings ranged from

- A thatched hut with a dirt floor and no furniture; it had a small cook stove in a corner
- A thatched hut with a cement floor, a few pictures on the wall, and a cook stove
- A 10-foot by 10-foot one-room apartment with a thin mattress on the floor and a cook stove
- Two apartments with three rooms each, and one with a refrigerator and a washing machine (clothes were hung on a line in a back room to dry)

Humble dwellings, all. The apartment with the washer and refrigerator was the nicest, though in America it would be the home of someone living under the poverty level. The other apartment was nice and airy and bright, and spacious compared to many that we saw, but still it was small by American standards and had relatively sparse furnishings.

But American standards are not Indian standards, and it is futile to compare the two, except to place them in context so you can envision the level or quality of living (again, against American standards). By the Indian standard of living, the latter two apartments were quite nice.

In all dwelling places – including the thatched huts – my wife and I were greeted sometimes shyly, but always with warmth and respect. The people were happy that we were in their dwelling places; there was no show of being embarrassed for their humble abodes (nor should there have been); there was only pleasure at making the acquaintances of two pasty-faced Americans who wanted to learn about their lives – and see not just *how* they lived, but *where* they lived. To them, it was an honor to have us in their house; to us, it was an honor to be there.

"I Will Be Your Left Arm"

On one such visit, I went to the aforementioned 10-by-10 apartment (Janet was nursing her sprained ankle at the hotel). The apartment was located in a back alley in a poor section of Chennai. It had rained hard the night before and the alley was filled with large puddles and potholes. Venkat, Viji, Sudha, and I had to be careful where we stepped as we made our way to the tiny apartment. It was painted an off-white on the outside, and had a thick curtain in the entryway. Kannan, the young man we were visiting, pulled back the curtain and we entered his apartment. It was dark – there was no electricity – and it took my eyes a few moments to adjust.

Inside, Kannan stood by his beautiful wife, Ambika, who cradled in her arms their newborn daughter. Ambika was very proud to show off her brand new baby. Kannan extended his right hand to me, and I shook it. It is the only hand he has; his left arm was amputated when he was a teenager, due to an accident involving an electrical wire in a field on the small farm he grew up on.

Kannan has learned to make do. He gets up every morning at 3 am to get on his motorbike – no easy trick learning to ride a motorbike, particularly on the streets of Chennai, with one arm – and ride to where he receives bundles of newspapers to deliver.

Kannan, in his early twenties, has faced more adversity than most people do in a lifetime. I learned that he faced some dark days after his arm was amputated. But he weathered that storm, and he moved from a rural village to the big city, and he met a woman who loved him for who he was. In fact, after many dates, during which they had grown quite serious about each other, he stopped Ambika as they walked down a street. It perturbed him that she had never mentioned anything about his missing left arm.

"Do you notice anything unusual about me?" he inquired.

"No," she said.

"You notice nothing at all?" he asked, incredulous.

"Well, I notice you are rather tall," she offered.

He rolled his eyes. "That is not what I mean," he said.

"I know very well what you mean," she said. "I am not blind. I know you have no left arm."

He looked at her soberly. "Does that bother you?" he asked.

"If it had bothered me, I would have said something," she said.

And then came the critical question.

"Can you marry a man with no left arm?" he asked, fearing the answer.

"Is that your idea of a proposal?" she responded.

Seeing the glint in her eye, he gained a bit of confidence. He could not help but grin.

"Yes," he said. "Will you marry me?"

She smiled. "I will marry you," she said. "And I will be your left arm."

Kannan and Ambika embody all that is good about the poor in India. Their stories, now melded into one story, are a mixture of hardship, bravery, hardiness, recreation, love, sacrifice, hope, and dauntless perseverance.

Those same qualities tie together all those whom we met in Chennai and the surrounding area. And because of those qualities, marketplace literacy education – giving people the skills, the marketplace understanding, the confidence, and the wherewithal to begin and sustain microbusinesses and to fashion a better life for themselves – is so fruitful and so empowering.

Coming Home

After ten days in Chennai, Janet and I flew to New Delhi. There, we played the tourists. We took a day trip to the amazing Taj Mahal, and though it rained all day, it was well worth getting wet and dealing with the crowds. We toured Delhi, seeing the Red Fort, built in the 1600s; the Jama Masjid, the largest mosque in India, also built in the 1600s; the Chandni Chowk, one of the oldest and busiest markets in Old Delhi, where we took a cycle rickshaw ride down the cobbled, twisting, and tight streets that were packed wall to wall with people; we shopped in various stores; we visited Gandhi's tomb.

And, truth be told, while we appreciated the beauty and splendor of all we saw in this great capital, we missed the heart and soul of the India that we embraced, and were embraced by, in Chennai.

After four days in New Delhi, we flew home, arriving exhausted, profoundly moved, and enriched by our time in India, and particularly in Chennai, where marketplace literacy is daily changing lives, and the people whose lives are changed are having a ripple effect on those around them and on the generations coming after them.

Made in the USA
Monee, IL
11 May 2022

96262974R00167